Sovereignty, Democracy, and
Global Civil Society

Sovereignty, Democracy, and Global Civil Society

State-Society Relations at UN World Conferences

Elisabeth Jay Friedman,
Kathryn Hochstetler,
and
Ann Marie Clark

STATE UNIVERSITY OF NEW YORK PRESS

Published by
State University of New York Press, Albany

For information, address State University of New York Press,
90 State Street, Suite 700, Albany, N.Y. 12207

Production by Diane Ganeles
Marketing by Michael Campochiaro

Library of Congress Cataloging-in-Publication Data

Friedman, Elisabeth J., 1966–
    Sovereignty, democracy, and global civil society : state-society relations at UN world conferences / Elisabeth Jay Friedman, Kathryn Hochstetler, & Ann Marie Clark.
        p. cm.
    Includes bibliographical references and index.
    ISBN 0-7914-6333-8 (alk. paper)
        1. Civil society.   2. Non-governmental organizations.   3. Environmental economics.
    4. Human rights.   5. Women's rights.   6. Sovereignty.   7. World politics—1989–.
    I. Hochstetler, Kathryn, 1962–   II. Clark, Ann Marie, 1960–   III. Title.   IV. Series.

    JC337.F75 2005
    300—dc22   2004045258

10 9 8 7 6 5 4 3 2 1

To Our Teachers

Contents

Tables

Acknowledgments

This project started as an idea for a conference paper. Ann approached Kathy to see if she would be interested in writing a paper on international state-society relations by comparing two UN conferences. Kathy suggested bringing Elisabeth in on the project, as she had recently attended the 1995 Fourth World Conference on Women. Nine years later, we have collaboratively written five conference papers, three articles, and, now, a book. Although coauthoring is no longer infrequent in our "home" discipline of political science, tri-author collaborations, particularly ones that are sustained over several years, are not exactly the norm. Some readers might be curious as to how we carried out this unusual endeavor.

We have been equal partners in this project. We structured our empirical work by deciding what the interesting question, or set of questions, might be asking those questions of different material, wherever it might be found—in UN conference documents and library depositories, nongovernmental organization (NGO) reports, or our own field research; and then coming back together, physically or virtually, to compare notes on our answers. We also generated long lists of secondary material, parceled it out for reading, and shared its insights. We started by focusing on the areas and issues closest to our individual research agendas, but soon branched into others. To put the various pieces together, we each took sections of first drafts to write, and traded them for rewriting . . . and rewriting . . . and editing. This was not always an easy process, and we certainly experienced our fair share of disagreement, miscommunication, and yes, even whining. But as an approach to research, we have found it has much to recommend it. The resulting comparative perspectives and theoretical insights are ones we simply could not have generated on our own. They have been illuminating and interesting to us, and, we hope, useful to others.

Besides accompanying each other on a fascinating intellectual journey, we have all benefited tremendously from the experience on a personal level—including support for and during our other research projects, tenure cases, several institutional moves, and other delightful and difficult life changes. The daily (or even more often) email exchanges, the occasional conference call, the even more occasional conference reunion, and one very memorable weeklong "workshop" in Fort Collins have provided us with companionship for what is so often the solitary experience of academic life. And so, we would like to take this opportunity to thank each other for the intellectual firepower, keen curiosity, patience, good humor, willingness to compromise and, at times, ability to endure that has made this whole thing possible.

We all have other debts of gratitude that we have collectively and singly incurred during the trajectory of this project. We are grateful to Michael Rinella at the State University of New York Press for his support in getting this book into publication. Our ideas were challenged and sharpened by a number of anonymous reviewers over the years as well as by interactions with colleagues at the International Studies Association, the American Political Science Association, the Latin American Studies Association, and in our present and past home departments at Barnard College, Colorado State University, Purdue University, and the University of San Francisco. We would particularly like to thank Jackie Smith and Dimitris Stevis, as well as our research assistants: Vania Brightman, Elsa Dias, Adriana Lins de Albuquerque, Eric Shibuya, and Jennifer Suchland. We are, of course, responsible for any remaining errors of fact or interpretation. We are also very grateful to those on the home front who have kept us going forward with our lives as well as with our work over the past nine years: Kathryn Jay, Roger Hoover, Jay McCann, and our cherished extended, and extending, families. We dedicate this book to our many teachers for their inspiration and guidance down this road, especially our graduate mentors Kathryn Sikkink and Terry Lynn Karl.

*   *   *   *   *   *   *

This book contains material published previously and used by permission: an earlier version of chapter 2 appeared as "The Sovereign Limits of Global Civil Society: A Comparison of NGO Participation in Global UN Conferences on the Environment, Human Rights, and Women." *World Politics* 51, 1:1–35; an earlier version of chapter 3 appeared as "Latin American NGOs and Governments: Coalition Building at UN Conferences on the Environment, Human Rights, and Women." *Latin American Research Review* 36, 3: 7–35; and a previous version of chapter 4 appeared as "Sovereignty Challenges and Bargains on the Environment, Human Rights, and Women." *International Studies Quarterly* 44, 4: 591–614.

Introduction

During the preparatory conferences for the 1992 United Nations Conference on the Environment and Development, several hundred nongovernmental organizations (NGOs) packed into a crowded sideroom in UN facilities every morning to coordinate their lobbying strategies. Individual NGOs were responsible for reporting on the current status of the negotiations in the various UN working groups; collectively, NGOs then came up with lobbying points and alternative language proposals and a schedule for the current day. While these proved to be efficient organizing meetings, some NGOs also used the time to complain about how the gatherings functioned—that all of the participants had to speak in English or find their own translator, or that business NGOs were able to participate alongside environment and development NGOs. Some NGOs, especially from the South, avoided the daily meetings altogether. A gathering of Latin American NGOs, for example, tried to launch a parallel dialogue (all in Spanish) with North American NGOs at one of the preparatory conferences about an alternative agenda to the governmental one that would pay more attention to issues like foreign debt and controls on multinational corporations.

At the 1993 World Conference on Human Rights, held in Vienna, NGOs fought an "upstairs-downstairs" sta-

tus difference that was only reinforced by the physical
layout of the conference facilities at the Austria Centre, where NGOs were relegated to the basement
while states conducted business upstairs. The contrast was not lost on participants, one of whom described the difference as a contrast between "grey car-
peted, grey walled, windowless ... rooms in which
black suited states delegates made longwinded
speeches" upstairs, just above the basement awash in
"a hive of activity and a vibrant mosaic of colour"
(Samuel 1994:59). On the official side, NGOs demanded to be heard, staging a walkout in protest of a
rollback of the participation privileges they had en-
joyed in the regional conferences and preparatory
meetings leading up to the conference. They achieved
limited access to informal sessions but were banned
from the critical closed-door sessions of the confer-
ence-drafting committee, forcing them to stand watch
for information filtering out secondhand from representatives of sympathetic governments.

The thirty thousand representatives of NGOs at the
1995 United Nations Fourth World Conference on
Women, held in Beijing, turned their energies to varied tasks. While some at the parallel NGO forum
heatedly debated the impact of UN conferences on
national women's movements, others eagerly net-
worked with other women's rights advocates from
across the globe, in workshops on issues ranging
from violence against women to improvisational art.
Still others used the forum time to strategize on how
to lobby governments on specific language in the official conference document, continuing their efforts in
hotel rooms scattered across Beijing. NGOs also
made their presence felt at the official conference itself: observing quietly from the back of delegates'
meeting rooms when allowed in; seizing the opportunity presented by coffee breaks to lobby particular
delegates on language changes; and even resorting to
forbidden protests inside the official conference hall
on issues they felt had been sidelined from the governmental agenda.

These are accounts of important moments in the recent development of global civil society. They may not be the images that come to mind first when considering non-state action at the international level, however. Instead, others seem to have replaced them:

> In late November and early December 1999, somewhere between 50,000 to 100,000 protestors from around the world, representing interests ranging from the environment to labor to business, descended on the third World Trade Organization Ministerial Conference in Seattle, Washington. Although the majority engaged in nonviolent protest of the negative effects of global neoliberal economic policies and the exclusionary nature of global trade negotiations, a small group became violent and started looting. A state of emergency was declared, and curfews, tear gas, pepper spray, and rubber bullets were used to subdue all protesters. Nevertheless, Seattle marked the beginning of regular demonstrations by thousands of protesters at international economic summits. Two years later, as well over 100,000 people protested at the 2001 economic summit of the major industrial democracies in Genoa, Italy, a 23-year-old protester died after being shot in the head. At least 100 people were seriously wounded during the protests. At the end of the summit, police raided the headquarters of the umbrella group that planned the demonstrations and left dozens injured. (Sanger 2001; Berlusconi says "No Cover-up" over Summit Violence 2001)

> On September 11, 2001, terrorists from the al Qaeda network crashed two hijacked U.S. airliners into New York City's World Trade Center towers, killing 2,870 people and destroying the towers and several nearby buildings. Another group flew a third plane into the Pentagon in Arlington, Virginia, killing 180 people and bringing down a wing of the building. Overwhelmed by passengers, a fourth group crashed their plane in a field outside of Pittsburgh, killing everyone on board.

In these more recent instances, non-state actors have visibly, and sometimes violently, demanded a role in world politics. Although their tactics and goals are wildly divergent, many of the actors have one thing in common: they operate largely outside of the sanctioned arenas of international negotiations. Clearly, some actors are not interested in entering such arenas, or in peaceful resolution of their grievances. But for those non-state actors who are determined to find sustainable solutions to the challenges inherent in an ever more global polity and economy, exclusion from global decision making is a serious obstacle. Recent attempts to enter many decision making processes have been met with resistance, if not outright repression.

These events suggest a global stalemate between governments and those who claim to represent the people in whose name governments rule—with the power still largely in the governments' hands. In contrast, the global UN conferences of the 1990s can be looked at as modeling global interaction among states and non-state actors willing to attempt peaceful solutions to global problems. The model of slower, more peaceful, and concerted negotiations among states and non-state actors may easily be overlooked, but continues alongside the more violent forms of interaction that marked the turn of the millennium.

This book offers an assessment of negotiated interactions among states and other actors at the global level. We provisionally use the term *global civil society* to refer to the non-state actors engaging in such activity, although our study includes an assessment of whether the quality of these interactions approaches a level that merits unreflective use of the term. To carry out this assessment, we examine the relations among members of global civil society and states at the UN world conferences of the 1990s, along with historical reflections on their predecessors. The world conferences, on issues ranging from human rights to the environment to housing, have offered one of the few examples of relatively open formal international negotiations, given both their wide-ranging agendas and the extensive and varied participation they permit. In particular, NGOs have gained increasing access to state-based dialogues throughout the conference processes of the last three decades. Thus, these conferences have offered a platform for sustained, peaceful challenge to the monopolization of global affairs by states. Moreover, the opportunity to compare global state-society relations across conferences on different issues allows for a more general overview and understanding of the form these challenges have taken and states' responses to them.

Historically, states occasionally accepted and sometimes

sought the incorporation of certain voluntary associations at international fora for the knowledge and other resources they could offer to help solve global problems. For example, states invited scientific and technical organizations to play a role in the 1972 Stockholm Conference on the Human Environment. Certain NGOs helped to write and negotiate preparatory conference documents, and the final document referred to their educational or technical role in issues such as environmental preservation and natural resource use. As members of global civil society, NGOs also claim that one of the key benefits of their inclusion in world politics is their ability to improve life in a particular issue area, whether it be women's rights, sustainable development, or racial equality.

The UN's Economic and Social Council gave NGOs a consultative status in recognition of these potential contributions, which include NGOs' representation of the populations of member states. While actual UN practice is another story, language in the charter suggests a vision of the UN that at least partly welcomes NGOs for their potential to democratize global governance processes. The UN conferences continue in this vein. In this study, we delve into the potential contributions of global civil society, as evidenced at the UN world conferences of the 1990s, to the democratization of global governance processes.

Democratization, and democracy, for that matter, are the subject of extensive conceptual debate. Three competing perspectives outline the contributions that global civil society can make to global democratization. One perspective stresses developments within the sphere of global civil society itself, analyzing the positive outcomes brought about through deliberation and exchange among global citizens, outside of formal politics and across national boundaries. A second perspective focuses on how the unique perspectives and resources of global civil society can transform diplomacy in the already-established realms of state-based international negotiation. Global democracy becomes the ability to formulate relations of accountability, representation, and citizenship between global civil society and states gathered at the international level. The final perspective is more skeptical, questioning whether global civil society can truly transform the international system, particularly given the elite, undemocratic nature of global associational life itself.

In order to assess the extent to which any kind of global democratization is taking place, the concept of global civil society itself must be defined. What is "global civil society"? Pose the question to an observer of world politics, and most likely the answer will include examples of well-known international NGOs that work on issues of global importance, such as the human rights organization Amnesty International, with its nearly one million members in 162 countries and territories (Amnesty International, nd). Others may mention transnational corporations, such as the Nike athletic company. Nike directly employs 23,000 people from nearly every world region, provides another one million with jobs in its supply, shipping, retail, and service network, and markets products in over 100 countries (Nike, nd). Yet others may point to explicitly political organizations such as Socialist International, the global organization of 141 social democratic, socialist, and labor parties and organizations (Socialist International, nd).

These examples illustrate the variety of actors and causes making their presence felt in international politics. Almost all definitions of global civil society agree that it is an associational sphere that excludes states and organizations that use violence to achieve their ends. Beyond those basics, the makeup of that sphere is heavily contested. Does it include market-based or -focused actors? Political parties? Other governing institutions? However the definitional boundaries are drawn, global civil society's impact is clearly dependent on the interactions of voluntary associations with economic and political forces.

As a way of shedding light on the development and impact of global civil society, our study examines the individual elements of global civil society—its global, civil, and social elements—as aspects of the UN conferences that have developed over time, throughout and between the conference processes. The *global* criterion asks if representation of NGOs, the official representatives of non-state actors at the UN conferences, is geographically diverse. Thus, we start by querying the extent to which all world regions are represented. But presence does not translate directly into influence. To assess the extent to which the presence of global civil society has an impact on the democratization of world politics, we delve further into the meanings of "civil" and "society."

The *civil* component of global civil society connotes both regularized non-state participation in global negotiations and NGOs' free access to states and other NGOs. We identify the *repertoires,* or patterns of engagement, of NGOs to assess the civility of global society. For example, we note that NGOs themselves are often divided on the most appropriate strategy for seeking global change, with some focusing on direct lobbying of governments while others prefer to network only with their fellow NGOs.

A full-fledged society, and thus, *social* relations, would be in evidence when members of the global society (both NGOs and states) act with reference to their ongoing relationships, based on the construction over time of common understandings of their identities, relations, and substantive issues. To assess the sociability of relations at the global level, we analyze the compatibility of the patterns in participants' beliefs about the causes of and solutions to contentious issues, among states and NGOs. Such beliefs are called *frames,* and they may be shared or contested among social actors. A prominent example of a shared NGO frame, for example, is one developed by NGO participants over the last three decades. They have come to see themselves as an essential element not only in the conference process, but also of world politics. They assert their importance as monitors of, if not replacements for, governments that they believe cannot or will not resolve global problems on their own.

How do we use these civil and social indicators to understand the extent of democratization? Assessing how NGOs build networks among themselves, and identifying their shared and contested frames, will indicate how developed the deliberative process of democratization is within global civil society. Examining the "official" NGO repertoire of NGO lobbying of governmental representatives, and the shared and contested frames between NGOs and governments, will indicate the extent of democratization within the governmental arena of world politics.

Analyzing the democratization of world politics brings into question the historically central role of states. Thus in this work we also take on the task of examining the challenges made to state sovereignty claims at UN conferences, and states' responses to them. States try to balance different dimensions of their sovereignty, weighing what they lose in autonomy by joining in international agreements against what they gain through additional international legitimacy or control over national problems. In the conference negotiations, states were sometimes—but not always—willing to strike bargains with other states and NGOs to achieve greater international coordination and oversight. We explore the bargaining process here, analyzing how different dimensions of sovereignty map onto contentious issues like national cultural values and development choices.

Overview of the Book

In chapter 1, we present an overview of the conceptual debates over the meaning of global civil society. We do so by first examining the concept of civil society, particularly with reference to its emergence as a subject of analysis during the worldwide processes of democratization in the last few decades, before turning to approaches to global civil society and its potential impact on global democratization. The chapter then explores to what extent statehood has changed in recent world politics by outlining the changing parameters of state sovereignty. The final section of chapter 1 introduces our theorization of global state-society relations and presents an overview of the cases that form the basis of our analysis. Our central cases include three of the largest conferences, including the 1992 United Nations Conference on Environment and Development (Earth Summit), held in Rio de Janeiro; the 1993 World Conference on Human Rights, held in Vienna; and the 1995 United Nations Fourth World Conference on Women, held in Beijing.

In chapter 2 we use these UN conferences as empirical "test cases" for the emergence and potential democratizing impact of global civil society. We find that NGOs have participated broadly at such conferences. They share many goals and offer diverse interpretations of important issues that often challenge states' own interpretations and interests. While the active presence of NGOs supports the potential of democratization at the international level, we find NGOs have faced significant opposition from states, especially when states interpret the issues of importance to NGOs as crucial to their own identities as states. Throughout all three conference processes—from the first drafts of working procedures, through the preparatory conferences (PrepComs) which negotiated conference agreements and action plans, to the final documents—governmental representatives continued to claim the sovereign rights of states to interpret and implement major issues according to national perspectives, denying the universal aspirations of much of global civil society.

In chapter 3, we use a regional case study of Latin American participation in the conferences to gain a perspective on our global findings. One criticism that has been made of some of the literature on global civil society is that it has tended to assume, without investigation, that state-society relations in the developing world will reflect, or progress toward, those of wealthier industrialized societies. Latin America's social, political, and economic characteristics bridge the developed/developing world dichotomy in many ways, making it an informative region in which to explore the presence and impact of global civil society. What we find is that despite some clearly regional dynamics, global civil society operates similarly in Latin America and at the global level.

In chapter 4, we show that, despite the wide range of issues states claim as subject to sovereign control, a comparison of the three conferences reveals three overarching sovereignty referents. Not surprisingly, independence in the use of economic resources emerged as one realm where states reserved the right to exercise sovereign prerogative. However, some states, particularly those where Catholic and Islamic belief is quite influential in the political sphere, also insisted on autonomous determination of national or cultural values. Finally, states debated the extent to which they would be accountable to international mechanisms. States invoked four dimensions of sovereignty while debating these claims. They were least willing to strike bargains on value-based claims.

Chapter 5 builds on and tests our exploration of UN conferences by turning to three more large-scale conferences: the 1994 International Conference on Population and Development, held in Cairo; the 1995 World Summit for Social Development, held in Copenhagen; and the 1996 Second UN Conference on Human Settlements (Habitat II), held in Istanbul. We assess whether states rely on the same sovereignty reference points as they had at other conferences, and whether such references became more or less prominent over time across the 1990s conferences. We see that sovereignty issues continue to shape NGO-state relations. As expected, sovereignty debates do indeed center on economic and cultural referents. The additional cases confirm that NGOs at the UN conferences of the 1990s exhibit an expanded global role, possessing more potential for independent agency and dialogue with states than at any time before. However, NGOs' agency is also shaped by the procedures and agenda that remain in the hands of states. We also find that money does not "change everything"; on issues of foreign aid discussed at the conferences, recipient states were not willing to have international agreements dictate the percentage of their budget dedicated to social programs. Few donor states were willing to bow to similar recommendations for the percentage of aid they should give for social needs.

Finally, chapter 6 presents our conclusions about the nature and impact of global civil society, particularly with respect to global democratization. We also summarize our findings about the nature of state sovereignty as revealed through state-society relations at the UN conferences.

This book provides a framework to analyze the nature of global civil society in the relatively self-contained world of the UN conferences. In doing so, it provides a basis from which to comment upon the extent to which democratization has taken place both within global civil society and in global state-society relations; and the impact that global civil society has had on perhaps the last realm of sole privilege for states, state sovereignty. Along with states, civil society actors at the global level are asserting their preferences, and basing the legitimacy of those assertions on the entitlements of those whom they claim to represent. The UN conferences have provided an arena, sometimes controversial, for negotiation of those preferences and assertions. In that contentious process, we find an exciting concentration of debate over the transnational basis of political claims and continued debate regarding the spheres of activity that are or are not reserved for state-based modes of action. Through the interactions there is a lot to learn about the nature of international politics and political claims in an emerging sphere where nothing less than enhanced democratic governance of the world is at stake.

CHAPTER 1

Global State-Society Relations

There is growing incongruity between the empirical evidence of global political actors and relationships, on the one hand, and the state-centric model of international relations, on the other. For several hundred years the ideal of the Westphalian nation-state system upheld a global politics based on the interaction, for good or ill, of sovereign territorial governments, with little room for other actors. But it is increasingly obvious that nongovernmental actors are claiming a larger role in global politics, and using their larger role to express both ideals and concerns that are not delineated by nation-state boundaries (Keck and Sikkink 1998; Smith et al. 1997; Wapner 1995; Sikkink 1993).

The most visible of the peaceful expressions of nongovernmental actors have come at the world conferences sponsored by the UN. From the 1970s until today, the presence of thousands upon thousands of nongovernmental organization (NGO) representatives at a wide variety of conferences has demonstrated their insistence on being present at moments of international debate over global issues. But of potentially greater importance, such representatives have sought an ever-increasing role in the process and outcomes of the negotiations. NGOs have sought inclusion from the beginning of the multiyear conference processes, often insisting on a modification of the UN rules that limit their conference participation. They have tirelessly lobbied governments—their own and others—on language for the final conference documents; they have sat quietly and listened, or loudly disrupted governmental meetings; and they have avidly used every opportunity to promote their own exchanges through expanding thematic, regional, and global networks.

States have not sat idly by during this upsurge of NGO activity. Whether through acceptance or rejection, it is clear that states have had to acknowledge the presence of new global actors. Some have actively promoted the inclusion of civil society actors. However, their inclusiveness has often been limited. State representatives have always possessed, and have often exercised, the option of excluding NGOs as debate approached issues perceived as impinging on state sovereignty. Beyond the traditional issues of economic development and military autonomy, these concerns have recently extended to social values. Human rights and gender relations, still perceived as domains in which states determine their very identities as states, have provoked the most conflict.

The increased visibility of NGOs and social movements at the international level along with states' continuing assertion of sovereign state prerogatives invite a thorough assessment of the current state of relations between states and other actors at the global level. It is undeniable that competitive and complementary actors crowd states' central position. But while the presence of such new actors is easily demonstrated, international relations scholars have debated their significance. Realists and their intellectual allies argue that states retain their central position; NGOs are a sideshow of international politics, if considered at all. At the other extreme, the literature on transnational relations asserts that global social interactions are important enough to represent a new sector of influence upon states—a "global civil society" circumscribing states' relative autonomy, or even creating alternate forms of global politics.

Our contribution to this debate comes from a more rigorous examination of its central subject. We argue that the concept of global civil society sets a more demanding standard for the evaluation of transnational political processes than has been applied in prior accounts of transnational activity. To provide a theoretical foundation for a systematic empirical assessment of transnational relations, the first section of this chapter develops the concept of global civil society.[1] To understand the impact of global civil society on world politics, the second section then examines the debate over its democratizing potential.

But in analyzing the changing dynamics of global state-society relations it is not only the concept and impact of "society" that demands more rigorous theorization. The characteristics of states cannot be left unexamined. In the UN conference venue, sovereignty is a unique resource that only states can mine for various purposes in defending their own positions and shaping debate. Some NGOs, on the other hand, find ways around this by using sovereignty as a legitimating benchmark. In other words, they ask sovereign states to act like states, with all the responsibilities that accompany the rights conveyed by sovereign status. We lay a basis for a deeper examination of how sovereignty is expressed in the course of the issue debates of the UN conferences in the third part of this chapter by starting with a review of the scholarly literature on state sovereignty.

The final section of this chapter turns to a discussion of our cases and approach to analyzing global state-society relations in the context of the UN conferences. The conferences of the 1990s followed a multiyear preparation process, with numerous preparatory committee meetings (PrepComs) and regional preparatory meetings for governmental delegations. In addition, each had significant NGO participation, both for lobbying the official conferences and for parallel nongovernmental conferences.[2] The conferences thus provided a forum for sustained debate and agenda setting on specific issues, as well as more general discussions of the role of nongovernmental actors and other principles of international organization (Fomerand 1996). In general, these conferences have been among the more open of formal international negotiations, both in terms of their agendas and in terms of the numbers and kinds of actors who participate. Specifically, NGOs have been more influential at these global conferences than in other UN settings (Willetts 1996:57-80). In other words, these conferences have been the settings for some of the most sustained recent challenges to traditional definitions of state prerogatives and interests. Comparing across different issue conferences allows us to identify and explain the form these challenges have taken and states' responses to them.

Global Civil Society

The presence of large numbers of non-state actors in international politics is now an empirical fact. Tens of thousands of nongovernmental representatives regularly attend UN conferences and summits, both to network among themselves at parallel fora and to seek direct impact on government-to-government negotiations. Yet even scholars who acknowledge this fact characterize the roles of those non-state actors in quite different ways. What is ultimately at stake in this debate are different understandings of the nature of global political processes and a possible global civil society. Part of the debate is an empirical one, as scholars struggle to map both the history and present occurrence of this phenomenon. The debate is also in part conceptual and theoretical, turning on differing interpretations of key concepts including civil society, democracy, and sovereignty. Although these concepts have been largely developed to discuss politics at the national level, we and other theorists of global civil society have relied upon them to aid in understanding international politics as well.

During the 1990s, the civil society concept moved to the forefront of a number of different research and analytic agendas, spurred by developments in world politics. In addition to the more-prominent presence of non-state actors in international politics, civil society was reinvigorated or even being created in Eastern Europe and Latin America (as well as in other parts of the globe) with the demise of various kinds of domestic authoritarian regimes there. Political theorists and philosophers responded by tracing the historical roots and debates surrounding the concept of civil society (e.g., Cohen and Arato 1992; Fine and Raj 1997; Hall 1995; Seligman 1992), while comparativists tried to map the rather complex new actors and relationships of transition politics onto these theoretical constructs (e.g., Diamond 1994; Friedman and Hochstetler 2002; Hall 1995; Pérez-Díaz 1993; Tempest 1997). Scholars of international relations have drawn heavily on such work in their own discussions of a possible civil society that transcends nation-state boundaries (e.g., Cox 1999; Wapner 1997, 2000).

Despite all of this analytic attention, serious differences remain on exactly how to define the object of study. While virtually all definitions include some notion of civil society as a voluntary associational sphere, the boundaries of what is included in that sphere are highly disputed. Perhaps the most common recent definition, which draws on the discourses and practices of the transitional experiences of Eastern Europe and Latin America, is one that identifies civil society as a third sphere, autonomous with respect to both market and state. Other definitions, however, draw in at least some parts of the other spheres. Both liberal and critical theorists often insist that economic forces and actors are central parts of civil society, although liberals simply grant that status to for-profit market actors as well as to other voluntary associations

(Pérez-Díaz 1993:56-58), while critical theorists see civil society as the site of a struggle between dominant and disadvantaged economic forces (e.g., Cox 1999). Another argument suggests that political arrangements and linking actors like political parties are so fundamental to the character of civil society that it is often difficult to understand the latter without considering the former (Foley and Edwards 1996); similarly, Antonio Gramsci argued that a hegemonic ideology could make state and civil society "practically indistinguishable" (Wapner 2000:269). These arguments are not only important to scholars. In the UN conferences we studied, NGOs and states also sparred over the definition of NGOs with real consequences for who was allowed to participate in NGO activities and to gain access to state actors.

Similar debates and divisions emerge among theorists of *global* civil society as well. Among theorists who speak of global civil society the most common definition is one that insists that this is a third autonomous sphere. Building on G. W. F. Hegel's vision of civil society as a free associational sphere, Paul Wapner (1995, 1996) asserts the existence of a world civic politics that is a public arena beyond the state. In this public sphere, politics emerges in power and knowledge, in acts of persuasion and understanding outside formal politics. In fact, Wapner reserves the label "civil society" for NGOs' political efforts that do not target states. Martin Shaw (1994) and Ronnie Lipschutz (1996) concur with this understanding, stressing the cultural mobilizing power of global civil society. Others, however, place economic actors within a global civil sphere (Cox 1999) or stress the ways in which the organizations of global civil society are themselves part of global economic relations (Colás 2002; Pasha and Blaney 1998). Finally, some see a set of non-state actors who are profoundly shaped by their relations with state actors and who find their primary importance in their ability to influence and interact with states (Willetts 2000).

We do not attempt to draw a final and consensual definition of the conceptual boundaries of civil society. The long history of the civil society concept means that there are theoretical antecedents and justifications for drawing the boundaries in a number of different places. The early theorists of civil society themselves conceived of it in remarkably different ways. In the current era, even if boundaries were analytically declared, numerous specific actors would be difficult to characterize because they inherently cross the boundaries—consider professional associations, for example—or because they cross the boundaries in practice, as when a nongovernmental organization accepts a government contract or when a union is linked to a political party. For our purposes, the crucial question about civil society is not how it is defined, but the impact that these voluntary associations have on world politics. This impact is quite clearly dependent on the interactions of voluntary associations with state and market forces, rather than simply a function of those associations' essential characteristics and unilateral actions.

Therefore, we begin here with the basic definition of civil society as a realm of voluntary association, more or less autonomous from state and market. Because our empirical focus is on the UN conferences and their parallel nongovernmental conferences, we concentrate on the boundary and interactions between state and civil society actors rather than the boundary between civil society and market actors. This focus does not imply that we think the civil society-market nexus is unimportant. In fact, the failure of the UN and the UN conferences in particular to address market-based social forces—and thus their implicit acceptance of a neoliberal market context—has already alienated some sectors of civil society. Some are choosing to redirect their attention from the UN to other fora that more directly confront dominant market forces and actors (Smith 2001a). Nonetheless, the stark contrast between the sometimes violent and dramatic street protests of Seattle and Genoa and the more placid and sustained engagements of state and society at the UN conferences further underlines the importance of understanding the latter: are these a desirable model for global state-society relations? If so, can they be replicated in some way in the more contentious economic sphere?

As we examine global civil society empirically, we are particularly concerned with the diverse set of nongovernmental and non-profit actors often simply called NGOs.[3] As Wapner (2000:268) says, "While the state system and the global economy provide a space for global civil society, as a phenomenon its existence rests on the activities of certain actors [NGOs] that actually constitute it and the quality of the relations that emerge between them." However, we think it is important not to assume that the simple presence of NGOs in the international system necessarily instantiates global civil society. In chapter 2, we outline a series of more specific empirical indicators that we believe are necessary in order to prove that a global civil society exists, and then to evaluate to what extent they are present at three major UN issue conferences of the 1990s. In this and in the subsequent chapters of the book, we also focus on the consequences of whatever global civil society does exist.

We envision at least three possible consequences of a more-developed global civil society. First, the new visibility and participation of non-state actors may have important implications for the democratization of global governance processes. Second, the development of global civil society may affect the nature of the state actors involved in world politics by limiting sovereignty. Finally, global civil society may have a substantive impact, with NGOs contributing to better outcomes in their issue areas of concern, whether they be environmental or human rights protection, the status of women, effective population policies, or a variety of other concerns. Because of our empirical focus on the UN conferences and on global civil society as a whole, in this book we extensively discuss only the first two proposed consequences of global civil society. At the UN conferences, negotiations among states and between states and NGOs provide ample evidence for assessing the extent of democratic processes and sovereignty claims and bargains. However, the actual impact on outcomes is a much longer-term process that would require substantially more issue-specific evidence and is beyond the scope of this book. The next two sections present some of the claims and debates about the potential impact of global civil society on global democratization and on state sovereignty.

Global Civil Society and Democracy

Like the concept of civil society, the related concepts of democracy and democratization have received new attention since the 1980s from political theorists and comparativists as well as from international relations scholars. Among democratic theorists, the 1990s brought a deliberative turn to understandings of democracy. As one of its proponents stated, "Increasingly, democratic legitimacy came to be seen in terms of the ability or opportunity to participate in effective deliberation on the part of those subject to collective decisions" (Dryzek 2000:1). Comparativists were once again inspired by the cases of the former Soviet bloc and Latin America to ask questions about the prerequisites of democracy and the conditions of its stability and deepening (e.g., Agüero and Stark 1998; Diamond et al. 1999). In international relations, observers questioned a "democratic deficit" in a wide variety of international institutions, from the European Union to the UN (e.g., Paolini, Jarris, and Reus-Smit 1998; Schmitter 2000), as well as in globalization processes as a whole (e.g., Held 1995; Rosow 2000; Shapiro and Hacker-Cordón 1999). At the same time, however, scholars recognized the capacity of NGOs and individual citizens to affect international politics (A. M. Clark 2001; O'Brien et al. 2000; Keck and Sikkink 1998; Rosenau 1997; Smith, Pagnucco, and Chatfield 1997; Willetts 1996). Jan Aart Scholte (2002) directly connects global civic activism and the question of democracy in global governance, delineating both the democratic possibilities of civil society and some of the characteristics that could cause it to fall short of that promise.

Although there is a long tradition of debate in numerous subfields about whether democracy rests in formal institutions and procedures or not, the debate about global civil society has advanced far enough that we focus on recent arguments relevant to that question among theorists of global civil society itself. These arguments address global civil society's potential impact on democratization at the global level and the nature of global democracy that might result. Two broad families of approaches assert that global civil society contributes to democratization at the global level. A third set of authors is more skeptical about this claim for a variety of reasons. The three approaches map onto the debates about the definition of civil society in interesting ways: one stresses developments among civil society actors themselves, independent of state and market actors; one stresses the changing relationship between civil society and state actors; and the skeptics of the third approach tend to focus on the relatively unchanged relationship between civil society and neoliberal capitalist forces.

Among theorists of global civil society, one of the most common visions of a potentially emerging global democracy suggests that NGOs alter political processes in fundamental ways, by adding a second sphere of governance to the one controlled by states (Wapner 1995, 1996; Lipschutz 1996). This alternative form of governance may transform the understandings of state actors as well as those of other parts of the public, but an impact on states is not required to call it governance or to call it political. The democracy that might be emerging, according to this conception, is akin to the deliberative turn of democratic theory, as it focuses more on deliberative and relational processes among citizens, outside of formal political systems and across nation-state boundaries. This international (Lynch 2000), global (Bohman 1998), or transnational public sphere (Guidry, Kennedy, and Zald

2000) is not free of conflicts and inequalities, but does allow civil society participants to directly engage each other, and even state and market actors, ostensibly outside the logic of profit and the boundaries of the state.

A second version of the kind of democratization associated with global civil society argues that the central contribution of NGOs to global politics lies in their (varying) ability to influence states and to find niches for taking part in international decision making. As Peter Willetts (2000:207) argues, "[t]he relationships between governments and international NGOs within intergovernmental organizations are a contribution to democratic global governance." In this view, governance continues to be largely associated with states and with their associated institutions, but NGOs help transform diplomacy in those realms with the unique bargaining resources and perspectives that they bring to international negotiations (A. M. Clark 2001). As they participate, NGOs may enhance the ability of states to govern (e.g., Raustiala 1997), fill diplomacy gaps that states cannot (e.g., Princen 1994), or operate as pressure groups to influence the content of state choices (e.g., Willetts 1996, 2000). Global democracy is reflected in the ability to formulate relations of accountability, representation, and citizenship between global civil society and formal political institutions above the nation-state level. Exactly how this will be done in a systematic way requires answering some fundamental questions, which David Held (1999:105) has succinctly articulated:

> At issue is the nature of a constituency (how should the proper boundaries of a constituency be drawn?), the meaning of representation (who should represent whom and on what basis?), and the proper form and scope of political participation (who should participate and in what way?). As fundamental processes of governance escape the categories of the nation state, the traditional national resolutions of the key questions of democratic theory and practice are open to doubt.

Theorists of global civil society argue that NGOs should be a part of the process of answering these questions and then actively engaged in a new global democratic politics with states, although they acknowledge that states often do not allow this (Knight 1999).

In contrast, a final set of scholars questions whether the emergence of NGOs as important new actors in international politics is likely to ever transform the international system in more democratic ways. The deepest skepticism comes from authors who argue that the failure of many proponents of global civil society to consider the economic positions and forces associated with new global civil society actors leads them to miss the inequality and alienation of the non-state sector (Macdonald 1994; Pasha and Blaney 1998). Frequently arguing from the perspectives of third world regions, they stress the exclusive and elite nature of global associational life: "Global civil society interactions reproduce the conflicts and contradictions of the domestic civil societies they emerge from, and also create new ones reflecting the dynamics of power at the international level" (Macdonald 1994:285). Undemocratic and unrepresentative itself, the participation and presence of global civil society cannot democratize the state system, according to these arguments.

The UN conferences we study here have been invoked as supporting evidence for all three of these arguments. John Dryzek (2000:130) and Iris Marion Young (2000:178), two prominent theorists of deliberative democracy, both cite the large mobilizations of the UN conferences as evidence of deliberative civic politics at the global level. Marie-Claude Smouts (1999:307–308) argues that the conferences show the new influence of civil society on states: "The proliferation of special conferences that devote part of their agenda to civil society and its major groups marks a basic transformation in multilateral activity. Henceforth the driving forces of civil society are involved in developing law; they have become incontrovertible partners in the elaboration, implementation and enforcement of recommendations that result from these big jamborees." Our own past work (A. M. Clark, Friedman, and Hochstetler 1998) raises doubts about whether NGOs have managed to use the UN conferences to democratize world politics, although we find the recalcitrance of states to be a key part of the explanation. In this book, we approach the question of the democratizing potential of NGOs at the UN conferences as an empirical issue, evaluating the evidence for each of these arguments.

Global Civil Society and Sovereignty

A second possible area of impact of global civil society is on its frequent target: the nation-state. Taking note of the real and potential influence of other global actors, scholars from varying theoretical perspectives have called for revisiting theories of sovereign state control (Sikkink 1993; Thomson 1995; Biersteker and Weber 1996; Litfin 1997). Few would argue today that sovereignty is a monolithic concept, or that states are the only actors to be considered in international politics. Instead, different dimensions of sovereignty are cataloged, debated, and revised. Moreover, these dimensions take on particular salience for scholars who have found that one dimension may well be traded off or compromised to capitalize on another in response to transnational challenges to state authority (Litfin 1997, 1998; Krasner 1999). For our analysis of the ways in which states assert, manage, and manipulate sovereignty at the global level, it is first necessary to review existing theoretical conceptions of sovereignty and to elaborate on the approach we will be using.

What is Sovereignty?

Sovereignty has been defined and redefined in the scholarly literature. Beyond the formal, juristic conception of sovereignty, which spotlights the international legal equality of states in the absence of formal overarching authority (B. C. Schmidt 1998:232), most definitions of sovereignty include some combination of internally and externally oriented attributes or capacities. The externally oriented components encompass states' relative freedom from outside interference, a negative feature rather than a positive ability to achieve a desired effect (Jackson 1990:27-28). On this view, states are defined by, and prize their legal independence from, other states, and will be reluctant to enter into binding agreements with them.

Internally, sovereignty is defined as a state's positive ability to act and to achieve the results it wants, especially within its territory (Jackson 1990:29-30). Scholars focused on the internal definitions of sovereignty have drawn on theories of the state in domestic politics, with references to pluralism (B. C. Schmidt 1998), postcolonial "quasi-states" (Jackson 1990), domestic preferences (Moravcsik 1997), the historical development of the state (Poggi 1990), and the state's implied link to a political community (Hinsley 1986). In all cases, as Stephen D. Krasner (1999) suggests, sovereignty is a complex affair that states achieve unevenly. At the domestic level, rulers coordinate and compromise internal aspects of sovereign control with actors in civil society.

Our observations confirm others' contentions that states negotiate between the two quite different positions of authority just described (e.g., Kocs 1994; Litfin 1998; Putnam 1988). On the one hand, the negative, juristic conception of sovereignty characterizes states' striving toward relatively autonomous action within the formal anarchy of the international system. On the other hand, states are accustomed to a role as centralized power-holders in domestic politics that may also play out internationally. In this capacity, at both domestic and international levels, states manage claims to sovereignty amid "a dense arrangement of disaggregated state and non-state actors interacting in a highly interdependent environment" (B. C. Schmidt 1998:238).

The dual image of sovereignty as expressed through external and internal dimensions raises the question of how to interpret and evaluate states' sovereign claims. Sovereignty status is partly descriptive and partly subjective. Which actors—states, or non-state actors (whether domestic or transnational), or both—bestow and withhold legitimacy on states' sovereign claims? Sovereignty must be assessed at least partly through how it is "performed" (Weber 1998), but the performance is reviewed by both states and domestic and transnational non-state actors. While earlier definitions of sovereignty have often focused on the legitimating relationship between states and their domestic civil societies, the role of actors from global civil society as potential legitimators of sovereign claims is not yet well documented or theorized.

Karen T. Litfin's conceptualization (1997), which finds sovereignty to be a composite of three dimensions—autonomy, control, and legitimacy—is helpful as a starting point. In this regard, the externally oriented aspect of sovereignty corresponds to a state's "autonomy," the aspect of sovereignty that connotes freedom in decision making relative to other agents. The internally oriented sovereignty concerns correspond to Litfin's "control": the state's power to execute its plans. Litfin adds legitimacy as a third dimension of sovereignty. This dimension asks which actors are socially recognized as having the authority to make, recognize, and enforce internal and external rules. The question of which actors participate in legitimating this authority merits further empirical examination in light of observations about the role of NGOs in international politics.

As corollaries to sovereign privilege, states have traditionally asserted that only fellow states may recognize one another's sovereignty, and that only states have the authority to participate fully in any global governance that may occur. Janice E. Thomson (1995) has argued that in practice states in large part do retain the ability to decide for themselves who else is sovereign and who has political authority within a territory. States have struggled to retain certain sovereign prerogatives while engaging in ever deeper dialogue with actors in global civil society. However, while a classic view of sovereignty suggests that states exist to guard the self-determination of distinct communities (Hinsley 1986:225), states' claims to sovereignty at the global level may also appear more or less legitimate based on an element of external, international social regard that autonomy, control, and even external, state-based legitimacy do not fully encompass.

We contend that it is important to recognize that sovereign legitimacy may in fact depend on two audiences: states and NGOs. Given the increasing influence of non-state actors on the development of international norms (Risse, Ropp, and Sikkink 1999; A. M. Clark 2001), states are not always able to define the extent of their sovereignty by themselves. To protect sovereign prerogatives states may cooperate internationally to box out societal actors, as Thompson suggest (1995), but others join with nongovernmental actors to express universal aspirations. In order to take into account this new potential source of legitimacy, we would suggest a fourth dimension to sovereignty: internal control, external autonomy, and legitimacy in the eyes of both other states *and* non-state actors. We will examine this multidimensional sovereignty empirically in chapters 2 through 5.

How Do States Claim Sovereignty in Global State-Society Relations?

The presence of multiple, interdependent, and potentially conflicting elements of sovereignty suggests that at times states may choose to trade one dimension of sovereignty for another—and not always under conditions of their own choosing. One example we find in this study is the trade-off between sovereign autonomy and control negotiated at the Rio conference whereby developing states agreed to limit their ability to make decisions over their natural resource use in return for monetary compensation from the developed world. Such choices, or bargains, will of course vary according to the issue at stake. If states are willing to strike bargains over sovereign prerogatives, we would expect to see such bargaining revealed at UN conferences. Because such conferences are among the more open of formal international negotiations, both in terms of their agendas and in terms of the numbers and kinds of actors who participate, they have been the settings for some of the more sustained recent challenges to traditional definitions of state prerogatives and interests.

Our Cases and Analytic Approach

The intense interactions between and among states and NGOs at the UN provide a microcosm of global state-society relations. As the UN enters its second half-century of existence, it continues to excite debate and controversy among scholars and political observers. James Rosenau catalogs twenty-three answers to the misleadingly simple question: of what is the UN an instance? (Rosenau 1998:253-255). The UN is both an intergovernmental organization of nation-states and an adaptive transnational organization that reflects emerging non-state-based values and interests (Cronin 2002; Rosenau 1998:255). As one result of its complex nature, the UN has been excoriated both for its international meddling at the expense of national sovereignty (e.g., Barr 2002) and for its inability either to act independently of, or to challenge the interests of, its more powerful members (Martin 1998). The variety of views of the UN also reflects the vast scope of its activities. It is one of the few social organizations outside of national governments that involves itself with security and economic growth concerns as well as issues of social concern as varied as educational practices, iodine deficiencies, human cloning, marital structure, pesticides, and genocide. These features of the UN, along with the simple fact that, like it or not, states turn to international organizations when they need to conduct common affairs (Abbott and Snidal 1998), support the argument that the UN will continue to reward in-depth study.

The highly visible global issue conferences supported by the UN have been called on an ad hoc, or nonroutine basis, and addressed a limited agenda within a single issue area (Willetts 1989:37). In the 1990s, nine UN conferences were held (see table 1.1). This book explores six of them. Because they addressed issues around which global social movements have arisen, we primarily analyze the 1992 United Nations conference on Environment and Development (Earth Summit), held in Rio de Janeiro; the 1993 World Conference on Human Rights, held in Vienna; and the 1995 United Nations Fourth World Conference on Women, held in Beijing. To assess our

Table 1.1 Major UN Global Conferences of the 1990s

Date	Title	Place
5-9 March 1990	World Conference on Education for All: Meeting Learning Needs	Jomtien, Thailand
29-30 September 1990	World Summit for Children	New York, United States
3-14 June 1992	UN Conference on Environment and Development	Rio de Janeiro, Brazil
14-25 June 1993	World Conference on Human Rights	Vienna, Austria
5-13 September 1994	International Conference on Population and Development	Cairo, Egypt
6-12 March 1995	World Summit for Social Development	Copenhagen, Denmark
4-15 September 1995	Fourth World Conference on Women: Action for Equality, Development, and Peace	Beijing, China
3-14 June 1996	Second UN Conference on Human Settlements	Istanbul, Turkey
3-17 November 1996	World Food Summit	Rome, Italy

(Source: UN 1998)

findings, we also use comparative information from three other conferences, the 1994 International Conference on Population and Development, held in Cairo; the 1995 World Summit for Social Development, held in Copenhagen; and the 1996 Second UN Conference on Human Settlements (Habitat II), held in Istanbul.

All of the conferences so far have shared similar goals and formats. A central focus of official business at each conference and at preparatory meetings leading up to the conference was the creation of a final conference document to be endorsed by state participants.[4] At regional preparatory meetings, governments developed regional positions on specific conference issues. Prior to each conference, a series of Preparatory Committee meetings (PrepComs) were global rather than regional, and focused particularly on drafting the conference document. The wording of the final documents was invariably the focus of intense politicking among states and between NGOs and states, which continued up to and through the final conferences.

Now that the decade of 1990s conferences is past, two nearly opposite interpretations have emerged. On the one hand, both observers and participants in the conferences have noted growing "summit fatigue." These concerns emerged with the disappointment at Rio+5, when the conference meant to mark five years of progress looked back on few new achievements since the 1992 Earth Summit (see, e.g., Sandbrook 1997). Such sentiments gained ground as ten-year anniversary summits for the 1990s conferences approached. Even the chair of the Rio+10 conference in Johannesburg, South Africa, in 2002 thought he was seeing the last environment summit of its kind (Meyerson 2002:1). In this view, the resources and time devoted to the conferences have not been repaid by the weak commitments to action that emerged from them.

The opposite point of view stresses the strong normative and agenda-setting functions of the 1990s conferences, which legitimated new ideas and actors rather than directly causing changes in state behavior (Haas 2002). Jacques Fomerand (1996:372) directly takes up the question of whether UN conferences are media events or genuine diplomacy, and concludes that "UN global conferences bring about new norms, new policies, and new modalities of action. They redefine problems by casting them in their global contexts and foundations. Their ultimate aim is to crystalize (*sic*) the existence of a majority will." Interestingly, this point of view has also caused some reluctance to hold additional conferences, as some advocates fear that government representatives might backslide on previously agreed norms and values. This has been the case for women's activists anticipating the ten-year assessments of the population and gender conferences (Center for Women's Global Leadership et al. 2003).

Our research starts out from the latter view that stresses the innovations of the conferences. While we acknowledge that large global conferences as a specific organizing phenomenon may be passing from the global scene, we focus on the conferences in order to understand more fully the new modalities of action and new actors that NGOs have represented in them. This includes addressing questions about the consequences of that NGO participation for broader global state-society relations and whether those consequences include the development of a global civil society and greater global democratization, as discussed earlier in this chapter. We believe that the consequences are likely to outlive the specific organizing framework of the UN conferences themselves, and may be a model for other kinds of global governance arrangements.

NGOs have not had standing equal to states in the UN conferences. But opportunities for issue influence and network building arose as soon as official preparations for the conferences began. NGOs attended both the preparatory and final conferences, some registering with the official conference and some not. A parallel NGO conference with a separate agenda, the NGO Forum, has been a feature of most UN conferences and their preparatory meetings since the 1972 conference on the environment in Stockholm. Supplementing the business of the Forum there was an extracurricular festival of NGO exhibitions and activities. In all of these ways, NGOs sought to influence the governmental agenda, to exploit news coverage of the event, and to carry on business among themselves.

As contributors to the wealth of transnational activity, NGOs are curious contenders for a role in international politics. Their most important claims for inclusion rest on norms of democracy and civic participation, which historically have been weak at the international level. The early UN institutionalized the ideal of social representation by creating a consultative status for NGOs within the Economic and Social Council (ECOSOC), but only 418 NGOs held this status in 1993 as the new UN conference cycle was getting underway (Bichsel 1996:241). Today, however, tens of thousands of NGOs participate in new ways, particularly during UN conference processes. Some avidly target intergovernmental politics as they lobby and help formulate, implement, and monitor the policies of states and intergovernmental organizations, while others supplement or eschew traditional political channels.[5] In practice, many NGOs adopt goals that straddle the division, coordinating dialogue with the grassroots sector *and* using lobbying tactics to target governmental and international policymakers.[6]

As just noted, our empirical investigation of the explosion of transnational NGO activity and states' responses to it seeks to answer three general questions. First, to assess the development and impact of global civil society, we ask how NGOs asserted a role for themselves as legitimators of, and participants in, global governance processes, and how states responded. Second, to assess the assertion of state sovereignty, we ask what kinds of sovereign claims states made at the conferences. Third, in a related vein, we ask what, if any, bargains were struck among the four dimensions of sovereignty when claims conflicted. These questions spotlight recent developments of global state-society relations from the perspective of state and non-state actors, and our research consequently is based on an analysis of textual representations and primary reports of their positions and agreements.

To answer the first question, it is important to analyze how NGOs sought a role for themselves in transnational negotiations vis-à-vis states and other NGOs, and how states responded to this assertion and, often, to NGOs' contestation of state positions. We rely on the public statements and private documents of NGOs, which express their assessments of states' claims, as well as the official documents of the UN and other primary and secondary sources, including participant observation in parts of all three conferences.[7]

To answer the second question, we rely on governments' public representations of their preferences throughout the conference processes. These are found in governmental representatives' plenary statements and in written, formal reservations to the final conference agreements. These sources are especially important for understanding the sovereignty claims specific states and groups of states make, and the responses of other states. Further evidence was gathered from secondary accounts and participant observation. We do not assume that such evidence constitutes the last word on states' views of sovereignty, but we do assume that it represents what the participants found fit for global consumption. Because global conferences show the most public faces of sovereigns and their critics, we may not be able to take their words at face value. But we can assume that they represent what the *participants want the world to believe* their priorities are, which means that states are likely to be especially conscious of how they construct the messages they send—as well as the precedent being set for later interpretations of sovereignty.

Finally, to assess the extent of sovereignty bargaining, we analyze primary and secondary accounts of conference negotiations and outcomes. We focus on evidence of diplomatic bargaining: negotiated verbal (and, in some cases, written) agreements in a public international forum that represent trade-offs among participants and their competing claims about sovereignty. The second step of converting those diplomatic bargains into substantive outcomes is beyond the scope of the present work, although we do offer some commentary on observed discrepancies between agreements and substantive outcomes. Evidence of sovereignty bargaining is to be found in the shifts, compromises, and refusals to yield on interpretations of state practices that make reference to sovereignty, in the process of arriving at the final conference agreements. Conference outcomes are the negotiated final texts and institutions created at the conferences. We assume, here, that they embody the sovereignty bargains that have (or have not) been struck by state actors.

CHAPTER 2

___

Global Civil Society:
Emergence and Impact

The day before the Rio conference opened, the international environmental group Greenpeace got the first word in by attempting to blockade the port of the Aracruz Celulosa company, a major Brazilian pulp producer and exporter. Hanging banners reading "Aracruz Plantations Kill Forests" and "Another Eco-farce," activists visibly contested Aracruz's top rating by the Business Council for Sustainable Development, a group of global executives seeking to promote the ecological responsibility of their firms. Instead, local Greenpeace activists used the opportunity of worldwide attention to environmental issues to hold the pulp producer responsible for destroying native forests and displacing native populations for over twenty years ("Earth Summit Battle Opened by Greenpeace," *Independent* 30 May 1992).

Nongovernmental organizations (NGOs) decided on the first day of the Vienna Forum, the NGOs' conference parallel to the official human rights conference, that they would refer to governments by name in their discussions of human rights violations. The decision, which threatened NGOs' permission to use the conference site because it flouted UN conference policy, dismayed conference organizers and created controversy among NGOs themselves. The Joint Planning Committee that was supervising Forum logistics bowed to the UN's decision to disallow preprinted copies of the Forum schedule because the schedule

31

named governments. The fact that the UN then footed the bill to print a "sanitized version" did not satisfy Forum participants, who protested that the UN had no right to intrude upon their independent activities (Inter Press Service Staff and InterNet 1993; Comeau 1994).

In the midst of the Fourth World Conference on Women, accredited NGO members from Latin America took over the central escalators in the Beijing International Conference Center. They were frustrated by the lack of effective discussion on the issue of economic development, and certain First World countries' reluctance to commit the material resources necessary to achieve gender equality. Holding up smuggled-in placards reading "Economic Justice Now!" and chanting "Justice!" "Justice!" they effectively blocked delegates' access to conference rooms and were immediately besieged by international media. Such demonstrations were strictly forbidden on UN premises.

As these anecdotes illustrate, nongovernmental organizations provided much of the color and controversy at the UN issue conferences of the 1990s. But what was the larger impact of NGOs' participation at these conferences? As shown in chapter 1, analysts have three distinct approaches to understanding the democratizing potential of an emerging global civil society. One approach focuses on the deliberative and relational processes among citizens across nation-state boundaries. A second sees the central contribution of NGOs to global politics in their influence over states and in their role in international decision-making. The third questions whether an inherently undemocratic global civil society can ever democratize the state system. In this chapter, we assess the extent to which any of these approaches approximates the actions of global civil society, using the rigorous definition of the phrase we present in the next section. The UN issue conferences on the environment, human rights, and women form our empirical domain for this assessment.

To describe the social relations among nongovernmental actors as *global* is to assume that the "complex network of economic, social, and cultural practices" forming global civil society is widespread enough that non-state actors from all over the world are involved in the interactions (Wapner 1995:313). Clearly, non-state representation that is geographically diverse is necessary in order to warrant the global moniker. This component speaks to one dimension of the emerging concerns about power and representation within the NGO community (Raustiala 1996; Willetts 1996). However global democratization is understood, the representativeness of NGOs is important for shaping the quality of the participation they provide.

The explosion in the number of actors is a minimal condition for the rise of global civil society, but deeper changes should be evident in the quality of nongovernmental access and proximity to global forms of governance. The *civil* component of global civil society connotes both regularized and open non-state participation in global interactions and NGO access to states and other NGOs. In other words, it cannot be assumed that greater numbers of non-state actors translate directly into more systematic participation in NGO-NGO discussions at the global level, or that states and international organizations uniformly respond to NGO "knocks" by opening the intergovernmental "doors." Examining to what extent "civility" is manifest among NGOs addresses the concerns of those who focus on the growth of a broad global community of non-state actors. Uncivil relations among NGOs would indicate that inequality still dominates their relationships and blocks development of a new democratic sphere of global networking. Examining to what extent civility is present in NGO-state interactions also speaks to the preoccupations of those who claim that NGOs' contribution to global governance must be assessed by evaluating their ability to influence states and state-based diplomacy. Here, the absence of vigorous civil relations at the global level would show limits to the democratization process in the state-based sphere.

Finally, the *social* component of global civil society presumes a quality of interaction among the relevant actors that goes well beyond the classic billiard balls analogy. Actors in society are actors in relationship with each other. These relationships are grounded in the presumption that participants "may care how they are regarded by others" beyond simple interest calculations (Lumsdaine 1993:25). In turn, they develop expectations of other participants and their actions. In relationship, they work toward developing common understandings of their relationship and of substantive issues, although complete agreement is not required for social relations. Once again, those concerned with democracy in a nongovernmental public sphere would be most concerned with the extent of sociability and common understandings among NGOs themselves, while those concerned with democratization of governmental spheres would focus on the understandings—or lack thereof—developed between states and non-state actors.

Bearing in mind these definitions, how do we empirically evaluate how "global" is the civil society we find participating in UN conferences? A newly *global* UN conference constituency should be reflected in the geographic diversity and numbers of nongovernmental participants in official and parallel UN proceedings.

The quality of *civil* participation can be determined by assessing the procedures governing NGO activity at global UN conferences. To regulate and channel increased participation and increased demands on the part of NGOs, we would expect, at a minimum, to see new rules facilitating NGO contributions as well as greater overall interaction. The indicators that we observe include matters such as conference accreditation, numbers of NGOs in attendance at the conferences, and the nature of contention over NGO participatory status.

We seek evidence of the quality of *social* interaction in current transnational politics by examining the substantive content of NGO participation, with the expectation that common understandings are developing both among NGOs themselves, and between NGOs and states. To what extent have NGOs at UN conferences been able to change the agenda and understandings of governments at those conferences through their participation? Do NGO achievements at the 1990s UN conferences show that a common society has emerged in the form of new networks and understandings among previously separate NGO actors?

While the global criterion is comparatively straightforward and easy to assess, our approaches to the civil and social dimensions require further explanation. Drawing on domestic theories of social movements (Traugott 1995; McAdam, McCarthy, and Zald 1996), we use the concept of *repertoires* to analyze the civil dimension of global civil society, and approach the social dimension through an examination of competing and coinciding *frames* used by participants.

The evolving NGO repertoire reflects the changes in state expectations about the NGO role. A repertoire is "not only what people *do* when they make a claim; it is what they *know how to do* and what society has come to expect them to choose to do" (Tarrow 1995:91). While UN conferences must use NGO consultative status to the UN Economic and Social Council (ECOSOC) as a baseline for NGO participation, in each conference process the specific rules for NGO attendance and involvement, controlled in the end by states, are freshly negotiated. At the same time, the NGO repertoire in all issue areas increasingly includes a "parallel repertoire" of NGO-to-NGO interactions, beyond that sanctioned by governments. To assess the impact of repertoire change on the "civility" of transnational relations, after tracing the NGO repertoires themselves we also investigate patterns of government responses to the different NGO repertoires.

We assess the social dimension by examining the frames used by different participants in the conferences to describe and motivate their own or others' participation. A frame is a concept that refers to a pattern in participants' beliefs about the causes of and solutions to contested issues (Snow and Benford 1992:137). The meanings, and thus the substance, of a particular issue are actively created and dynamically reinforced by the frames that participants use. In the milieu of a UN conference there will be varying degrees of alignment between the frames being used by different participants. The development of common frames suggests more complete democratic relations among NGOs and between NGOs and states. If there is a development in social relations, we would see similar or related patterns of understandings from the governments in the different conferences, not only among the NGOs themselves. Alternatively, differences in NGO input, participation, and reception at the conferences may suggest an incomplete shift to a coordinated "society." Thus our analysis of the substance of NGO participation asks to what degree NGOs have managed to construct a shared frame among themselves and, then, to what degree their participation in UN conferences has helped to realign the frames of governmental participants with their own.

Table 2.1 summarizes these definitions and their empirical indicators.

At the UN conferences, we found that of all the components in

Table 2.1 Global Civil Society: Empirical Indicators

Term	Definition	Empirical Indicator
Global	Geographically diverse and balanced representation	Number of NGOs from different world regions
Civil	Regularized participation in global interactions; NGO access to global forms of governance	Procedures and repertoires
Society	Existence of social regard; mutual behavioral expectations; shared substantive understandings	Substantive understanding and shared frames

our definition of global civil society, the global component was most nearly achieved. By the 1990s conferences, NGO participation was much more widespread than at earlier conferences, although Northern NGOs still dominated many interactions among NGOs and were numerically overrepresented. With respect to civility, we found NGOs embodying exactly the two alternative roles identified by scholars (see chapter 1): some focused on networking with other NGOs in an alternative global public space, while others, which we call lobbiers, sought to influence governments. States offered the lobbiers some new channels for participating in the 1990s conferences, but also set arbitrary limits to their participation; the networking took place at parallel NGO fora largely ignored by states. Thus there were clear advances in global civility compared to earlier UN conferences, but both states and some non-state participants resisted the development of democratic interaction anticipated by some theorists. Interactions among NGOs showed some development of social relations, and the possibility of a democratic public sphere of shared understandings beyond the state. However, states were slow in acknowledging the existence of this sphere, and strongly reasserted their sovereignty as unique global and national decision makers.

Global Civility? The Changing Repertoires of NGO Participation in UN Conferences

From the late 1960s to the 1990s, there were significant advances in both the quantity and the quality of NGOs' participation in UN thematic conferences. Less than 300 NGOs attended the Stockholm Conference on the Human Environment in 1972 (Morphet 1996:144, footnote 35). In 1992, 1,400 NGOs registered with the Rio conference, and 18,000 NGOs attended the parallel NGO Forum (Weiss, Forsythe, and Coate 1997:239). Only 53 NGOs in consultative status sent representatives to the 1968 Tehran International Conference on Human Rights, and four others attended at the invitation of the conference Preparatory Committee (United Nations 1968:Part I: Para. 2, and Annex I, Parts V, VI). For the 1993 Human Rights Conference in Vienna, a UN source lists 248 NGOs in consultative status and 593 as participants (United Nations 1993i:908); NGO reports estimated that 1,400 to 1,500 NGOs attended.[1] At the 1975 Mexico City Conference for International Women's Year, 6,000 people attended the NGO Forum and 114

NGOs gained access to the official conference; at the 1985 closing conference of the UN Decade on Women in Nairobi, 13,500 people registered for—and many more attended—the NGO Forum, and 163 NGOs were accredited to the official meetings. Ten years later over 30,000 people attended the Beijing NGO Forum, doubling previous attendance records. But equally as impressive, 3,000 accredited NGOs gained access to the UN Fourth World Conference on Women, an increase of 2,500 percent in twenty years (Fraser 1987; United Nations 1996c).

Beyond their expansion in sheer numbers, NGOs from all three issue areas also became increasingly involved in every stage of the conference process. The types and goals of NGOs expanded, along with the increases in size and extent of NGO participation. More NGOs representing local interests and NGOs from the developing world were able to take part in the processes. For example, NGOs from Latin America were overrepresented with respect to their share of global population at two of the three 1990s conferences (see chapter 3). Partly due to this broader representation, the repertoires of NGOs expanded. While some focused on lobbying the official conference proceedings and affecting its documents, others deliberately used the UN conferences as a convenient locus for networking with other NGOs.

After an overview of NGO participation in early conferences, the remainder of this section focuses on the differences among NGOs over their ideal procedural involvement, as well as the changes that occurred in the forms of both lobbying and networking strategies in the 1990s. Finally, a section on governmental responses to NGO strategies show that while inroads were made, governments were unwilling to allow broad NGO participation, especially when it seemed to threaten their dominant position in negotiations. Thus, the procedural element of a democratic global civil society has yet to be firmly established through shared state and NGO expectations concerning procedures for participation and access.

Early Conferences

At the early UN conferences NGOs had a limited ability to lobby governments. At the 1968 International Conference on Human Rights, the few NGO representatives who attended were observers only. The then-nascent international human rights community lacked lobbying experience on human rights themes at the UN, but human rights NGOs in consultative status formed a coalition to publicize the need for international human rights protection (Tolley 1994:107-108). Amnesty International, for example, was focused mainly on campaigning for the release of individual prisoners of conscience rather than on affecting UN policies. At early conferences on other themes, the repertoire of NGO participation was also markedly small when compared with current roles. On the environment, governments gave primarily scientific and technical NGOs a role to play. Certain hybrid NGOs—part governmental and part nongovernmental—attached to the UN Educational, Scientific, and Cultural Organization (UNESCO) helped draft and negotiate preparatory conference documents at Stockholm (Morphet 1996:116-125). In the Women's Decade conferences, NGO participation was initially limited in size and few NGOs made official interventions.[2] NGOs were not involved in preparatory processes leading up to Mexico City and Copenhagen; however, they were included in both national and regional preparatory conferences for Nairobi (Stephenson 1995).

In the final official statements of the early conferences, governments recognized NGOs not for their contributions to the conferences, but for their ability to help implement conference recommendations through education and publicity. The 1972 final environmental documents referred to NGOs in their educational role or as specialty groups on single issues (see Appendixes II, III in Rowland 1973). The documents from the first women's conference in Mexico City also mentioned the educational role of NGOs (United Nations 1975:27, 185). The Proclamation of Tehran did not mention NGOs, although in a resolution on measures to eliminate racial discrimination, the conference appealed to NGOs and the media to publicize "the evils of *apartheid* and racial discrimination" (United Nations 1968:7, Res. III).

Despite their limited lobbying capacity at the official conferences, NGOs did engage in forms of collaborative activity to develop both relationships among themselves and joint positions vis-à-vis governments. Prior to Tehran, both lobbying and networking opportunities were somewhat limited, but there were seeds of NGO organizing on both fronts. In 1965 at the UN, a committee of human rights NGOs possessing consultative status in the ECOSOC began meetings to prepare for Tehran. There was no NGO forum in Tehran, but an independent de facto network of groups separate from the UN committee came together in 1968, in anticipation of the conference. This coalition of 76 NGOs and 50 independent experts drew up NGO recommendations for the official conference. Both groups were coordinated by the former Irish diplomat Sean MacBride, who held simultaneous leadership positions in two major human rights NGOs.[3]

At the 1972 Stockholm environmental conference NGOs held their first parallel forum, concurrent with the official governmental conferences (Willetts 1996:67). Similar to all later NGO fora, the first parallel conference gathered a wider variety of NGO participants than did the official conference. One observer characterized the Stockholm NGOs as "a colourful collection of Woodstock grads, former Merry Pranksters and other assorted acid-heads, eco-freaks, save-the-whalers, doomsday mystics, poets and hangers-on" (Rowland 1973:1). These NGOs were quite different from the more sober and scientific NGOs contributing to the official documents. Also presaging future NGO fora, participants in the Stockholm parallel conference spent much of their time simply getting to know each other, which precluded much impact on the official conference outcomes.

The NGOs attending the fora at the three conferences of the UN Decade on Women also brought together a diverse set of participants. The women's fora provided a kaleidoscope of activities from artistic performances to prayer meetings. At Mexico City and Copenhagen, vigorous political debates often overtook discussions of women's common concerns. By Nairobi, the increased representativeness among participants—and the shared conference history of some—allowed for more expanded and integrated dialogue in the hundreds of workshops and meetings held.

NGO Differences over Repertoires in the 1990s: Lobbying vs. Networking

By the 1990s, NGO participation had expanded in both the official conferences and parallel fora to the point that NGOs were divided over the procedures that they should follow: lobbying or networking? NGO lobbiers would spend much of their time at the site of the official conferences, participating in meetings or haunting the hallways around the meetings from which they were excluded. The NGOs more interested in networking, or without official accreditation, took advantage of the fertile ground for NGO exchange provided by the fora. The strongest, most active, and most effective lobbying organizations came from the North, while the South, often represented by Latin American groups, spearheaded the NGO networking.[4] In the words of one NGO newspaper, writing about Rio, "the Africans were watching, the Asians listening, the Latin Americans talking while the North Americans and Europeans were doing business" (Terra Viva, No. 12, 15 June 1992, *Earth Summit: NGO Archives*). In general, the lobbiers' and the networkers' repertoires were mutually interdependent, although not always harmonious.

Each side of this division was split on its views of the other. Some on each side viewed each of the roles—accepting the boundaries set by governments and pushing them—as necessary complements. Others on each side had much more critical views. For example, although lobbiers at Rio made a concerted effort to represent a wide range of geographic positions, some of the lobbiers saw new participants, who tended to focus on networking, as "lost in the process," distracting, and, above all, potentially threatening the access of all NGOs to the conference process (Centre for Applied Studies in International Negotiations Issues and Non Governmental Organizations Programme 1992a:10). Some of the networkers saw the lobbiers as legitimating an illegitimate process and wasting time and resources on useless governmental proposals (Finger 1994). Many of these individuals did participate in some of the lobbying activities, but they tended to spend more time discussing issues that had been left off the governmental agenda. They set up various kinds of NGO-meets-NGO activities, like dialogues between Northern and Southern NGOs. Unlike the lobbiers, networkers justified these alliances in and of themselves rather than as a strategy to influence governments. While the networkers did not use the exact language of those theorists who posit a "deliberative" global civil society outside the realm of state-focused interaction (Lipshutz 1996; Shaw 1994; Wapner 1995, 1996), they shared the same vision of an international political arena of debate and persuasion not subject to state-controlled negotiations.

NGO Networking: Expanding the Parallel Repertoire

The networking repertoire of NGOs could be summarized as a process parallel to government negotiations, involving NGO-to-NGO policy discussion supplemented by informal networking. Each NGO forum produced its own formal statement, had its own program and newspaper (or newspapers), and offered a multitude of activities for daily visitors. Workshops and other participatory activities and educational displays formed part of the common repertoire of NGOs.

At Rio, computer records tallied 450,000 daily visitors over the 14-day celebration (Yole 1992:8, *Earth Summit: NGO Archives*). Participants selected from 350 scheduled meetings and even more informal gatherings sponsored by a wide array of environmental, educational, business, and religious organizations. They could visit the Kari Oka village, an indigenous village constructed at the edge of the Tijuca Forest in Rio, add a leaf-shaped pledge to make a positive contribution to the environment to the "Tree of Life," be a delegate to the International NGO Forum—Commitments for the Future, which held daily discussions, or learn ecological bodysurfing. Visitors could also watch the official daily conference proceedings on closed-screen television. The newspaper *Da Zi Bao* celebrated the many voices of the NGO community by simply publishing short "environmental personals ads" contributed by NGOs attending the conference. In issues of the newspaper with titles like "Tropical Fruit Salad" or "Rebuild Civilization," participants announced meetings, told stories, exhorted each other to action ("When governments fail to govern for the benefit of life on earth, GOVERN YOURSELF!"), and demanded the removal of furniture with sponsor Coca-Cola's insignia.

In Vienna, groups crowded the basement halls of the Austria Centre, the official conference center, with their displays, and expanded into an adjoining outdoor pavilion. According to one estimate, approximately 255 NGOs held about 400 "parallel events" at Vienna, in which nearly 3,000 people participated (Nowak and Schwartz 1994:5, 7). This produced "a hive of activity," covering "everything from rape to racism; development to democracy; self-determination to sisterhood, nationalism to networking; communication to children; Bosnia to Burma; [and] Cuba to China," with multiple music, dance, and theater offerings in the evenings (Samuel 1994:60). NGO workshops vied with one another for inadequate meeting space, with double-booking of rooms and a lack of chairs a frequent problem.

Every forum associated with the women's conferences held workshops whose numbers (and issues) multiplied at an astonishing rate. In Mexico City (1975) there were 192 sessions in all; by Copenhagen (1980) 150 were held each day; at Nairobi (1985) there were a total of 1,200; and at Beijing there were 3,340, an average of 371 per day (Fraser 1987:60, 147, 199; Chow 1996:187). These covered a wide range of topics, ranging from economy to spirituality, and included meetings diverse as "National & International Armed Conflicts & Their Effects on Women," hosted by the Lebanese Council of Women; "Psychology & The Environment," held by the Mexican Academy of International Law and "Sound, Color, Movement: Exploring Wholeness Through Improvisational Arts," offered by the Children's Express and Women With Wings.

The most important results of the NGO activities not aimed at governments cannot be as easily quantified as the scheduled events. The format of these conferences, which brought literally thousands of NGOs together, facilitated face-to-face discussions, debates, and celebrations among very different nongovernmental actors from across the globe. As will be discussed in the section on "social" understandings these encounters were divisive as well as unifying among NGOs. But as NGOs lunched together, gathered in plenaries, and simply talked, the parallel fora proved to be especially intense loci of the world civic politics of persuasion and mobilization that some scholars anticipate as part of a global civil society. And as the NGOs went home to their many different homes, they took the insights of their global interactions with them, transforming national discourses and understandings as well (e.g., Friedman 1999).

NGO Lobbying: Expanding the Official Repertoire

NGOs began to push for an additional set of procedures at the early conferences, notably at the Stockholm environmental conference in 1972. The real strategic innovations came in the later conferences, however. NGOs in all of the issue areas expanded their procedural repertoire in the 1990s, but women's NGOs were especially creative. Many of the same NGOs, even small ones, attended multiple conferences. This suggests that cross-mobilizations and cross-references between the conferences may be an elusive source of regularity in NGO repertoires. Some of the shared lobbying strategies across conferences included participating in preparatory processes at the national and regional levels; coordinating lobbying on a daily basis at—and between—the official meetings; circulating information through conference-based newspapers; and increasing contact with official delegates and media representatives.

RIO: Environmental NGOs used several different strategies for influencing their official conferences. Many of them participated in their national and regional preparatory processes, following the UN General Assembly's directive to national governments to include NGOs (UN General Assembly Resolution 44/228). A few were even included as members of their national delegation to the official conference processes, giving them unprecedented access to, and information about, the conference negotiations. The vast majority of NGOs followed the process from a greater distance, however. They were allowed to distribute proposals and even speak in conference sessions—but only where and when governmental delegates permitted it.

These lobbiers began their days at the United Nations Conference on Environment and Development (UNCED) and its Prepatory committee meetings (PrepComs) with a strategy session, where they coordinated lobbying, debriefed each other on the previous day, formulated joint interventions, and discussed substantive issues. They set up working groups on each of the agenda issues of the conference and worked at influencing language and country positions on the formal documents. Fifteen different NGO-edited newspapers helped NGOs—and even government delegates—accompany the many rings of the Rio negotiations. They could turn to *Cross-Currents, the Earth Summit Bulletin,* or *Terra Viva* to find daily schedules and the status of ongoing negotiations, including exactly which documents were likely to be discussed at particular negotiating sessions. These newspapers carried interviews with prominent governmental decision makers and aimed to provide accurate information about governmental debates and positions. The first issue of *Terra Viva* (3 June 1992) at the Rio summit, for example, contained Conference Secretary-General Maurice Strong's analysis of the U.S. position on the biodiversity treaty, as well as an interview with the World Bank's Environment Department Director about the World Bank's positions on the funding issues still being hotly negotiated.

A major issue for the environmental lobbiers was how to incorporate the growing stream of NGOs. Only a few dozen NGOs attended the First PrepCom, but participants gradually increased through the process to the eventual total of fourteen hundred registered NGOs. Many new participants knew little about the process and what had been done so far, why some compromises were necessary, and so on. The lobbiers produced periodic reference books to bring NGO representatives up-to-date. But they worried that uninformed and inexperienced NGOs hampered their own influence efforts. In one direct confrontation during the Fourth PrepCom, fifty grassroots activists hijacked a formal reception that the U.S. Citizens Network had organized for the U.S. delegation, singing, shouting slogans, and confronting U.S. Ambassador Bob Ryan with criticisms of U.S. positions. A reporter noted, "A few MEMBERS of the Citizen's Network were quite pleased with the outcome, but some expressed reservations, saying that it could destroy their careful cultivation of the US delegation" (Chatterjee 1992a:25). At other times, experienced lobbiers felt a need to reassure newcomers, using the Earth Summit Bulletin near the end of the Fourth PrepCom to tell them that there would eventually be some agreement:

> As negotiations at this PrepCom come down to the final hours, the combination of stress, fatigue, and an unfamiliarity with the process of UN negotiations have led some observers to dramatize the state of affairs, as seemingly intractable as they may be. Word from veterans of these UN "cliff-hangers" is that collapse, despair and the "dark times" are just part of the process as played out here in the UN. . . . The style, they say, is that when "crunch-time" comes and a failure seems to be in the offing, the time is right for a deal to be struck. (Goree, Chasek, and Bernstein 1992:5-6)

The expansion of the lobbying process to include unprecedented numbers of NGOs was thus a learning process for both the newcomers and the UN veterans.

VIENNA: In the Vienna conference process, many of the larger and older human rights NGOs defended the principles of universality, interdependence, and indivisibility from possible retrograde movement, while pushing concrete proposals for better implementation of human rights measures. International NGOs had attended the regional NGO parallel forums in the lead-up to Vienna, where they and their regional counterparts coordinated and conducted initial lobbying efforts (cf. Azzam 1993:92-93). In a division of labor at the Vienna conference itself, the large international NGOs, already skilled at lobbying the UN, individually advocated particular proposals. For example, Amnesty International revived the idea of a High Commissioner for Human Rights who could oversee an integrated UN response to human rights violations; the International Commission of Jurists advocated the creation of an International Criminal Court on human rights (Nowak 1994:217).[5]

Human rights NGOs also coordinated working groups to discuss lobbying strategies during the official conference in Vienna, but their limited access to drafting meetings forced them to seek alternative sources of information. Amnesty International "mounted a constant 'guard' outside the drafting meetings," closely following progress on issues of concern (Cook 1996:195). When NGOs were excluded from drafting meetings, NGO representatives serving on official delegations also began to report regularly to their colleagues at the Forum, "gaining their input and involvement in turn" (Gaer 1996:59). Although some grassroots NGOs felt that the Joint Planning Committee (JPC), charged with making arrangements for the Forum, was too deferential to the UN hierarchy, the confabulation at Vienna allowed grassroots NGOs who attended the conference to become "familiar with the major players in the international NGO community" on their own. The recognition afforded by proximity made it easier "to connect without having to go through the JPC mafia," according to Reed Brody, then-representative of the Washington-based International Human Rights Law Group and member of the Liaison Committee that eventually replaced the JPC (Brody quoted in Human Rights Internet 1993).

BEIJING: Women's NGOs used all of the repertoires developed in the other conferences, and also innovated an additional set of strategies in the 1990s. Because of their experience with multiple conferences on their own theme (three instead of one), and the opportunity to engage in conference procedures on other themes between the 1985 and 1995 conferences on women, women's NGOs were exceptionally well prepared to engage in lobbying. They had been frustrated at conferences during the United Nations Decade on Women (1975-1985) because NGOs were neither involved in the crucial drafting stage of the main conference documents nor sufficiently organized at the conferences themselves. Women improved their lobbying in three ways between Nairobi and Beijing. First, they built coalitions through a caucus mechanism. Second, they participated "early and often" in preparatory meetings and in development of new preparatory strategies. Third, they increased contact with the media and with national delegations. Women's NGOs developed many of these innovations at the UN conferences on other issues.

Before Rio, the Women's Environment and Development Organization (WEDO) sponsored the largest-ever NGO preparatory conference for a UN meeting, with fifteen hundred attendees. It resulted in the Women's Action Agenda 21, a gender-sensitive lobbying document based on the official conference document drafts. One of the most important mechanisms to come out of the UNCED process was the establishment of the Women's Caucus, a lobbying group (with specific task forces) to channel women's demands at UN conference processes. It applied what became the highly successful strategy of assembling "precedent-setting" information from previous UN documents to support women's positions, to show how women's positions were built on accepted norms within the UN, not "new rights." Whereas individual NGOs had been limited in the past to presenting single position papers and lobbying individual official delegates, the Women's Caucus presented joint concerns to the conference as a whole (Chen 1996).

Before the Vienna human rights conference, women's NGOs and human rights organizations formed the Global Campaign for Women's Human Rights. This group of ninety NGOs focused on violence against women as a global human rights issue, working to make it a special theme of the conference (Bunch and Reilly 1994). The Global Campaign's efforts culminated at the NGO Forum with a Tribunal on Violations of Women's Human Rights, where women presented testimony of human rights abuses to a distinguished panel of judges. The Women's Caucus coordinated lobbying on women at Vienna and was able to make six plenary presentations at the official conference.

In advance of Beijing, women's own conference, women's NGOs used strategies developed at earlier conferences: large numbers participated in preparatory meetings, formed new caucus structures, and negotiated with national delegations.[6] WEDO coordinated a Linkage Caucus to advance gains made by women at prior UN conferences, and circulated three advocacy documents that served as the basis for NGO lobbying efforts. In Beijing up to fifty issue-specific caucuses met daily on conference grounds to discuss lobbying strategies. A group called the Equipo (Team), representing the major caucuses, coordinated a daily NGO briefing session. Despite their inability to make statements, NGOs were allowed to attend most of the meetings of the governmental Working Groups debating the text remaining to be negotiated. Since NGOs were kept out of many of the smaller, more sensitive negotiations, most lobbying was done in the halls, with more organized caucuses circulating draft language for the final document. Longtime working relationships with delegates, particularly NGO members who belonged to official delegations, facilitated communication. In addition, NGOs made fully one-third of the plenary speeches, in contrast to the Rio conference where environmental NGO representatives made only three speeches to the plenary. Some 67 percent of NGO recommendations on bracketed text were eventually incorporated into the final governmental document (Women's Environment and Development Organization 1995b). One area where NGOs led the way was in fulfilling their promise to make Beijing a "Conference of Commitments." Although governments refused to hold themselves accountable for promises made at the conference in the official document, NGOs did so by publicizing every promise made by an official delegate (Women's Environment and Development Organization 1995a).

Lobbiers at the Beijing official conference, while much more involved and successful than at previous women's conferences, still faced considerable difficulties. As at Rio, veteran lobbiers quickly grew frustrated with the difficulties of absorbing the huge influx of NGOs that had not participated in the preparatory process but that now wanted to join the lobbying efforts. The geographic separation between Beijing, site of the official conference, and its distant suburb of Huairou, the site of the NGO forum, exacerbated the distance between NGOs focused on networking at the forum and those focused on lobbying at the official conference. Moreover, the lobbiers at the official conference, like those at Rio, tended to be coordinated by Northern NGOs, who had disproportionate control over NGO resources such as paid personnel, travel funds, data, and computers, as well as the experience required to guide lobbying efforts. However, there were concerted efforts to integrate individual representatives of Southern NGOs in lobbying strategies.

Government Responses

If established lobbying NGOs had trouble incorporating the rising floods of NGO participants, governments were even less prepared for them. From Rio on, NGOs without ECOSOC consultative status could be authorized for accredited participation in the PrepComs. As a result of this potentially greatly increased access, the PrepComs turned out to be a major arena of contention over NGO participation. During the preparations for all three conferences, we identified a "Fourth PrepCom phenomenon." At this point in the process, the grudging government inclusion of NGOs changed to exclusion. In each case, the limitations placed on NGOs at the final and arguably most important Fourth PrepCom indicated the degree to which governments were still unwilling to legitimate global civil interactions when they most mattered: during the crucial final stages of drafting the conference documents.

RIO: The level of NGO admission to the official environmental conferences diminished over the course of preparations. At the early PrepComs where the discussions focused on procedures, the meetings were formal and NGOs had access.[7] As the actual summit approached, meetings became substantive and informal, with less NGO access. Task-oriented Working Groups at the PrepComs varied in the level of NGO access. The narrowing of participatory opportunities coincided with an increase in the number of NGOs seeking to participate as the conference drew nearer, leaving many quite frustrated. At the Third PrepCom for Rio, even the Working Groups that had been most liberal in terms of NGO access decided in the last week to keep NGOs out of informal negotiations—using the conference guards to usher them out—ostensibly to speed negotiations. When NGOs objected, they were told to consider their exclusion a "reprieve from terminal boredom" by governments who worried that an explicit discussion of NGO participation in the informal negotiation sessions would take too much time—and possibly result in even greater levels of exclusion (Goree IV et al. 1991:9-12). In the first days of the Fourth PrepCom, the chairs and coordinators of the governmental committees pledged to maintain free access to as many meetings as possible, but retained important blocks: NGOs could not speak at informal sessions and could not attend the country-to-country bargaining sessions of "informal-informal" meetings (*Earth Summit Bulletin* 3 March 1992:2-3). NGOs were frustrated by the exclusions, and lashed out at government delegations, but took the closures as a sign of their own impact:

> having cleared the ["]competence and relevance" hurdle, NGOs have spent a lot of money and time in following the UNCED process only to find that the UN is not ready to incorporate them in its workings and accept them as partners. The UN seems to feel that by allowing the NGOs into the corridors, it has created a Frankestein [*sic*], and that the monster is out of control. Hopefully, that is correct. (*CrossCurrents* 6-9 March 1992:4)

By the actual summit, there was little formal access to negotiations.

VIENNA: NGOs were also marginalized at the Fourth PrepCom

for the World Conference on Human Rights. Initial participatory capacities included the opportunity to observe, submit written statements, and make oral statements at the discretion of committee chairs (Nowak 1994:208). But at the April 1993 Fourth PrepCom, where governments were unable to complete the task of drafting a Final Statement in preparation for the conference, Asian governments led an unabashed effort to limit the NGO participation arrangements for drafting at the upcoming conference itself. The Western and East European delegations came to the actual conference with instructions to permit NGO participation in the conference drafting committee, an arrangement that the Asians continued to oppose (Guest 1993:173). The Latin Americans and Africans were said to be "leaning towards NGO participation" as the discussions progressed (Ibid.). According to a contemporaneous report, those governments were wary that the conference would lose credibility if NGOs were barred from substantive participation; and for their part, "NGOs from Latin America and Asia made it clear that they [would] not let their governments exploit their presence to claim credibility for the conference, and then bar them from participating" (Ibid.:175). NGOs, nerves raw over the Joint Planning Committee's decision to give in to the UN policy that the human rights abuses of individual governments should not be mentioned in the Forum program, could not agree to use the JPC as a formal channel to lobby governments in unison over the issue of drafting participation (Ibid.). In a compromise, NGOs were permitted to observe plenary sessions and to make presentations to the Drafting Committee, but were excluded from even observing actual drafting (Azzam 1993:95). Access to the Drafting Committee, characterized by one observer as "without a doubt the most important committee at the Conference" (International Commission of Jurists 1993:110), would have permitted NGOs to observe individual governments' positions, but now they were effectively excluded from meetings where the real work occurred (Cook 1996:192).

BEIJING: Exclusion also characterized the later stages of the Beijing preparatory process and threatened to mar the World Conference on Women itself.[8] In the General Assembly resolution on NGO accreditation for the preparatory process (UN General Assembly Resolution 48/108), the degree of government ambivalence was indicated by the fact that NGO participation in the official conference was not mentioned. At the Fourth PrepCom in New York in March 1995, NGOs were again effectively excluded from the real work of the meeting, since most of the discussions on text took place in closed sessions. The conference Secretary-General, Gertrude Mongella, was said to have described the arrangements as a situation in which "the delegates, as hosts, invited the NGOs into their sitting room, but then disappeared into the kitchen to cook, keeping their guests waiting and hungry" (*ENB* 10 April 1995). NGO members from across the world hurriedly sent out faxes and email messages condemning their lack of access to the meeting and asking for allies to put pressure on their governmental delegations to the concurrent ECOSOC meetings. In an unprecedented use of its assembly procedures, ECOSOC challenged the conference delegations' exclusion of NGOs. Meeting in New York, it adopted a declaration on the matter halfway through the Fourth PrepCom that extended the NGO application period for accreditation, gave NGOs the chance to appeal denials, and held that NGO conference participation rules should match those of the PrepComs (United Nations 1995a).

To varying degrees, the governmental obstacles to NGO participation at drafting sessions continued throughout the official conferences themselves. Accredited NGO representatives did have access to some of the larger Working Group sessions, set up to hammer out the remaining differences over issues in the final documents left unresolved in the preparatory process. But as with the PrepComs, the more delicate the negotiations, the more exclusionary the meetings. NGOs rarely were able to attend the so-called informal sessions at which the most contentious language was argued over by those countries with most at stake.

Governments also had an impact on NGO-focused networking. Host governments struggled with the logistics of the rather unwieldy parallel fora, although national and international NGOs did most of the planning and fund-raising with the UN Secretariat. The Chinese government threatened to throw planning for the women's NGO Forum off course altogether. In moves that observers attributed to a fear of radical activism and criticism of its human rights record (Zheng 1996:196), the government not only delayed visas for many participants in the women's NGO Forum until the last minute (or after) but also switched the site of the Forum from Beijing to Huairou a mere four months before the conference. The switch was justified by the dubious claim that the Beijing site could not support the expected number of participants. The new site, an hour's drive from the capitol, was never finished, did not provide meeting spaces that could accommodate more than fifteen hundred people at a time, and located meeting rooms far from each other or in flimsy tents that collapsed under the constant rain (Morgan 1996).

The Brazilian and Austrian governments proved to be more willing hosts. The Brazilian national government focused nearly all of its attention on the official conference, neither interfering with nor doing much to support the parallel conference. Although the Rio Forum site was also an hour's trip from the official conference, its setting was the much more congenial and centrally located Atlantic beaches of Rio de Janeiro. The human rights Forum was conveniently held at the Austria Centre, the same building as the official conference.

Nonhost governments had a variety of responses to the parallel fora. Some dismissively focused on their colorful and festive qualities, seeing them as not very serious sideshows to the governmental negotiations. Others recognized their power, as either a negative or positive force. The Chinese government and other governments that felt the sting of NGOs' willingness to name names and to forego diplomatic niceties sometimes reacted with angry counterattacks. For example, the Malaysians and a Brazilian General lashed out at NGOs for their open criticisms of those governments at the third environmental PrepCom (CrossCurrents, 1991: Nos. 4, 10) Other governments, in contrast, credited NGOs with putting the conference issues on the global agenda: Brazilian President Fernando Collor credited the "determination and even . . . the sacrifices made by nongovernmental organizations" for advancing the cause of environment and development in his closing statement, before characterizing the parallel NGO forum as "a great and magnificent event" (United Nations 1993e:Vol. II:61).

In sum, NGOs broadened their repertoires for participating in the UN conference processes, establishing a relatively shared notion of "civil" procedure—at least among themselves. NGO privileges and substantive access were trimmed at the whims of governments. For Rio, the trimming went on as preparations progressed, while the Vienna preparations exhibited a fairly stable openness until the last PrepCom considered upcoming conference privileges. At Beijing, ECOSOC resolution procedures external to, yet binding upon, the conference proceedings were used to protect the gains that had been made. Thus states excluded NGOs from negotiation over the most important formal outcomes of the conferences—the final statements—and hindered NGO-to-NGO interaction. The changes from the 1970s to the 1990s notwithstanding, govern-

ments still refused to allow substantial democratization of the procedures of the conferences.

Global Society? The Substance of NGO Participation

Despite the undeniable profusion of nongovernmental actors
and activities at UN conferences, there is much less consensus on
the long-term consequences of these global interactions for the substance of international politics. In this section, we evaluate the
ways in which the participants framed or interpreted NGO participation and the substantive content of their participation. First, we
assess the extent to which NGOs themselves have constructed
shared frames—or find themselves acting "socially"—with regard
to the substance of their issues and the nature of their role. This
framing is based on considerable agreement, though unaligned
frames remain to some degree based on geographic (and geostrate-
gic) differences. The sustained debate among NGOs supports the
argument that a parallel political sphere of democratic deliberation
is emerging alongside the political sphere dominated by states. Second, we analyze the governmental framing of the NGO role and
state-society relations, as shown in the official conference documents and in governments' treatment of NGOs. This framing continues to manifest state dominance over key sovereignty-related issues, casting doubt on whether states and NGOs find themselves in
a democratic sphere of global governance, and on whether NGOs
have achieved the influence over states that some desire.

NGO Frame Alignment across Issue Areas

One potential area for shared frames between NGOs lies in the
substantive content of each issue network's agenda. In other words,
to what extent have the substantive concerns and frames of each of
the NGO issue networks been incorporated by the others? The answer to this question shows two levels of frame alignment. On the
one hand, there are close two-way connections between women's issues and each of the other two issues. On the other hand, environmentalists and human rights activists, while not antagonistic, did
less to incorporate each other's concerns into their own more specific agendas at global conferences.

ENVIRONMENT-WOMEN: The earliest documented conference
link between environmentalists and women's activists was in

Nairobi in 1982, when the United Nations Environment Program held a special meeting to evaluate the achievements of Stockholm, ten years after the conference. Although this was not a global conference on the scale of Stockholm or Rio, about a hundred NGOs met to accompany the process. A women's caucus met twice, and established a network "to increase the involvement of women's organizations in environmental issues" (ELCI Global Meeting on Environment and Development for NGOs—Nairobi, nd). The ongoing caucus raised women's issues for environmentalists at the 1982 meeting, and then immediately followed up by raising environmental issues at the women's conference in Nairobi three years later. The caucus was aided by environmentalists from the Environment Liaison Centre International (ELCI), an international organization of environmental NGOs permanently located in Nairobi.

After a decade of such cross-mobilizations, the 1990s conferences show quite a bit of mutual influence. In their final documents, environmental NGOs stressed the specific needs and resources of women, while women made environmental justice one of the rallying cries of the Beijing Forum. The women's tent at Rio, Planeta Femea, was among the most crowded with fifteen hundred people registered there (Centre for Applied Studies in International Negotiations Issues and Non Governmental Organizations Programme 1992b:25), and environmentalists and indigenous activists organized busy workshops at Beijing. Many participating NGOs, such as WEDO, made the distinction between environmental and women's NGOs irrelevant by being both.

HUMAN RIGHTS-WOMEN: Similar kinds of ties have also developed between human rights activists and women's rights activists. Ongoing relationships between key players within large human rights groups and women's rights activists in different countries had solidified in the late 1980s, and were bolstered by conference preparations for Vienna (Keck and Sikkink 1998:183). This fostered the mainstreaming of women's rights within human rights discourse and action, leading to the emergence of the women's human rights movement (Friedman 1995:25-27).

Women's organizing at Vienna was mirrored in the preparations of human rights organizations for the Beijing Conference on Women. To coincide with the Beijing conference, two major international human rights organizations staged campaigns and issued publications on women's human rights.[9] By this time, "women's rights as human rights" had become a dominant frame for NGOs in both issue networks. The NGO documents from both conferences show substantial cross-fertilization: for example, one of the "Strategic Objectives and Actions" of the Beijing Platform for Action is the "Human Rights of Women."

ENVIRONMENT-HUMAN RIGHTS: Between environmentalists and human rights activists, the connections are much looser. Among environmentalists, indigenous activists have been the most frequent users of rights language. "Human Rights and International Law," for example, was the first section of the final document of the World Conference of Indigenous Peoples on Territory, Environment, and Development, held in Rio immediately before the UN conference (Kari-Oca Declaration 1992), but other NGO declarations written during various parts of the environmental NGO Forum were less focused on human rights. In less formal activities, the Sierra Club Legal Defense Fund sponsored an all-day seminar on human rights and the environment at Rio.

Conversely, the atmosphere of attack on basic human rights assumptions at Vienna was not conducive to an ambitious expansion of the concept of human rights. Human rights NGOs on the lobbying front anticipated the difficulties and steeled themselves to defend existing rights (Riding 1993a:11). Some environmental issues pertaining to the right to development were considered at Vienna, but no working group at Vienna's NGO Forum focused solely on environmental issues.[10]

NGO Frames on Global State-Society Relations

In over three decades of participation in UN issue conferences, NGOs have fashioned one clear, shared, presumption about their participation: they have come to see themselves as an irreplaceable part of the conference process—and of global politics itself. Their self-perceived importance resides in their role as monitors of, and/or alternatives to, governments they consider unlikely to resolve global problems. In the issue areas of the environment, human rights, and women, NGOs view governments as among the causes of current problems while they themselves are a part of the solution. As the Vienna NGO Forum report concluded, "in the face of government inaction or duplicity . . . it was up to NGOs to take a stronger stand" (Nowak 1994:105).

For many NGOs, this conclusion led to the corollary that governments need to be monitored by NGOs. The frame has long been shared by human rights NGOs, and was evident in the preparations for Vienna. Amnesty International, for example, adopted the assertive theme, "Our World: Our Rights," for its publicity materials, and prior to the Fourth PrepCom circulated a strongly worded yet sophisticated proposal for reform of the existing system of human rights protection.[11] While it was not universal among NGOs, the government-monitoring frame was prominent across the entire range of human rights groups. Both larger, established NGOs and smaller grassroots ones treated governments with suspicion. The chair of the Rainforest Foundation, Franca Sciuto, noted, "if NGOs give into governments, they lose their soul" (Inter Press Service Staff and Internet 1993:172). In a speech given between the Fourth PrepCom and the Vienna conference, Amnesty International's Secretary-General, Pierre Sané, asserted, "It is governments themselves who are in the dock" (Sané, nd.). At other conferences as well, this frame motivated both NGO-to-government activity and NGO-to-NGO exchange, with lobbiers seeing their presence as necessary to prod governments to take positions they would not otherwise take, and the networkers offering their parallel conferences as alternatives to governmental conferences that glossed over key issues. Both kinds of participants also saw their continued activism as critical for holding governments accountable at home for the promises they made at the conferences. Some networkers at the Rio conference did not wait for the end of the negotiations to begin holding governments to higher environmental standards. Bella Abzug of the Women's Congress for a Healthy Planet and the women's caucus read a statement to the Fourth PrepCom plenary in protest against the arrest of leaders and supporters of India's Chipko movement and Kenya's Green Belt Movement and of Andy Mutang of the Sarawak Indigenous People's Alliance in Malaysia. Governments were outraged in turn, especially because of UN norms against naming individual countries in UN debates (*CrossCurrents* 6-9 March 1992:1-2). A few days later, indigenous lobbyists asked governments to designate indigenous nations as a UN advisory council that would give governments an "annual report card" on their progress toward meeting the Rio commitments (*CrossCurrents* 9-11 March 1992:1).

The rise in sheer numbers of NGO participants in all issue areas attests to the emergence of the frame that sees NGOs as key actors in global governance. Tens of thousands of participants spent time and money that showed a commitment to action at the level of global processes. Further evidence is provided by the fact that since the 1990s conferences, NGOs have shown a commitment to following up on the promises they and governments made at their conferences. Human rights NGOs were quick to criticize governments for the modest achievements of the Vienna conference

(M. Schmidt 1995:599). WEDO issued its first report on government commitments a year after Beijing (Women's Environment and Development Organization 1996). NGOs in all three issue areas were a critical audience for the governments' five-year reviews of post-conference achievements.[12]

At Rio, NGOs also wrote a series of NGO treaties designed to specify what citizens could do themselves to reach the conference goals. Thousands of NGOs signed treaties on topics ranging from education to consumption and poverty to biodiversity and biotechnology. In the Alternative Non-Governmental Agreement on Climate Change, for example, NGOs came to much quicker agreement on the serious nature of the climate change problem and recommended a series of specific NGO commitments to action, in conjunction with scientific groups, local communities, and governments. Among other commitments, they pledged to do things like "support citizen activism at all levels including choices with regard to transportation and waste treatment; and the adoption of full social and environmental pricing of natural resources" (Alternative Non-Governmental Agreement on Climate Change 1992:3). While this can be taken as further evidence of the government-monitoring frame at work, it also suggests the emergence of a frame that recognizes the need for active NGO initiatives in their own right. This marked a significant change from the role of NGOs at the earlier conferences, where they were passive observers of governments. The alternative treaty process created at Rio oriented NGOs around the idea of independent action, and was designed to incorporate NGOs who were unable to attend the conference but who shared the commitment to global NGO action. NGOs did not have to be present to sign the treaties, and signatory NGOs were to develop plans to implement the treaties at home with other groups unable to attend. Implementation has not been fully successful, even within the NGO community, because NGOs largely stopped working collectively with the treaties after Rio. Women's energetic coalition building, described earlier, supports the centrality of an NGO dialogue frame among women's groups as well. In the human rights area, NGOs already share a frame of unity in opposition to state repression, making coordination easier.

Unaligned NGO Frames

Using the language of frames draws attention to the fact that the substantive content of particular issues in world politics is not simply inherent in the issue, but is constructed by the participants involved. Understandings of the philosophical and procedural content of human rights claims changed considerably between 1968 and 1993, and the same can be said of environmental protection and women's rights. Although NGOs share many frames and definitions, as outlined in the previous sections, they have also actively disputed meanings with each other. One of the ironies of the global conference phenomenon is that by bringing so many divergent NGOs together, conferences also provide a forum for NGOs to discover their disagreements. Perhaps the sharpest divisions among NGOs have come along geographic lines, with Northern and Southern NGOs prioritizing different dimensions of these issues. However, airing differences within a single conference, or across several conferences, can result in further understanding and collaboration among NGOs, even those from very different national contexts. A second difference among NGOs relates to the varying autonomy of NGOs with respect to their national governments.

NORTH-SOUTH DIFFERENCES AMONG NGOS: The experiences of NGOs at the Rio conference illustrate the types of struggles over frame alignment that may occur during the conference process. Northern NGOs were disproportionately involved in the early preparations for the Rio conference, lobbying official delegates on the conference agenda. This agenda reflected many of the traditional environmental concerns of the North, stressing specific sources of pollution or resources in need of preservation. When Southern NGOs showed up in larger numbers at the Third Prep-Com, they disrupted this lobbying by focusing on issues on the periphery of the official agenda, such as the ways in which international debt and multinational corporations contributed to environmental degradation. One Northern NGO reported after the Rio conference that issues dividing Northern and Southern NGOs included Southern assertions of national sovereignty over decision-making and resources versus Northern support for a global decision making body and the concept of a global "common heritage of resources" (Centre for Applied Studies in Internet and Negotiations Issues and Non Governmental Organizations Programme 1992a: 16). On these issues, some NGOs had more in common with their home governments than with each other.

At the same time, the final conclusion of this report stresses the ways in which NGOs gradually aligned their environmental frames through the remaining PrepComs and throughout the actual Rio conference. The experiences of trying to work together across traditional divides, and the raised awareness among Northern environmental NGOs of issues of concern to Southern NGOs, and of development issues generally, may change the way in which NGOs work in the future. Some Northern NGOs simply picked up the rhetoric of the development debate, but others began changing their policies in response to what they learned through UNCED (Centre for Applied Studies 1992a:11). While differences on many of these issues remain among NGOs, the North/South divide does not delineate the sides as neatly after the Rio process as before.

North/South divisions characterized the women's conferences in the beginning as well. However, the repeated encounters and growing experience in negotiation made possible by the four women's conferences resulted in the blurring of what had been a sharp dividing line. The timing of the conferences was also a factor: as the tensions among nations fostered during the Cold War receded from the mid-'70s to the mid-'90s, so too did the tensions between Northern and Southern women. At Mexico City, women from the South were more concerned about development and imperialism, whereas women from the North focused on sexism to the exclusion of other political considerations (Stephenson 1995:143). At Copenhagen the conference-wide debate over whether to declare Zionism as a form of apartheid was reflected in the near-pitched battles fought among NGO representatives. But the ever-growing web of women's connections that developed over the course of the Decade on Women resulted in more agreement on issues of common concern. In the area of development, in particular, interaction between Northern and Southern feminists became increasingly fruitful. Critical engagement with gender-biased development practice led theorists and practitioners to recognize the need to take into account women—and men's—location within larger economic structures as well as in the social relations of gender. By Beijing, women from all regions had found international economic policies increasing their burdens—although Southern women linked economic concerns to other problems such as gender-based violence, while Northern women tended to see such issues as separate (Bunch, Dutt, and Fried, nd).

In some contrast to the other conferences, North-South differences were present at Vienna but did not impede agreement among NGOs for long. The early dispute over the makeup of the Joint Planning Committee not withstanding, one commentator remarked on the "depth of common understanding" of values, goals, and policies, "expressed by human rights activists from both the South and the North of the world" (Boyle 1995:91). The evidence suggests that NGOs developed this common understanding before preparations began for the Vienna conference. By 1993 Latin American NGOs, in particular, were strong advocates of civil and political rights, with experience advocating such rights in international fora. Although one might expect Southern NGOs to be stronger proponents of economic, social, and cultural rights, as well as the right to development, the importance of such claims is widely recognized even by the larger Northern-based NGOs that tend to have the most experience at the UN. For example, the International Commission of Jurists, based in Geneva and dedicated to promoting human rights as a manifestation of the rule of law, determined in 1959 that the rule of law included economic justice; in 1986 the organization helped to promote UN recognition of the right to development (Butler 1996:20; Dolgopol 1996:34; Tolley 1994:144-145). Amnesty International also recognizes the interdependence and indivisibility of all human rights (Amnesty International 1997:355).

With the universality of human rights under attack at the Vienna conference, NGOs set aside any remaining differences over extending the human rights agenda. Efforts to defend the universality of rights and to create stronger monitoring powers were "strongly supported by delegates from over 1,000 nongovernmental organizations, many from Asia, who dismiss the third world's 'relativist' arguments as nothing more than excuses for authoritarian regimes" (Riding 1993c:5). At a plenary session of the conference, a group of African NGOs went further, calling for an independent global monitoring body and affirming that human rights standards should be applied "regardless of the political, economic, or cultural systems" (da Costa 1993:187). Contrary to participants' forecasts, there was little evidence of a North-South split over the right to development at Vienna.[13] The unity of Southern and Northern NGOs in favor of limits to national sovereignty at Vienna contrasted with the Southern NGOs' occasional defense of sovereignty at the Rio conference.

This evidence suggests that although NGOs disagree among themselves on many issues, the North/South divide may not always be the most important one among NGOs. In all conferences, this divide partially overlaps more persistent divisions between the newer generation of small grassroots organizations focused on local action[14] and the more professional, often larger and older, organizations with long-standing activities at the UN.[15] These divisions lead to the differences in repertoire already noted, but are also reflected in different substantive orientations. Older NGOs tend to follow the substantive agenda of the UN more closely than do the newer ones, much as they tend to work within the established mechanisms for NGO participation.[16]

NGO AUTONOMY FROM STATES: Another issue that divides NGOs is their varying autonomy from their national governments. Many governments offered some form of support for NGOs, from allowing NGO participation on governmental delegations to providing funding for national NGO conferences and NGO travel to particular international conferences (Centre for Applied Studies 1992a:26). For the Rio conference, the French government hosted and financially supported an entire alternative preparatory NGO conference in December 1991 (Kingham 1991). The Brazilian organizers of Rio's parallel Global Forum received funds from governmental agencies of Canada, France, the European Economic Community, and the Netherlands, as well as from the UN Development Program-Brazil (Fórum de ONGs Brasileiras 1992:4). The Venezuelan Ministry for Women's Affairs hosted a national preparatory NGO conference prior to Beijing, and the U.S. Agency for International Development was designated as the main external funder for Latin American participation around Beijing (Alvarez 1998:314). Such support brings with it the possibility of compromising NGOs' independence, and is often debated among NGO participants. However, it also indicates that governments may be accepting certain roles for NGOs.

The more serious threat of wholly government-sponsored NGOs has also arisen as a subject of debate. Rules governing ECOSOC consultative status prohibit such groups, but some states have taken advantage of the relaxed rules for affiliation with UN conferences. Countries such as China have either declared party organs (e.g., the All China Women's Federation) to be NGOs, or established new organizations (e.g., the Human Rights Society of China) in order to participate in the NGO fora at international UN conferences (Ching 1994:34). These "GONGOs" (government-organized NGOs) are regarded with suspicion by NGOs that fear government diffusion of disinformation and encroachment of their relatively autonomous arenas of debate (*On the Record* 3:1). Conditions other than outright government sponsorship could inhibit NGO independence in some developing nations. A Moroccan NGO representative at Vienna was quoted as saying that, in parts of Africa where human rights organizations are relatively new, some NGOs were populated with "former ministers or ex-ambassadors who have a political discourse that does not correspond to a vision of independence worthy of an NGO" (Naji Jamal Eddine, quoted in Bouabid 1993:173). But even the move to exert control over NGOs can be seen as reflecting the increasing strength of NGO activity, to the point where governments feel a need to monitor it from within.

Governmental Responses to NGO Frames

Governments retain the ability to respond selectively to the new NGO frames, adopting some and firmly rejecting others. One way to assess the diffusion of shared issue definitions among NGOs and governments, and thus the extent of democratization in the area of values, is to look for documentary evidence of the impact of NGOs mobilizing for the first time at conferences outside their own issue areas, for example, women participating at human rights or at environment conferences. We refer to such impact as cross-fertil ization. If evidence of cross-fertilization shows up at conferences where NGOs rather than governments have linked concerns across issue areas, we contend that it can plausibly be attributed to the growth of global civil society.

Indeed, impressive evidence of women's cross-fertilization appears in the documents of Rio and Vienna. Women and women's concerns are thoroughly absent from the various documents of Stockholm. The words *women* or *woman* never appear, and the "generic" man is the main actor. Population issues receive ample attention, but even here there is no suggestion that women bear children. Neither do women appear in the first agenda for Rio. Women were added to the agenda of the Rio conference only at the Third PrepCom, after a large lobbying group of women showed up at the Second PrepCom (Centre for Applied Studies 1992a:26). Women lobbied for the Women's Agenda 21 that detailed exactly what language about women they wanted, and they largely succeeded in having that language included in the final document. In turn, there is at least a coincidence between the presence of environmental NGOs at the women's conference in Nairobi and the fact that this was the first women's conference that produced a document with an entire special section on the environment. With respect to links between women and human rights, observers also counted women as the most successful NGO coalition at Vienna, noting that they were able to get whole paragraphs on women's rights and violence against women in the final document (Azzam

1993:95; Ottaway 1993). In contrast, a single resolution had referred to women in the Tehran Final Act (United Nations 1968: Part III, Res. IX).

Environmentalists and human rights activists did not form the same kind of united front at any of the conferences, and there is less evidence of cross-fertilization on their issues. The Vienna document does adopt the language of sustainability when discussing the right to development for the first time—and environmentalists attended that conference, while they did not participate in Tehran (United Nations 1993f:Part I, Para. 11).

Based on these conferences, the evidence suggests that NGOs making a concerted effort to lobby across conferences may achieve more than if they lobby exclusively at their own conferences. The experiences of women indicate that influencing governments may even be easier at conferences on other issues. One reason may be that at a conference on a specific issue, both proponents and opponents are mobilized, while only one side may mobilize for a conference on a seemingly unrelated issue. For example, conservative governments and NGOs mobilized for the population and women's conferences but largely ignored the environmental conference, and so women faced less opposition there.

NGOs met special resistance from at least some governments on several issues that remained remarkably consistent between all of the conferences from 1968 to 1995. First, governments strongly resisted NGO challenges to a key nation-state prerogative: the choice of economic development models. While developing states had objected most strongly to any expansion of the NGO role, developed states also exercised their vetoes on this issue. The United States and the European Union played key roles at both Rio and Beijing in bracketing language questioning dominant economic models, and ensuring that no "new resources" would be promised for conference document provisions in Beijing (*ENB* March 1995, September 1995). At Vienna, strong NGO statements about the "compatibility" of structural adjustment programs and human rights precepts were not reflected in the final governmental documents (Nowak 1994:83).

In addition, with the growth of attention focused on issues of gender equality through the women's conferences, this arena also has become one in which certain states assert claims to "national" (often "cultural" or "religious") sovereignty. At Beijing, representatives of the Holy See, Guatemala, Honduras, Argentina, Malta, Sudan, and Iran frequently used the language of sovereignty to object to certain formulations of women's and girls' rights that they saw as somehow undermining family or national cohesion and morality. When unsuccessful at blocking inclusion of such rights, they placed reservations on them when signing onto the final conference document. As will be shown in chapters 3, 4, and 5, women's status—or the structure of gender relations more generally—has become one of the main contested issues in debates over sovereignty.

How did governments respond to NGOs' central claim of importance as global actors? After half a decade of global conferencing with active NGO participation, we identify lingering differences between governmental and NGO frames on their relations. While governments have agreed to a certain level of NGO involvement at the international level, they still seek to bar NGO participation in procedures or issues that in some way restrict state sovereignty or threaten states' monopoly of formal global governance.

On its face, the evidence supports the argument that governments have recognized the fact that NGOs form a new part of global society. Here, the contrasts between the documents of the earlier and late conferences are especially telling. In all three issue areas, NGOs were virtually ignored at the earlier conferences, meriting only a passing comment in conference documents. In the 1990s, all three sets of final governmental documents found extensive roles for NGOs. They are expected to implement, educate, and even help formulate new approaches to all of the issues. The UNCED final document dedicates an entire chapter to the role of NGOs, while NGO references are integrated throughout the Vienna Declaration and throughout the final Beijing document. The new Commission on Sustainable Development, created at Rio, also finds a place for NGO participation similar to the active NGO role in the Human Rights Commission (Imber 1994:102).

Despite this language, governments were in fact seriously divided over the issue of NGOs' role both at the conferences themselves and in global politics more generally. The clash came in the "promising but difficult marriage of an essentially American model of democratic lobbying and a forum [the UN] with a built-in democratic deficit," wrote an observer of the women's Fourth PrepCom (*ENB* 10 April 1995). Even governments accustomed to American-style lobbying at home drew limits to the roles of NGOs abroad, although developing countries took the lead in excluding NGOs.

Governments did not accept the new NGO frame on global governance entirely, maintaining their own dominant role especially at home. The most common kind of reference to NGOs in the Rio conference's Agenda 21 depicts NGOs as secondary collaborators with states, as in this example: "The United Nations system . . . in cooperation with Member States and with appropriate international and nongovernmental organizations, should make poverty alleviation a major priority" (United Nations 1993e:Vol. 1:32). Other language in the documents also reasserts the central role of nation-states. Mark Imber notes that "whereas the Stockholm Declaration postponed the party-pooping affirmation of states-rights until paragraph 21, the Rio Declaration affirms national rights over resources in paragraph 2" (Imber 1994:102). This affirmation is backed up with a shift in the language from that of "man's" to "states'" responsibility for the environment. In Beijing, religiously influenced governments attempted to assert their religious and cultural sovereignty over both NGOs and international organizations. When unsuccessful, they used reservations to the document to make their displeasure felt. At Vienna, while the principle of the universality of human rights was upheld, governments waffled on protections for human rights NGOs at the national level. The final document from the 1993 World Conference on Human Rights cites national law as the relevant standard for the protection of NGO activities, which was seen by NGOs as a setback for the impartial application of international standards of human rights (Posner and Whittome 1994:491). In summary, many (but not all) governments acknowledge that NGOs have a new role to play in global politics, but most resist the transnational implications of their full participation. Chapter 4 expands on these sovereignty claims and debates.

The Changing NGO Role in ECOSOC

The conference-based struggles to define the limits of global civil society have had an impact on the UN beyond the conference arena. The 1996 revision of the terms of NGO consultative status within ECOSOC reflects the progress of, as well as the remaining obstacles to, NGO access to official UN business.[17] The new rules continue to confine NGO consultative status to ECOSOC rather than to the entire General Assembly, and NGOs may not circulate written statements as official documents or play "a negotiating role" at conferences (Willetts 1996:74-75).

However, several changes reflecting the growth of NGO participation in conference processes indicate government acceptance of NGO importance and strength. First, more NGOs are allowed involvement in the consultative and conference processes. In contrast to earlier stipulations, regional and national NGOs' participation is now actively solicited, particularly from countries with developing economies.[18] Second, conference and preparatory process participation rules have been eased. In language borrowed directly from the resolution on women's participation at Beijing (Resolution 48/108), rules have been adopted to expedite NGO inclusion and to assure continuing NGO participation in conference follow-up. An entirely new section has been added extending UN Secretariat support to facilitate the wider range of activities in which NGOs are now involved.[19]

Conclusion

Is global civil society contributing to the democratization of global governance, as evidenced by the UN issue conferences? The answer depends on the starting assumptions about the potential contributions about global civil society. There is some evidence that an additional sphere of global debate and possibly global governance was emerging among NGOs during the 1990s conferences, as NGOs gathered in unprecedented numbers to meet each other in their own parallel Forums. Nonetheless, the NGO sphere is fraught with tensions and inequality, not unlike the state sphere. NGOs also showed up as a substantial new lobbying force at the 1990s conferences, offering some support for the existence of a global civil society pressing for representation of its interests and values in international governmental diplomacy. However, states presented equally substantial resistance to this new force. Table 2.2 summarizes these results.

Paul Wapner (1995:316), writing of a second sphere of world civic politics, posited that his analysis of the parallel activities of Northern NGOs on the environmental front might be extended to all NGOs. We find that at the UN conferences, NGOs' shared expectations for dialogue and networking do exemplify the norms of conduct one would expect to find among NGOs if such a global civil society is emerging. A shared substantive cross-conference agenda may also be emerging, if the women's example can be viewed as a prototype. Framing NGO activity as an alternative sphere of global governance leads us to observe that steps toward mutual agenda

Table 2.2 Global Civil Society: Expected Characteristics and Empirical Findings

Term	Expected Characteristics	Empirical Findings
Global	Increase in number of participating NGOs; balanced geographic representation	Significant numerical increase but skewed geographic representation; imbalance still favors Northern NGOs
Civil	*NGO-NGO:* new ways of participation (repertoires); greater overall interaction among NGOs; *NGO-State:* New rules facilitating NGO access and participation; greater interaction between NGOs and governments	*NGO-NGO:* greater interaction; *NGO-State:* New rules, but NGO repertoires met by state-imposed, sometimes arbitrary limits; amount of NGO-state interaction circumscribed by states
Society	*NGO-NGO and NGO-State:* Development of mutual understandings (frames) regarding both behavior and substance, both among NGOs and between NGOs and governments	*NGO-NGO:* Ongoing development of mutual understandings among NGOs; *NGO-State:* lack of shared NGO-state frames; sovereignty claims pose significant obstacles to substantive NGO-state agreement

formation taken by non-state actors have intrinsic rewards, whether or not they have an impact on state actors. Even so, we find that there are important differences in experience and goals among NGOs that fall roughly along geographic lines and will challenge the unity of any alternative political sphere. North-South differences and concomitant differences of philosophy remain a nontrivial source of "unaligned" NGO frames, or social division. These differences support to a certain extent the arguments of those who doubt that democracy can be forged among non-state representatives from substantially different backgrounds, even when states are left out of the equation. Chapter 3, which traces the participation of Latin American NGOs and governments in the 1990s conferences, helps us to understand some of the dynamics in a "bridging" world region, and what those regional dynamics may mean for the future development of a truly global alternative sphere of politics among NGOs.

When states enter the equation, as they do in the state-focused version of global civil society, civil procedures and social understanding are also in question. States do allow greater roles for NGOs in the 1990s conferences compared to earlier generations of conferences, but they hasten to maintain their control over that participation. When they reach the point of real decision-making, NGOs are shut out of the room (the "Fourth PrepCom phenomenon"). This finding also casts doubt on the extent to which democratization is possible at the global level. States clearly delimit a secondary role for NGOs, especially on a key set of issues that they see as central to their own sovereignty. The choices that states protect from direct NGO influence—of economic development models and of domestic gender relations—are a rather puzzling mix of issues that do not include some of the issues that international relations theorists see as central to state sovereignty. What is even more puzzling is that states sometimes do make agreements among themselves on these issues. We address these puzzles in chapters 3 and 4. After a regional assessment of global civil society in chapter 3, chapter 4 focuses more directly on states' claims and bargains on issues they deem central to sovereignty, and traces the emergence of a new and more subtle NGO role in these bargains. Chapter 5 extends this analysis to states' choices and interactions with NGOs in three more 1990s conferences that highlight economic and/or gender issues.

CHAPTER 3

Global Civil Society and Latin America
in the UN Conferences

To further assess the extent and impact of global civil society we turn in this chapter to an evaluation of Latin American participation at UN world conferences: does it reinforce traditional divides between state and society in global politics or does it transform state-society relations in ways that suggest a democratization of the international system? We focus on Latin America because in the current world context, it occupies a unique, bridging position across many international divides—in particular the North/South division. This division plays an important role in the debates between advocates and critics of the concept of global civil society. On the one hand, advocates assume, often without presenting empirical evidence, that the experience of Southern nongovernmental organizations (NGOs), and Southern state-society relations in general, will mirror or progress toward the situation in the North. They frequently do not distinguish among the very different types of NGOs that exist, or take into account countries' varied structural locations vis-à-vis other nation-states in the world system. On the other hand, critics argue, again often without empirical investigation, that structural differences among geographic world regions necessarily mitigate against any similar set of experiences across the "development divide." They find Northern dominance of transnational relations, whether through resource-rich NGOs or hegemonic state power, and dismiss the transnational arena as a meaningful locus of intervention for Southern NGOs or states. To evaluate these very different claims, research is necessary.

The Latin American region is well situated as an object of such research, since it occupies an intermediate position with regard to many of the criteria that are often used to differentiate between countries in the Northern and Southern regions. Politically, it shares a recent authoritarian past with many countries, especially those of the South. However, its recent democratic transitions are joining it to the community of primarily Northern liberal nations. Economically, the region is also in transition. By many indicators, it remains mired in severe poverty, inequality, and structural ineffi- ciencies. Yet while Latin America saw some economic improve- ments in the 1990s, other regions of the world continue to face even more daunting challenges. Socially, regional values continue to be a hybrid of "traditional" and "modern" ideas from every world region.

As a result of the region's bridging nature, the different posi- tions taken by Latin American actors on international issues are especially important in evaluating current international relations debates developing at the level of global politics. The interactions among Latin American NGOs and states at UN conferences will show us whether global civil society is truly "global," at least with regard to one important region outside the wealthy North.

In many ways, Latin Americans used these conferences to col- lectively develop their positions on the conference issues. The nov- elty of the issues as subjects for state-society debate made the posi- tions taken by Latin Americans somewhat more fluid and changeable than those of both state and civil society actors in other regions. In one particularly graphic example, Brazilian NGOs met with their national delegation in a special briefing at the environ- mental Fourth PrepCom and were astonished to hear then-Secre- tary of the Environment José Lutzenberger take up their own argu- ments and voice strong criticisms of some Brazilian government positions at the conference and of the agencies he himself headed. A few days later, he was fired from his position and the Brazilian government returned to positions dominated by the foreign min- istry, Itamaraty (*Earth Summit Times* 23 March 1992). Such exam- ples notwithstanding, certain patterns in Latin American positions emerged at these conferences, which we explore in the next section.

Based on the description of the global civil society concept pre- sented in chapter 2 (see table 2.1), it is possible to hypothesize about the observations we would expect of the Latin American case if an international society that is global, civil, and social is reflected in, or advanced by, regional interactions (see table 3.1).

First, to confirm the *global* component of global civil society, we

Table 3.1 Global Civil Society: Global Definition and Regional Expectations

Dimension	Global Definition (from Chapter 2)	Empirical Indicator for Latin America	Expectations for Latin America
Global	geographically diverse and balanced representation; includes non-state actors	NGO participation proportional to regional population (10%)	Latin American NGO participation lower than share, especially compared to Northern NGOs
Civil	regularized [NGO] participation in global interactions; NGO access to global forms of governance	inclusive regional procedures; relative independence of NGOs from governments	governmental inclusion of NGOs; NGO efforts to guard independence from governments
Social	existence of social regard; mutual behavioral expectations; shared substantive understandings	shared issue understandings among NGOs and states in region	NGO-state differences on economic models (neoliberalism); rights

should find NGO representation in proportions that match Latin America's share of the global population, approximately 10 percent. Economic difficulties and the comparatively recent appearance of NGOs in the region led us to expect that Latin American participation would lag behind this proportion, confirming the predominance of NGOs from wealthy, Northern regions in global civil society that we observed in chapter 2.

The *civil* component is seen in the NGO *repertoires* or procedures and forms of participation, including how these are influenced by the extent to which governments accept the legitimacy of NGOs' participation. We expected recent democratization processes in Latin America to have helped shape the identities and priorities of Latin American NGOs as international actors. More democratic governments would be expected to expand their citizens' opportunities to participate in domestic and global politics. At the same time, in all three issue areas examined here, Latin American NGOs began to organize under, and in opposition to, authoritarian rule. This marked the actions and attitudes of the groups profoundly, not least in their shared ambivalence toward cooperation with the state (Alvarez, Dagnino, and Escobar 1998; Jaquette 1994). Although such ambivalence is not an uncommon trait among nongovernmental actors in general, the degree to which it affects groups in the region is high due to their history of state repression. In the Latin American context, confirming evidence for the existence of democratizing relations at the global level would include the presence of regional procedures to incorporate NGO perspectives in governmental documents and to permit NGO participation during conference processes. However, we also expected Latin American NGOs to assert their autonomy from their governments at the global conferences, both by devoting more time to building a deliberative sphere independently with other NGOs and by devising national and transnational strategies to confront their governments.

In evaluating the *social* component of global civil society, chapter 2 has shown that NGOs and governments *framed* issues and their relationships in differing ways. This in itself is not surprising, and still less does it constitute an inherent threat to the social aspect of global civil society. One would expect, however, that in a global conference process some similar frames—mutually understood interpretations that form through social interaction—should develop concerning substantive issue areas in order for productive dialogue to ensue. Given the broad picture sketched in chapter 2, of governments defending sovereignty and its prerogatives from encroachment by NGOs, and NGOs committed to monitoring state behavior, we expected the values component of our investigation to evidence a big divide between NGOs and governments in Latin America. In particular, given recent government policies, we expected to see a pronounced split on the acceptability of the neoliberal economic model, with states supporting it and NGOs in opposition. Second, we expected that rights would be a significant issue, with governmental support for universal rights a critical measure of the degree of democratization of political practices and values in Latin America.

To evaluate the extent to which the Latin American region conforms to the emerging general patterns of global civil society, we drew on the actions and documents of Latin American states and NGOs at the UN conferences on the environment, human rights, and women. However, we also incorporated information from the regional gatherings held in conjunction with the global conferences. Prior to the Earth Summit, the UN's Economic Commission for Latin America sponsored a regional discussion among governments and NGOs in Mexico City, 4-7 March 1991. Prior to the human rights conference, governments and NGOs met at San José, Costa Rica, 18-22 January 1993. In preparation for the conference on women, the Latin Americans met in Mar de Plata, Argentina, 20-25 September 1994. The region's NGOs and governments each drew up their own official statements at the preparatory meetings on human rights and women; prior to the environmental conference, a group of eminent Latin American environmentalists wrote a regional response to a major UN report on the global environment (Latin American and Caribbean Commission on Development and Environment 1990; World Commission on Environment and Development 1987). Regional actors also met in the global PrepComs which preceded the final conferences, and then reengaged while participating in the actual conferences themselves.

Before moving on to the details, we briefly summarize our findings here. As regards the *global* aspect, we find that Latin American NGOs are remarkably vigorous and well-represented members of international society on the issues examined here. At the *civil* level, as with other global nongovernmental actors, Latin American NGOs' repertoires include both interaction with governments (lobbying) and building alliances with NGOs (networking). Our findings suggest that Latin American NGOs, both nationally and in regional fora, have developed some level of trust in their governments. Nonetheless, the slow pace of reforms and the ambiguous nature of current Latin American democracy produced an ongoing NGO debate at the conferences about whether it is more appropriate to target governments as worthy adversaries through direct lobbying, or to refrain from engaging governments in favor of building alliances with civil society. As for the *social* nature of Latin Americans' participation in the conferences, we found, to our surprise, that Latin American NGOs and governments participating in all three issue conferences wrote regional documents that spoke of a broadly shared backdrop of regional conditions, indicating a shared framing of regional problems. As we demonstrate in the next section, both sets of actors stressed the ways in which international economic pressures limited regional choices and prevented the resolution of poverty and other chronic social issues in Latin America. Both also spoke of the newness of regional democracy and the need for deepening its hold in the region. Still, we found that substantively, regional NGOs were quicker to embrace universal norms, particularly on human rights and women's rights, than were their governments. In addition, governments and NGOs often disagreed on the solutions to the problems they all acknowledged.

Whatever we might conclude about the extent to which a global civil society exists and its impact on states gathered at the international level, Latin Americans are full participants. Their experiences at the 1990s issue conferences closely track those of the Northern region, notwithstanding the much more recent appearance of NGOs in Latin America. At the same time, perhaps more than participants from other regions, Latin Americans bring a regional sensibility to their participation in UN conference processes. The recent political liberalization in Latin America brought state and civil society actors closer together at home and in the global negotiations, but both sides evidenced wariness as they maneuvered through a number of regional "firsts": the first time that governmental negotiators invited large numbers of nongovernmental participants to a regional conference, the first time that nongovernmental actors helped write governmental position papers, and so on. That regional sensibility produced more regional agreement on the substance of the conference negotiations than was present in other world regions; continuing disagreements reflect ongoing Latin American problems and debates. We turn now to the individual conferences and show how they manifest the global, civil, and social dimensions of global civil society.

The United Nations Conference on Environment and Development, Rio de Janeiro, 1992

The Rio conference on environment and development set a number of important precedents as the first of the 1990s' major UN conferences. Its eighteen thousand exuberant NGO participants seemed to embody the emerging concept of global civil society. Latin American NGOs were full participants in this conference, the only one of the 1990s conferences to be held in the region. Their multiple forms of participation reflected ongoing regional NGO debates about the desirability of collaborating with national governments—and their assessments of the "civility" of regional governments also varied accordingly. Substantively, Latin American NGOs and governments shared an emphasis on the links between environmental degradation and regional poverty, although the most vocal NGOs thought their governments had failed to push the issue far enough.

Global Dimensions of NGO Participation on the Environment

The *global* dimension of the Rio conference was strongly affected by the fact that the conference was held in a Latin American country. In Rio itself (after four PrepComs in other parts of the world with less regional participation), Latin American NGOs predominated. Latin Americans made up 41 percent of the participants in the NGO conference held parallel to the governmental conference, the Global Forum. Their numbers nearly totaled the participation of North America (22 percent) and Europe (20 percent) combined, while dwarfing the participation of Asians (12 percent) and Africans (4 percent) (Centre for Applied Studies in International Negotiations Issues and Non Government Organizations Programme 1992b). They were not only present, but dominant in the activities of the Global Forum, sponsoring 41 percent of the meetings and 52 percent of the exhibitions (*Information on the '92 Global Forum* [6]:6).

The Latin American participation did develop slowly. While some national-level organizations had had strong international links to Northern NGOs before the UNCED process, there were few regular contacts among environmental NGOs within the Latin American region before 1990. As a result, early NGO participation was rarely representative of the entire region. At one of the earliest meetings, for example, only 16 South American NGOs and 1 Norwegian one met in Santiago, Chile, on 23-27 October 1989. A final outcome of the meeting was the creation of the South American Ecological Action Alliance that aimed to mobilize larger numbers of regional participants. Even so, only about 100 NGOs attended the regional governmental forum held in Mexico just four months before the Rio conference itself (Ortiz 1992); unfortunately, the regional conference coincided with the Fourth PrepCom. As a result, Latin American environmentalists never developed comprehensive networks or statements that spoke for the region as a whole, although they developed (multiple) characteristic patterns of participation.

Civil Dimensions

The Rio conference expanded a number of existing mechanisms for nongovernmental participation in UN activities as outlined in chapter 2. The General Assembly resolution authorizing the conference directed national governments to hold broad consultations while preparing their national reports on environmen-

tal conditions. NGOs were also allowed to lobby government negotiators during the conference process, with their access depending
on the stage of the negotiations. Nonetheless, civility was unevenly achieved among Latin American participants in the environmental conference process. NGOs' participation in the national reports varied widely, suggesting that not all governments in the
region took the UN's admonitions for broad public consultation seriously. Regional governments were willing to include NGOs in
certain stages of conference decision making, and lobbying NGOs
took advantage of these opportunities. Nonetheless, a significant
number of NGOs were themselves hesitant to enter into more sustained cooperation with their national governments on the conference issues.

An early test of the civility of Latin American state-society relations in the UNCED process was in the writing of the national reports on environmental conditions. The range of experiences was
wide, as shown by several illustrative examples. At one extreme,
Central American NGOs reported playing a very active role in
preparing their national environmental reports, with the Costa
Rican NGO Neotropica writing its entire Country Report (*Cross-
Currents* 9-11 March 1992:20). At the other extreme, Uruguay completed its Country Report very late and with minimal consultation
(Panario 1992). Perhaps most typically, governments were selective
in their consultation. The Brazilian government drew on the contributions of about seventy technical collaborators, but opened the
document for public comment only a week before formally submitting it (Ferreira 1992:45), while the Mexican government selected
just some thirty NGOs to discuss its Country Report in a public
forum (Salazar 1992:13).

In the conference negotiations themselves, governmental openness was similarly mixed, according to NGOs. At their regional
preparatory meeting for UNCED in March 1991, Latin American
governments prepared a statement setting out their regional priorities for the conference. In this document, the governments nodded
to the role of NGOs in preparing for and helping to implement conference agreements (United Nations 1991:118-127). NGOs ap-
plauded the intention of this conference, noting that "It is the first
time in the Latin American subregion that NGOs are invited to
participate and contribute resolutions in a governmental meeting"
(Ortiz 1992:3). NGOs were less contented about the actual conference, with the primarily Mexican attendees rejecting the "joke of a
'dialogue'" and the South American Ecological Action Alliance issu-

ing a statement of support for the Mexicans (Acuerdo de los Andes 1991:1).

Latin American NGOs themselves took a variety of stances toward their governments' efforts—or lack thereof—to include them in conference decision-making. Even before the March 1991, regional governmental meeting, participants in the South American Ecological Action Alliance issued a statement noting that Latin American governments had shown little capacity to implement previous UN agreements. This failure prompted them and other NGOs to develop a strategy of action that prioritized alliances between Latin American NGOs and citizens and NGOs from all over the world. Strategies for relations with their governments, in contrast, were to prioritize independence, while maintaining a constant dialogue (Encuentro de los Andes Taller del Cono Sur 1991:Sections 2, 9). As the PrepComs progressed, these NGOs joined in protests and joint press releases to indicate their dissatisfaction with the pace and content of the governmental negotiations. The protests allowed for networking with like-minded organizations of the South, such as the Third World Network, NGONET, and SONED (Southern Networks for Development), as well as with more radical Northern organizations.

At the same time, other NGOs eagerly interacted with their governments. Several governments, including Brazil and Venezuela, had included environmentalists on their national delegations. Many of the governments held at least occasional briefing sessions for NGOs. During the Fourth PrepCom, an assortment of NGOs from Central America and the Andean region formed networks to better lobby Latin American governments. They worked to develop common positions on biodiversity, climate change, poverty, financial mechanisms, debt, and the Rio Declaration (CrossCurrents 9-11 March 1992:20). These lobbying NGOs worked closely with their governments, as well as with other NGOs engaged in lobbying on the official conference agenda. Global NGO networks worked on a biodiversity conservation strategy, recommendations on forest principles, and transnational corporations.

Not surprisingly, Latin American NGOs drew a variety of conclusions about the openness of their national governments to their participation. The lobbiers tended to stress areas of congruence with their national governments. Dr. Roberto Troya of Ecuador's *Fundación Natura* observed, "The official delegates of each country and the national NGOs may have distinct focuses, but we come from the same region." Maria Eugenia Bustamante, an NGO member of the Venezuelan UNCED planning committee, concurred: "In the close collaboration between NGOs and the government, Venezuela is an exemplar of the popular participation they are discussing in the sessions of PrepCom 4" (*CrossCurrents* PC4(7), 23-25 March 1992:12). In contrast, the more critical NGOs were frustrated by both their fellow NGOs and their national governments. A report of Latin American NGO networkers at the Fourth Prep-Com complains that only nineteen people attended their first meeting because too many NGOs were investing all of their energy in the governmental processes instead of in the parallel process, "which is really our event." The report also notes that while official delegates came to address their group, they stayed only a short time and "in response to questions about the official position, argued that there wasn't time to give a detailed explanation, but we should be assured that this group of official delegates was progressive and they would raise sustainable development policies for the governments we were worried about" (Acta de las Reuniones del Foro Paralelo de la UNCED Celebrada entre los Groupos Latinoamericanos y del Caribe 1992).[1]

In the final summit segment of the Rio conference, sixteen of twenty Latin American heads of state made statements, but most failed to acknowledge the contributions of the NGOs. The Brazilian, Chilean, and Uruguayan leaders did credit NGOs as one of the driving forces behind the conference, but none of the Latin American leaders at the summit spoke of an NGO role beyond it (United Nations 1993g:Vols. II, III). This silence was more than filled by statements from two different Latin American NGO fora in those final days, which loudly criticized the governmental efforts. One lamented the fact that regional governments had failed to include interested independent organizations, as directed by the UN, and concluded that this meant that the governments themselves were exclusively responsible for the documents they had allowed to be written (*Informe "R"* 1992:12; Declaración del Pacto Acción Ecologica 1992).

Social Dimensions

Despite the frequent criticisms from some NGOs, there were areas of substantive frame alignment among Latin American governments and NGOs in the Rio process. The most consensual issue was the emphasis on poverty, debt, and lack of development in the region, and the corollary argument that environmental problems could not be resolved without also addressing these development issues. In the report *Our Own Agenda,* the regional response to a major UN report on the global environment, the Latin Americans emphasized the complementarity, and not the commonality, of global environmental conditions (Latin American and Caribbean Commission on Development and Environment 1990). The report highlighted the role of poverty, and its root cause in foreign debt, in creating distinct Latin American environmental problems and solutions. Both governments and NGOs singled out this issue in their final analyses of the UNCED, concluding that it had not been adequately addressed. Only the heads of state of Uruguay and Costa Rica failed to stress the importance of regional poverty in addressing environmental issues in their statements in the summit part of the Rio conference (United Nations 1993g:Vol. III).

Nonetheless, most of the Latin American heads of state stressed technical and economic solutions to their environmental and poverty problems, notably fairer trade, environmental technology granted on concessional terms, and new financial resources. Only Cuba's Fidel Castro cast his statement in terms of a wholesale attack on consumer societies, in terms comparable to those of many NGOs. While several of the leaders noted that their countries had not paid enough attention to the environmental impacts of their economic production, none of them suggested that his or her own country's economic model needed substantial revision.

The final statement of the NGO Global Forum, the NGO conference held parallel to the governmental conference, echoed the Latin American NGO position, which criticized the official conference for paying insufficient attention to models of development. In the words of the People's Earth Declaration (1992:1), "While [political leaders] engage in the fine tuning of an economic system that serves the short term interests of the few at the expense of the many, the leadership for more fundamental change has fallen by default to the organizations and movements of civil society. We accept this challenge." As this declaration makes clear, the poverty-based critique of the UNCED served both to unite and to divide NGOs and governments, in Latin America and globally. Beneath the uniting concern about poverty, governments and NGOs continued to differ on the kinds of measures needed to overcome it. For many Latin American governments, a quantitative increase in resources in the region was enough to address poverty, while the NGOs generally argued for qualitative changes in the development model as well.

Consensus was blocked on many issues by the conference's dual agenda of environment and development. NGO participants included not only environmentalists but a whole set of development-oriented actors, and governmental delegations also included representatives from environment and development agencies, as well as diplomats. The divide was evident, for example, when the eight Amazon nations decided collectively to make national sovereignty the centerpiece of their regional position on the Amazon, which blocked the negotiation of a proposed global treaty on forests (MacDonald and Nielson 1997:273-274), and NGOs could not respond with one voice for environmental protection. Inside the twelve hundred-organization Brazilian Forum, some labor and development organizations insisted that sovereignty and jobs were in fact the proper lens on the Brazilian Amazon, stymieing environmental and indigenous activists who wanted to reject their government's position.[2] Finally, as just noted, NGOs were divided on what their role in the process should be, and states were as well. Thus the end of the Rio conference did not bring a new regional framing of the proper role of non-state actors in global environmental politics.

The World Conference on Human Rights, Vienna, 1993

The human rights NGOs occupied a potentially antagonistic position vis-à-vis regional governments because in most cases their own governments had recently been, or still were, the sponsors of large-scale human rights abuses. Having been tested at home, civil society actors from Latin America participated forcefully on the global human rights stage. Governments shared many of the NGOs' interpretations of the sources of former and continuing human rights difficulties, but did not necessarily accept the responsibility that NGOs wanted to attribute to governments for the redress of human rights problems.

Global Dimensions of NGO Participation on Human Rights

Of the registered NGOs participating at the Vienna NGO Forum in the three days preceding the official conference, 236 out of 1,529 organizations (15 percent) came from Latin America.[3] As mentioned in chapter 2, during the NGO Forum, the liaison committee of NGOs that had officially facilitated overall NGO participation during the preparatory process was dissolved and reorganized—after criticism that planning had been dominated by international NGOs based primarily in Geneva and New York—to reflect stronger representation from local and regional NGOs across the globe, including Latin America (Azzam 1993:96-97; Elliot 1993; Korey 1998:282-283, 291).

Latin American human rights NGOs already shared a history of strong links to their global NGO counterparts. Some, like Argentina's Mothers of the Plaza de Mayo, had formed continuing relationships with external human rights groups (Brysk 1994:52-53). Regional federations had also formed, such as Service, Peace, and Justice in Latin America (SERPAJ-AL), an NGO whose purposes include, but are not limited to, the promotion of human rights concerns, and the Latin American Federation of Associations of Relatives of Disappeared Detainees (FEDEFAM), a regional organization of national-level groups. Such NGOs had a good deal of experience working with other international actors, inside and outside of the UN structure, and they played a networking role in preparations for the Vienna Conference. Several had previous UN conference experience, having attended UNCED, although there were newer, smaller NGOs, which had less prior exposure to international human rights fora. Two of the larger global human rights organizations, Amnesty International and the International Commission of Jurists, sent international-level staffers to Latin America's regional preparatory conference who were themselves Latin Americans.[4] This may be taken as a further indicator of the integration between Latin American and global NGOs.

Civil Dimensions

While NGOs and Latin American governments did not always see eye-to-eye, the legitimacy of procedures providing for their interaction during regional preparations for Vienna was not in dispute. At the regional preparatory meeting for Latin America and the Caribbean, governments and NGOs met separately. NGOs already in consultative status with the UN's Economic and Social Council were permitted to observe the government proceedings, and those without consultative status but based in Latin America could also designate accredited representatives as observers in consultation with the regional governments (United Nations 1993e). This level of access was itself the result of global lobbying by NGOs since the start of the preparatory process (Korey 1998:278-279).

NGOs also submitted written materials to the governmental conference. The Inter-American Institute of Human Rights, based in San José, Costa Rica, conducted an "orientation session" for NGOs the day before the opening of the regional preparatory meeting in San José in early 1993.[5] At that session, NGOs coordinated lobbying strategies (Azzam 1993:93). NGOs were able to comment on the governments' proceedings during the San José meeting. Jointly and individually, the NGOs had prepared detailed, analytic statements that were entered into the conference record. Their written and oral responses to items on the governmental agenda formed the basis of a joint NGO document for presentation at the final global PrepCom and at the World Conference itself. In a meeting with the governmental drafting committee, NGOs also commented on the draft governmental declaration (Preparatory Meetings: Latin American and Caribbean Regional Meeting 1993). The governments' call for a UN High Commissioner for Human Rights, the need to strengthen the UN Centre for Human Rights (now the Office of the High Commissioner for Human Rights), and the need to protect vulnerable groups can be traced to NGO input (Azzam 1993:93). Notably the role of NGOs in the protection or advancement of human rights was not mentioned at all in the governments' regional declaration.

Social Dimensions

There was a degree of shared framing evidenced among the statements of Latin American NGOs and governments throughout the Vienna preparations and throughout the conference itself. The governments supported new requests for resources to be devoted to human rights at the international level, along with newly inclusive rhetoric. The governments emphasized support for international human rights mechanisms, but were quiet about their own responsibilities to investigate and prosecute abuses. Instead, they stopped with the recognition that "rupture of the democratic order threatens human rights in the country concerned"(United Nations 1993c, 1993f). The issue of dealing with past violations at home was muted by the Latin American governments.

NGOs forthrightly invoked the linkages among differing conceptions of human rights. At San José, looking back to the Rio summit and forward to the Vienna and Beijing conferences, they stressed the need for better protection of all forms of rights, including the rights of women and environmental considerations.[6] With the San José meeting sandwiched between the African and Asian regional meetings, where human rights' universality was questioned,[7] the Latin American NGOs stood up for the importance of implementing the historical consensus for universal human rights. But they also pushed for expansion of the meaning of those rights in light of the North's impact on the region's economic, social, and cultural history, and they carried their regional concerns to Vienna. They criticized neoliberal economic models not just for marginalizing some social groups and for concentrating wealth, but also for causing harm to the environment. From their own governments, they wanted stronger domestic implementation of international human rights commitments, as well as measures to counter impunity for past violations. They also criticized militarism as an obstacle to full realization of human rights, emphasizing that armed forces should submit to civilian authorities at all times and that the judicial measures of habeas corpus should be upheld even during states of siege. The NGOs also wanted *developed* governments to work toward closing the developed/developing country gap and invoked the Proclamation of Tehran, issued twenty-five years earlier at the UN's only previous world conference on human rights, on that point. In addition, they adopted declarations on the status of women and on indigenous peoples (Annex II:1993). While a North-South split was in evidence in the backlash against the NGOs' planning committee at the start of the Vienna conference, Southern NGOs found themselves united with their Northern counterparts in the desire to lobby governments for strong human rights commitments (Korey 1998:291).

In contrast, the debate among governments at San José centered on democratization and resource issues, such as the right to development and Latin America's history of unequal economic relations with the North (Azzam 1993:93). In that respect, they were open to expanded conceptions of human rights while retaining an emphasis on implementing democratic reforms. They also were receptive to further guarantees of protection for "vulnerable social groups." However, governments could not come to an agreement on whether or not they should endorse a stronger human rights enforcement capacity for the UN. Cuba, Mexico, Colombia, and Peru blocked such a proposal by Costa Rica at the San José meeting (Payne 1993). Latin American governments also blamed their international debt obligations for interfering with their ability to comply with international human rights standards (Lewis 1993b). Unlike their NGO counterparts, governments protested human rights-related sanctions: "when democratic Governments are making determined efforts to resolve their human rights problems, such problems should not be used for political ends or as a condition for extending assistance or socio-economic cooperation" (United Nations 1993c:Item 12). Their characterization of "obstacles to the observance of human rights," which was one of the agenda items, emphasized the international factors, with only a nod to domestic failings such as "the lack of genuinely independent systems of justice" (Ibid.:Item 10). The San José governmental statement did not include any version of the phrase "national and regional particularities," which the other regional governmental statements used as a veiled questioning of universalism, but instead emphasized international cooperation.

The NGOs at the Vienna conference itself addressed their concerns in topical working groups at the NGO Forum. Five had been planned, and five more were established at the site. One of the latter groups addressed the connection between military forces and human rights violations, including specific forms of repression such as disappearances and torture. It also addressed impunity, a main concern of the Latin American NGOs (Nowak 1993:87-88). Even though their range of concerns had expanded from the older issues of torture and other threats to physical integrity to encompass greater attention to the rights of the poor, women, the disabled, and indigenous peoples, the Latin American NGOs wanted to maintain external pressure upon the governments of their own region to investigate and punish the perpetrators of past violence. For their governments, however, the issue of impunity appeared only in a list of obstacles to human rights with no comment as to where prosecutory responsibility rested (United Nations 1993c:Item 10).

The Latin Americans appended an addendum to the final NGO statement at Vienna because the Forum had not had time to deal with all of their concerns. The addendum did not mention Latin America in particular, but it did offer a detailed analysis of the way in which the legacy of North-South economic inequality contributes to human rights violations of all kinds: "grave violations of human rights still occur; in past decades dictatorial regimes were mainly responsible, but in recent years they have been witnessed in restrictive neo-liberal democracies under new forms of authoritarianism engendering corruption, violence and impunity," characteristically appearing with "harsh adjustment policies" (Addendum 1 to the Final Report of the NGO-Forum 1993:95).

Beyond the shared interpretations of the economic pressures on Latin America (although there might be disagreement about the proper solution), a striking manifestation of a shared Latin American perspective among NGOs and governments was the combination of support for universal conceptions of human rights in tandem with an opposition to external intervention, particularly from the United States. For NGOs, regionally shared resentments came to a head when U.S. President Jimmy Carter addressed the NGO Forum at Vienna. He had championed human rights in U.S. foreign policy, but the Latin American NGOs remembered that U.S. security policy in Latin America had often trumped human rights rhetoric by aiding or abetting authoritarian governments in their region. Carter was shouted down with cries of "Carter No," and "Go Home" and had to abandon the rostrum ("Hecklers Stop Carter Speech" 1993; Prinz 1993; da Costa and Johnson 1993). One news report quoted an Argentine protester's comment that "the shouts were 'the cries of thousands of people killed with American guns sold to Latin American armies'" (Riding 1993b: 23).

Latin American governments were not as vocal as Latin American NGOs in addressing intervention issues or their own complicity in human rights violations. Neither did they join the overt opposition to internationally applicable concepts of human rights articulated by Asian and African governments prior to and during the Vienna conference, but journalistic and academic accounts of the conference are curiously silent about the positions of the Latin American governments. In the set of government statements upon the adoption of the Vienna Declaration and Program of Action, only Argentina and Chile are represented from the Latin American region, but the Chilean delegate gave a surprisingly blunt statement indicating regrets at governments' role in limiting the procedures and substance of achievements at the conference (Declaración de la delegación de Chile, nd). The Latin American governments did not associate themselves publicly with the strongly universalist positions of the Western governments, led by the United States, nor with their anti-universalist opponents.

The Fourth World Conference on Women, Beijing, 1995

Participation in a more established global civil society, particularly on the part of Latin American NGO representatives, was evident at Beijing. Women participated in large and diverse numbers throughout the process, with representation itself a major preoccupation of regional organizers. They had frequent opportunities to develop civil relations among themselves, and eventually agreed to extend their efforts into the governmental realm. There they were widely accepted as legitimate participants. However, on the issue of gender relations a deep division among some governments and NGOs showed an incomplete development of social values in the region as a whole.

Global Dimensions of NGO Participation on Women's Rights

It is hard to estimate exactly how many Latin American women took part in the Beijing process, but they participated in large and fairly representative numbers throughout. The national-level preparations incorporated hundreds of women from diverse backgrounds in local and national meetings in order to develop national NGO documents on women's status. This widespread involvement was reflected in the 1,200 people who attended the NGO parallel forum of the regional preparatory meeting (NGO Forum on Women 1995:95). In far-flung Beijing, Latin America (and the Caribbean) sent 5 percent (1,500) of those attending the NGO Forum at Huairou, compared to 2 percent from Western Asia, 8 percent from Africa, 40 percent from Europe and North America, and 45 percent from Asia and the Pacific (Ibid.:16). Moreover, all but one of the Latin American countries had accredited NGOs at the official conference, altogether making up 147 (8 percent) of all accredited NGOs.[8]

Prior to Beijing, regional relations among Latin American NGOs and individual activists had been fostered through the feminist *Encuentros* or "meetings" held every few years for the last two decades (Ibid.:14; Sternbach et al. 1992). International links had also grown from former exiles' experiences in Europe and the United States during the decades of repression. These links were further enhanced by Latin American activists' more recent participation in UN world conferences from the mid-'70s to the 1990s (Alvarez 1990, Lamas et al. 1995).

Civil Dimensions

Reflecting the historical dynamics of the region, the development of civil interactions among NGOs and governments was contentious although ultimately successful. During the conference process NGOs found many opportunities to interact, albeit often to debate their different points of view. The issue of cooperation with governments was itself one of the central points of debate among NGOs, somewhat resolved by the incorporation of nongovernmental strategies into governmental fora.

Regularization of NGO participation in the preparatory process benefited from the implementation of the regional organizing strategy developed by the UN-based NGO coordinating committee for Beijing (NGO Forum on Women 1995:9-10). "Focal points" in each country coordinated nongovernmental evaluations of the status of women, the results of which were gathered first in six subregional meetings, and then brought to the NGO forum of the official regional preparatory meeting in Mar de Plata, Argentina, in September 1994. Thematic networks also organized cross-nationally (Vargas Valente 1996:45, footnote 2).

Funding for such participation was fiercely debated. Due to the U.S. Agency for International Development (AID)'s controversial history in the region, many women's groups disagreed over accepting the funding proffered by the agency, which had been made financially responsible for much of the NGO regional preparatory process. This debate was especially heated in the large Brazilian women's movement, where AID funding was eventually turned down. Organizers in other countries decided it was high time the United States gave money for a worthy cause, and took AID up on its offer. And even the Brazilians found alternative external funding; their "Articulation" organizing group was supported by $40,000 from the Ford Foundation, as well as by UNIFEM, the UN Fund for Women (Mello 1994:28-29; Sant'Anna 1994:5-6).

A central goal of the nongovernmental organizing was to insure the widest possible representation. The NGO coordinating committee's urging to incorporate traditionally underrepresented groups, such as indigenous and young women, was widely heeded, particularly when funders insisted. "NGOs and women's movements" were equally welcomed, and usually both invoked, during the regional discussions in Mar de Plata. This drew attention to women's different organizing approaches, which were the subject of considerable discussion in the region (Alvarez 1998:308). Virginia Vargas, a central coordinator of the regional process, repeatedly stressed the participation of women in all their diversity. Her goal for an inclusive global movement of women was to seek "equity in order to develop differences," and Beijing was seen not as an end in itself but a way to strengthen women's movements (Vargas, n.d.).

However, the emphasis on hearing different women's voices resulted in charged discussions throughout the workshops and plenaries. In one plenary response period at Mar de Plata, a Catholic activist asked the panel participants why nonfeminist NGOs were excluded from the meeting panels—to which the moderator responded that she would be happy to discuss the power of the church. In another plenary discussion a Bolivian radical feminist accused NGOs of establishing new power hierarchies among women, using their outside funding to promote clientelistic relationships with poor women, and a Bolivian peasant representative chided NGO panelists for engaging in complex discussions of gendered citizenship while peasants were still having trouble registering to vote. Moreover, due to their sense that the dominant Argentine political party was too tightly controlling the NGO parallel conference, independent Argentine feminists, along with activists from Bolivia and Mexico, held a three-hundred-person parallel-to-the-parallel forum with a set of meetings off-site.

The debate over different forms and expressions of women's activism resulted in little attention paid to lobbying governments at the regional meeting. This result could not be wholly blamed on the dynamics of the meeting; only one of the three documents prepared for general discussion at the conference mentioned lobbying strategies directly. Moreover, the issue of nongovernmental/governmental cooperation was itself a contentious proposition. Despite a move in the last few decades from a stance of confrontation to one of negotiation vis-à-vis governments (Vargas Valente 1996:45), many women's rights activists in the region are not convinced that democratizing governments are sufficiently committed to the democratization of gender relations. Not surprisingly, women in civil society disagreed over the extent to which they were willing to ally themselves with their governments during the conference preparations. Many NGO members and independent feminists cooperated with governmental women's agencies in the national-level assessments of women's status (Alvarez 1998:303; Faccio 1995:4; Ramírez 1995:8). Their contribution was recognized by governments: the regional governmental document refers throughout to the role of both NGOs and women's movements in achieving gender equity (United Nations 1995d). But other nongovernmental actors were deeply concerned about the potential for state cooptation (Aguila 1995:15-16).

By the time of the Beijing conference, however, Latin American activists, particularly regional leaders, began to focus on lobbying. They had become mobilized by the overall exclusion of NGOs at the

Fourth PrepCom in March 1995 (see chapter 2; Valdés 1995), and the bracketing of language that they supported in the final document, the Platform for Action. Increased participation in "North American feminist-controlled global mega-networks" also helped to bring Latin American perspectives to global organizing, as well as to orient Latin American activists to the lobbying process (Alvarez 1998:310; NGO Forum on Women 1995:14; Vargas Valente 1996:54). As the conference approached, women focused on the makeup of the official delegations. Feminists in Guatemala, Argentina, and Paraguay objected when their governments appointed Catholic activists focused on a traditionalist gender agenda to the delegations (Amado 1995:3; Asturias 1995:2; Rodríguez A. 1995:5). By Beijing, NGO representatives were appointed to the majority of Latin American delegations (Alvarez 1998:303; NGO Forum on Women 1995:15).

However, as had become apparent from preparatory organizing, there was a general division between those who came to Beijing to lobby governments, and those who came to network among fellow activists. It was in the Latin American and Caribbean "tent"—one of several regional meeting spaces at the NGO Forum—where those particularly identified as movement activists aired objections to lobbying. According to one activist, "'Feminism has ceased to be marginal and is now institutional . . . the cost of this institutionalization has been great . . . it seems that we have forgotten about process . . . the most urgent of our problems will not be resolved here [in Beijing].'" NGOs appeared to another participant to be "'legitimated by the patriarchal powers'" (Alvarez 1998:312-313). The distance between the site of the official conference and NGO Forum (at least an hour by bus) exacerbated the different orientations of the participants. But particular leaders made a great effort to be in two places at once, giving regular reports on the official conference at the regional tent. As a result of their efforts to bridge the governmental and nongovernmental division, the closing declaration from the tent celebrated the vast efforts, both historical and current, which made possible the actions taken at Beijing, particularly the growing emphasis on negotiation or lobbying ("Declaración de América Latina y del Caribe" 1995).

Moreover, the techniques used at the official conference to solicit governmental response pushed the boundaries of lobbying techniques to include more movement-oriented strategies. The lobbiers found allies in many of the delegations (Hernández Carballido 1995:4; Navarro 1995).[9] But those accredited to the official conference also took more direct action, particularly around the issue of economic justice, which they found neglected. After she gave only the opening sentences of her prepared speech to the governmental plenary, Virginia Vargas unfurled a banner displaying the following words: "Transparency—New Resources—Economic Justice." Holding it, she stood in silence for the rest of her allotted time. In an incident described in chapter 2, Latin American activists took over the central escalators in the conference center, holding a forbidden demonstration on economic justice.

Social Dimensions

Latin American NGOs were largely able to come to agreement on the issues the conference addressed. Regional governments shared some frames with them, particularly on the need for economic development. But there was frame disalignment between NGOs and half of the regional governments over the issue of how much to challenge the structure of gender relations. This conflict became evident at the regional preparatory meeting and continued in Beijing.

The regional governmental document focused on eight priority areas, including gender equity; development with a gender perspective; elimination of poverty; women's equitable participation in decision making in public and private life; human rights/peace/violence; shared family responsibilities; recognition of cultural plurality; and international support and cooperation (United Nations 1995d). Economic development issues in particular were highlighted at Beijing. Government representatives from Ecuador, Venezuela, Honduras, Haiti, and Cuba used their plenary time to point to the problems stemming from structural adjustment, and/or the insensitivity of the First World to the Third World's economic problems. Other governments drew attention to the problem of poverty in the region, but did not overtly question development policies promoted by First World governments and international and regional multilateral lending institutions.

Regional NGO documents attest to NGO agreement with many governmental perspectives; however, the NGOs' language is often stronger or more precisely targeted. The regional NGO meeting's summary document on development, for example, was focused in its entirety on "structural adjustment." It claimed that "[p]eriods of adjustment continue to leave women as the most beaten down [*golpeadas*] by these programs and moreover with their capacity to fight back diminished" (Cuales 1994:1). In the closing declaration from their tent at the NGO Forum in Beijing regional activists recognized that structural adjustment policies had controlled spiraling inflation in the region, but emphasized their "enormous social costs," finding that they "sustain[ed] the concentration of wealth and cause[d] the fragmentation and the exclusion of wide sectors of the population, weakening the social fabric" ("Declaración de América Latina y del Caribe" 1995).

Very significant differences between nongovermental and governmental perspectives appeared in the area of gender relations. Throughout the conference process, Latin American NGOs promoted a universal women's rights agenda[10] that included aspects perceived as contravening Catholic or socially conservative beliefs, such as the protection of reproductive rights as well as gay and lesbian rights, and the decriminalization of "voluntary interruption of pregnancy" (Faccio 1994:8-10). NGOs indicated their opposition to the position of the Vatican and its allies on these issues by suggesting that Latin American states "detain the expansion, diffusion and impact of religious and political fundamentalism" (Ibid.:9) and that the whole conference reconsider the fact that the Holy See holds governmental rather than nongovernmental status at the UN (NGO Forum on Women 1995:88).[11]

Among the allies of the Vatican, NGOs found half of their own regional governments. These joined the Holy See and governments influenced by conservative Islamic thought in defending a more traditional conception of gender relations. This defense was illustrated by the often amusing, yet quite serious debate over the use of the word *gender*. During the preparatory process, the Vatican objected to the feminist understanding of the word *gender,* which makes a distinction between biological sex and the roles, expectations, and actions of socialized men and women. Such a definition challenges the church doctrine on gender role "complementarity" and opens the door to accepting different sexual orientations. The Archbishop of Tegucigalpa and President of the Latin American Episcopal Conference, Oscar Rodríguez, went as far as to assert that the goal of Beijing was "to force society to accept five types of gender: masculine, feminine, lesbian, homosexual and transsexual" (quoted in Franco 1998:282). At the final PrepCom, Honduras took the lead in insisting that "gender" be bracketed throughout the Platform for Action, pending a satisfactory definition (*ENB* 3 April 1995). Mysteriously, when Spanish-speaking delegates arrived in Beijing, they found that their version of the Platform for Action substituted "sex" for "gender" all the way through. While this "mistake" and the conflict over the term were resolved in favor of keeping the term *gender* in the document, the larger debate continued throughout the conference. Plenary statements from Ecuador, Peru, and Argentina, and Platform for Action reservations from the Dominican Republic, Guatemala, Honduras, and Peru affirmed that life begins at conception.[12] A plenary statement from Chile and reservations from Argentina, the Dominican Republic, Honduras, Peru, and Venezuela opposed legalizing abortion and, frequently, its use as a method of family planning. In the Platform for Action negotiations Peru and Guatemala insisted that women leaders also be referred to as mothers (*ENB* 9 September 1995). Argentina and Ecuador objected to language giving women the "right" to control their fertility because it would give women new rights (Ibid.:6 September 1995). In reservations, Argentina and Peru defined the family as based on the relationship between a man and a woman; Paraguay and Guatemala declared gender to refer to both sexes; and Peru held that "sexual rights" only applied to heterosexual relationships.

During the entire Beijing process Argentina, Chile, the Dominican Republic, Ecuador, El Salvador, Guatemala, Honduras, Nicaragua, Peru, and Venezuela followed the Vatican framing on gender relations—and opposed the ideas of their own NGOs—to some extent. On the other hand, Bolivia, Brazil, Colombia, Costa Rica, Cuba, Haiti, Mexico, Panama, Paraguay, and Uruguay were either supportive of NGOs or silent on such issues.

Conclusion

What do the findings from Latin American participation at the three UN conferences tell us about the existence and impact of a global civil society? Table 3.2 summarizes the results of our study and compares them to both the global results and our expectations about the regional findings.

First let us consider the globality of Latin American participation. Overall, there was substantial regional NGO participation across the set of conferences. At both Rio and Vienna, the numbers of Latin American participants rose above the Latin American share of global population. The predominance of Latin Americans at the NGO Forum of the one conference in their own region (Rio, 41 percent) and their relative scarcity in faraway Beijing (5 per-

Table 3.2 Global Civil Society: The Global and Regional Evidence

Dimensions	Empirical Findings: Global (from chapter 2)	Expectations: Latin American Region	Empirical Findings: LA Region
Global	Northern imbalance in numbers of NGOs	Latin American NGO participation lower than share, especially compared to Northern NGOs	Latin American NGO participation disproportionately high at Vienna and Rio, lower at Beijing
Civil	new rules and heavy interaction; rules and limits imposed by states	governmental inclusion of NGOs; NGO efforts to guard independence from governments	mixed govern-mental inclusion of NGOs; Cooper-ation among Northern and Sourthern NGOs; independent lobbying at all conferences, with lobbying-network-ing debate at Rio and Beijing
Social	development of common frames among NGOs; lack of shared NGO-state understandings	NGO-state differences on economic models (neoliberalism) and on rights	similar NGO-state frames on economic models; mixed interpre-tations of rights

cent) illustrate that there are still practical and financial limits on the ability of regional NGOs to participate in global fora. Nonetheless, Latin Americans made up 8 percent of the NGOs accredited to the official conference in Beijing, and were 15 percent of the Forum representatives in Vienna, numbers that show that Latin Americans are likely to be a part of any global civil society that forms.

Civility was manifest in the growth of regional networking among NGOs through all of the conference processes, as well as in Latin American NGOs' strategic alliances with other Northern and Southern NGOs. Latin American governments' influence on NGO repertoires was manifest in their qualified acceptance of NGO participation at both regional and global conferences: they were more eager to incorporate NGO delegates in conference processes than to promise future collaboration. Meanwhile, NGOs in the environ-

mental and women's sectors were split as to the degree of cooperation they sought with governments, with many more interested in
talking to each other than focusing possibly futile efforts on altering governmental agendas. But some compromises were struck,
with an infiltration of nongovernmental strategies into governmental arenas at Beijing. The lobbying/networking division was not as
deeply at issue for NGOs at Vienna, perhaps because a major goal
was to achieve stronger rights guarantees from governments, virtually requiring a lobbying approach. In all three issue areas, however, Latin American governments still carry the burden of proof to
show that they are willing to accept civil society actors as partners,
both at home and abroad.

When it came to the social component, NGO representatives
sought to push issues farther than governments, whether it meant
promoting sustainable development, punishing human rights violators, or challenging traditional gender relations. But there was a
surprising amount of frame alignment among representatives of
civil society and governments as well: at Rio, the development/envi-
ronment connection was upheld by all, as was a focus on the need
to address poverty; at Vienna, the Latin American governments did
not dispute the universalism of human rights, as governments
from Asia and Africa did; and at Beijing, half of the countries
seemed to be not openly opposed to NGO perspectives on gender relations. Along with their NGOs, almost all Latin American governments seemed to be more interested in criticizing neoliberal economic models, and their impacts on populations, than in
supporting the recent economic changes.

What light do these findings shed on our initial questions concerning the extent to which Latin American participation in global
fora reflect global patterns of civil society development? As can be
seen in table 3.2, the Latin American NGOs have successfully
struggled to increase representation in global civil society. Representation in, and access to, global fora remain difficult for participants from developing countries, though effective regional preparatory processes can help in this regard. As to the extent of civility,
we did indeed find, as predicted, that NGOs continue to insist on
independence from their governments, partially in response to the
inconsistent welcome from those quarters. But two other central
influences emerge in NGO repertoires: strong internal debates over
the focus of NGOs' efforts (the lobbying vs. networking debates), as
well as the crucial support for Latin Americans' actions and positions from extraregional NGO networks. Thus, the qualified de-

mocratization of procedures on the part of governments was met by
ambivalence on the part of NGOs, many of whom preferred to create dialogue among themselves. Finally, while the extent of the society created by Latin American NGOs and governments at the
conferences was limited by real differences over the framing of issues, particularly in the rights arena, more agreement was evident
regionally than at a global level.

It is clear from this analysis that regional dynamics do have a
profound impact on participation in global civil society. The contention among NGOs over the most effective use of energy and resources can be easily traced to a history of civil society/state confrontation in the region, as well as to the uncertainties about the
extent of national democratization. The issues on which shared understandings are difficult to craft at the global level reflect ongoing,
deep-seated regional problems that governments have proved unwilling or slow to address: environmental degradation in the context of economic inequality, impunity for human rights violators,
and lack of full equality and autonomy for women.

But the growing numbers of participants, and perhaps unexpected agreements on procedures and substance, revealed in this
study of Latin American participation in global civil society also tell
another story. Even when deeply split at home, governments and
NGOs can make common cause at the global level, especially to
press home issues that continue to disproportionately affect the
global South. Simultaneously, NGOs have used their growing networks of allies in the North and South to advocate positions that
remain highly contentious at home. Thus, for very regional reasons, Latin Americans' involvement in global civil society has become stronger than we anticipated. Latin Americans are participants, and not laggards, in the reworking of global politics, but
further democratization of global politics depends on deepening
democratic relations at home.

CHAPTER 4

———

Sovereignty in the Balance

Sovereignty is a key set of privileges that states, and no other kind of international actor, possess. The principle of sovereignty provides the rationale behind a state's legal equality with other states, and protects its capacity for authoritative action vis-à-vis other actors. Assessments of the relative importance of state and non-state actors in international politics, therefore, have depended in large part on assessments of whether and how sovereignty may be eroding as a guarantor of state power in certain domains. In this chapter, we examine how sovereignty has been challenged and reformulated in the specific domain of the UN conferences.

The general debate over changes in sovereignty and their permanence and significance is far from settled. Scholars attempting to articulate the practical and theoretical purview of the state have always found international rhetoric and practice to be riddled with the kinds of contradictions that naturally arise in response to contingent political events. Rather than settle the potential conflict between state power and transnational links, astute political actors attempt to make the most of the indeterminacies. As we observed in chapters 1 and 2, in some cases, particularly economic, environmental, and social issues with transnational components, sovereignty appears both more vulnerable and less relevant than it used to be (Wapner 1995; Sikkink 1993; Litfin 1997). Globalizing economic influences coexist and sometimes collide with the power politics of the nation-state, but debate over the manner in which each form of influence will endure continues (see Waltz 1999).

Norms of sovereign autonomy may protect differing national

ways of life at the same time that international norms of human rights seek to preserve minority practices from the assertion of state control (Jacobsen and Lawson 1999). On social issues such as women's rights that used to be considered far from affairs of state, "advocates have found it both necessary and expedient to find allies across national borders" (Friedman 2003:316). Women's rights activists, as well as human rights advocates more generally, have worked transnationally to frame, politicize, and position women's issues with respect to the international human rights framework (Ibid.; Joachim 2003; A. M. Clark 2001). States have used sovereignty both instrumentally and symbolically at different times to negotiate the management of global environmental commons such as oceans and the atmosphere (e.g., Mitchell 1998). And finally, without much fuss states themselves have ceded some measure of autonomy to manage other common affairs through intergovernmental organizations (Abbott and Snidal 1998), with the result that states' own understandings of their interests may be redefined in the process (Finnemore 1996).

Stephen D. Krasner (1999:40) suggests that states have long employed various forms of compromise in the exercise of their sovereignty, asserting that "rulers have invited violations of their de facto autonomy of their own polities" for instrumental purposes. In this view, sovereignty has always involved "organized hypocrisy." While our study is compatible with such an assertion to the extent that we analyze outcomes as potential trades of aspects of sovereignty, it is important not to assume that sovereignty is so flexible that it is whatever states decide that it is. We believe that the "organized hypocrisy" view does not fully account for why states assert sovereign rights so strongly in the face of the particular challenges that arose at the UN conferences. States protest too much.

Sovereignty in and of itself is not necessarily the "enemy" of environmental protection or other transnational issues (Litfin 1997:168), although states and nongovernmental organizations (NGOs) at the UN conferences often occupied opposing positions that hinged on whether states should have autonomy over these issues. On this basis, it must be noted that in large part, governments still strive to protect and consolidate their sovereign privileges as they debate such issues with one another and with non-state actors. While Southern and Northern NGOs joined with some Northern governmental conference delegations at Rio, Vienna, and Beijing to propose new understandings of environmental sustainability, universal human rights, and women's roles, both

Northern and Southern states—especially the latter—continued to use the language of sovereignty to respond to transnational challenges to their authority. Governmental representatives articulated claims to the sovereign rights of states throughout all three conference processes: from the first drafts of working procedures, through the PrepComs that negotiated conference agreements and action plans, to the reservations on the final documents. As we observe in this chapter, states tried to claim and manipulate sovereignty in ways that would preserve some aspects of their sovereign capacities. However, in the UN conference arenas, sovereign states faced concerted challenges to their claims from members of global civil society. Patterns that we observe in the content of compromises and controversies at the conferences allow us to hypothesize about the meaning and import of sovereign claims as they appear in international practice.

In this chapter we analyze states' sovereign claims and non-state actors' challenges to those claims at the UN conferences on the environment, human rights, and women. Following the discussion in chapter 1, we investigate sovereignty as a multidimensional concept whose elements are bargained and traded by states—not always freely. In this view, states value control, autonomy, and legitimacy in the eyes of other state and non-state actors; however, when all cannot be had at once, states may have to make compromises. Thus, the interaction at the conferences potentially tells us what states deem appropriate content for sovereignty claims. While this content can vary widely, it is not random or arbitrary. The UN conferences provided an arena in which shared understandings about what constitutes supportable sovereign claims were hammered out, amended, and sometimes reinforced through give-and-take among states and between states and NGOs. By separating sovereignty into four elements, we are able to analyze the nature of such claims and their implications for democracy at the global level (cf. Litfin 1997). Taking sovereignty apart in this way and applying it to the statements and actions of states and NGOs in comparable, well-defined venues allows us to recognize sovereignty's malleability and to analyze any changes over time.

We start with a brief review of the four aspects of sovereignty we have identified: autonomy, control, legitimacy among other states, and legitimacy among non-state actors. The first dimension of sovereignty, autonomy, refers to states' ability to make independent decisions for their own territory and citizens. It is an externally oriented dimension of sovereignty, which highlights states' right to make such decisions without interference from outside actors. The second dimension, control, refers to states' ability to achieve the results they seek, usually inside their boundaries. The final two dimensions both relate to legitimacy, the recognition by other actors of states' sovereign authority. We posit that the actors bestowing or withholding legitimacy on states' sovereign claims may be other states or non-state actors. While sovereign legitimacy, as external recognition of a state's sovereign authority, is formally granted or withheld by other states, it may take into account the quality of a government's internal relations with its own citizens as well as government capacity to exercise authority.[1] This is the dimension of sovereignty we refer to as legitimacy among other states. And, as we have observed in chapters 1 and 2, non-state actors at the global level also see themselves as monitors of states. In this capacity, they have the potential to play a transnational legitimating role in global politics. Thus, global non-state actors' activities as a transnational audience for states' sovereignty claims may also influence state sovereignty and bargaining. This is the dimension of sovereignty we refer to as legitimacy among non-state actors.

In this chapter we attempt to do two things: first, establish a foundation for the premise that legitimacy appears to incorporate this non-state dimension in our cases; and second, investigate whether the cases reveal patterns in the ways in which states negotiate among the four components of sovereignty. There are many potential trade-offs available. The choices among potential trades provide different ways for states to assert and manage their sovereignty, and offer legitimating actors—both state and non-state—differing degrees of influence over states. Accordingly, we would expect the politics of different issues to influence the content of the bargains that are or are not made. Table 4.1 elaborates on the types of bargains that could be struck among the four posited dimensions of sovereignty.

Our study of sovereignty claims in these areas produces two main findings. First, although states continue to assert sovereign privilege, reserving the right to decide when to compromise their sovereignty, they do face new, external legitimating audiences. To the extent that nongovernmental organizations are able to demand accountability at the international level, they expand the external sources of legitimation for state sovereignty from states only to both states and non-state actors. Sometimes this external legitima-

Table 4.1 Potential Tradeoffs among Components of Sovereignty: The Nature of the Bargain and the Relevant International Actors Involved

	Component Gained			
	Autonomy	*Control*	*Legitimacy (Non-state)*	*Legitimacy (Other States)*
Autonomy	—	state trades autonomy to gain control; e.g., receiving international resources with conditions attached; may involve international monitoring	state trades autonomy to enhance legitimacy with non-state actors; e.g., responding to pressure or informal monitoring activities of non-state actors	state trades autonomy to enhance legitimacy with other states; e.g., conforming with international norms promoted by the community of states
Control	state trades internal control for autonomy; e.g., refusing to receive international resources with conditions attached because conditions reduce decision making autonomy	—	state trades internal control to enhance legitimacy with non-state actors; e.g., granting transnational actors powers to act domestically, or introducing formal mechanisms of accountability to non-state actors	state trades internal control to enhance legitimacy with other states, e.g., allowing environmental resource protection by other states
Legitimacy (Non-State)	state trades approval of non-state actors for autonomy; e.g., state unilaterally pursuing aims without consulting or responding to non-state actors	state trades approval of non-state actors to gain internal control; e.g., repressing domestic activities of non-state transnational actors	—	state trades approval of non-state actors to gain approval of other states; e.g., joining with other states to exclude non-state actors from international negotiations

(continued)

Table 4.1 *(continued)*

		Component Gained			
		Autonomy	*Control*	*Legitimacy (Non-state)*	*Legitimacy (Other States)*
Component Traded Off	Legitimacy (Other States)	state trades approval of other states for autonomy; e.g., state pursues domestic preferences over conformity with external standards	state trades approval of other states to gain internal control; e.g., violating international rights norms in order to control domestic protest or promote economic goals	state trades approval of other state actors to gain approval of non-state actors; e.g., by supporting the preferences and participation of non-state actors over the objections of other states	—

tion is invited (Krasner 1999), but it may also be uninvited. NGOs, for their part, place demands on state legitimacy both internally and transnationally. Indeed, they often condition their acceptance of state authority in global governance on a larger governance and oversight role for themselves. If states are actually bargaining with uninvited, external legitimating agents, sovereignty as we know it is indeed at stake and potentially diminished.

Second, in the cases under study, bargaining over interpretations of sovereignty has shaped sovereign claims and the responses of legitimating actors in a patterned way. Our findings show that sovereignty compromises are more likely when the potential for material gain is high, and less likely when states perceive core identity issues, such as values asserted by governments as central to particular national or cultural ways of life, to be at stake. In other words, for states seeking resource concessions on certain issues, sovereignty is used as a bargaining chip. Outside of the realm of military power, sovereignty emerges as less central to states' material interests and more central to their asserted social identities than standard arguments over sovereignty suggest. In this chapter, we present our evidence for these claims based on the environment, human rights, and women's conferences. We further test and refine our findings in chapter 5, with an analysis of three more conferences on different issues.

Sovereignty Claims

Three main conflicts over sovereignty claims emerge from a comparison of debates at Rio, Vienna, and Beijing: on discussions of economics, national values, and monitoring mechanisms. First, at Rio, the strongest claims were made for autonomy and control over national economic development and resources. China and the vast majority of the G-77, as the bloc of developing states is called, joined in the economic claims, with a few Northern countries—notably the United States—also stressing national economic autonomy. Second, at Vienna and Beijing, states argued strongly for autonomous determination of "national" or "cultural" values. Countries in which conservative Catholic and Muslim beliefs and/or leaders wield political influence articulated many of the cultural autonomy claims, against universal rights understandings strongly supported by Northern countries and by NGOs around the world. Finally, at all three conferences, states debated the extent to which they would be subject to new legitimating mechanisms of international monitoring and accountability proposed both by other states and by non-state actors. While engaging in debates around these claims, states invoked arguments that map onto conflicts among the conceptual dimensions of sovereignty just outlined.

NGOs entered the debates at all three of the conferences, where NGOs from Northern *and* Southern global regions consistently opposed most state sovereignty claims, and expressed skepticism about the bargains states made to shore up at least some dimensions of their sovereignty. NGOs joined with governmental delegations primarily from the North to propose global rather than national initiatives on environmental sustainability, universal human rights, and equality in gender relations. At all of the conferences, NGOs stressed the importance of meeting the needs of people around the world, rather than the needs of political and economic elites. NGOs' presence at the conferences and their substantive claims were intended to remind states that non-state actors were prepared to hold them accountable for their conference promises. In the next sections, we interpret states' claims to sovereignty over economics, national values, and international monitoring—and NGOs' counterclaims—using a multidimensional concept of sovereignty.

Economics: Rio

Countries at all three conferences claimed the right to make their own economic choices, but at Rio's Earth Summit bargaining focused on economic issues. The environmental bargaining invoked both the autonomy and control dimensions of sovereignty, centering on the potential trade-offs between choices over who directs states' environmental and development planning (autonomy) versus how states would gain the resources to act on those plans (control). Nearly all of the 103 statements made by heads of state or government at the Rio conference stressed that global cooperation was necessary in order to solve common environmental problems (United Nations 1993g:Vol. III), and environmental NGOs agreed (*Earth Summit: The NGO Archives* 1995), suggesting that legitimacy considerations supported negotiating an agreement for greater environmental protection.

At Rio, Northern and Southern states struck a bargain over the international mandate to conserve natural resources and states' ability to use natural resources for development. The bargain is evident in the Rio Declaration, a statement of principles written near the end of the conference process (United Nations 1993g:Vol. I). Leading principles of the declaration place sovereignty concerns at the forefront, affirming sovereign control over natural resources and the right to autonomous development (Principles 2 and 3, respectively). Other principles listed in the document, however, join national rights to control resources with new responsibilities to exercise them sustainably, with sensitivity to the physical and social environment.

The bargain, in sovereignty terms, amounts to the following. New obligations to implement sustainable development, that is, development policies limited by environmental and other social considerations, could be seen as violating states' claims for autonomous decision making on economic issues. For many Southern states, the new responsibilities were accepted only as a direct trade for Northern financing of sustainable development programs (Imber 1994). Thus while ceding a measure of autonomy through the trade-off, Southern states could potentially enhance their domestic control over both national economies and environmental outcomes. The President of Guatemala made this autonomy/control bargain clear in his statement to the Summit. He claimed national sovereignty over the use of Guatemala's forests, but added the caveat that "[f]orests are not in themselves a global resource, but they can become so provided that the social cost of maintaining or promoting them is shared" (United Nations 1993g:Vol. III:248).

The members of the G-77 justified the new Northern financial obligations implied by such a bargain with explicit arguments that Northern industrialization had itself created the current environmental problems. They argued that most of the resources for correcting existing environmental problems should be Northern as well. If the South were to prevent additional environmental degradation by forgoing heavy use of its own resources, the North should pay. Members of the G-77 also argued that the structure of international economic trade patterns, debt, and development institutions forced them into ecologically unsustainable models, diminishing their economic and environmental control and autonomy. Not every Southern country asserted all of these claims, but countries as diverse in other ways as Gabon, Cuba, Saint Kitts/Nevis, Azerbaijan, Iran, Colombia, Pakistan, and Malaysia, raised at least some of them (United Nations 1993g, Vol. III:19-20, 38-39, 40-41, 58, 82-83, 109, 153-154, 231-233). NGOs of both North and South supported many of these claims, with final NGO documents stressing the governments' inadequate treatment of issues of poverty, foreign debt, and multinational corporations: "The urgency of our commitment [to global environmental activism] is heightened by the choice of the world's political leaders in the official deliberations of the Earth Summit to neglect many of the most fundamental causes of the accelerating ecological and social devastation of our planet" ("People's Earth Declaration" 1992:1).

Financial arrangements were the most contentious part of negotiations over Agenda 21, the nonbinding action document of the Rio conference. They were settled only after high level representatives gathered face-to-face in Rio de Janeiro. Most Northern participants, including Canada, the United States, the Netherlands, Sweden, Japan, Austria, Norway, France, Ireland, Switzerland, Luxembourg, and the European Union, eventually pledged additional financial resources to help less wealthy countries meet their new environmental commitments (United Nations 1993g:Vol. III:73, 78, 106, 157, 163-164, 183, 191-192, 194, 199, 222, 246, 219). The cost of implementing Agenda 21 in developing countries was calculated in the document at $600 billion annually for 1993-2000, with grants and concessional loans to make up one-fourth of the

total amount (United Nations 1993g:Vol. I:417). However, this estimate far exceeded actual levels of official development assistance
from the countries that belong to the Organisation for Economic
Co-operation and Development, which reached only about $55 bil-
lion annually in the early 1990s, leaving a huge shortfall that neither North nor South wanted to fill (Grubb et al. 1993:174). Thus,
while more financial commitments were made at the Rio conference than later at Vienna or Beijing, the new resources pledged at
Rio fell far short of the actual costs of the promises and agreements
to protect the environment.

The trade of Southern autonomy over sustainable development
issues for Northern resources that would enhance Southern control
over those same issues was critical for achieving the Rio conference
results. Two counterfactuals illustrate the importance of such a
trade between elements of sovereignty for the bargain reached at
Rio. The first is the experience of the United States, which made
similar economic autonomy claims but was not in a position to receive the control-enhancing resources that facilitated the trade for
Southern states. The second is the ensuing negative outcome of the
Rio conference bargain itself, where the agreement collapsed when
neither side was willing to uphold its side of the bargain.

First, the United States, like the G-77, was especially persistent and forceful in asserting claims about its national economic autonomy and health throughout the conference process. Presented
with the promise of new resources, the G-77 did join in the global
bargain just described. The United States, on the other hand, with
no carrot of enhanced domestic control through international cooperation at stake, was tarred as one of the most recalcitrant participants, a "lone renegade" (Raustiala 1997:51; see also Middleton,
O'Keefe, and Moyo 1993). George H. W. Bush's administration refused to sign either of the accompanying treaties on biodiversity or
climate change, and the United States submitted the longest statement of written reservations of any country (United Nations
1993g:Vol. II:17-19). In this statement, the United States continued
to maintain its autonomy, taking special pains to deny that it was
bound by obligations implied by concepts like "the right to develop"
(Ibid.:17) or "the special leadership role of the developed countries"
(Ibid.:17-18) or by resource pledges (Ibid.:19).

Second, the longer-term results of the Rio agreement itself illustrate how central the proposed trade-off was to the diplomatic
bargain. Successive follow-up meetings of the Commission on Sustainable Development (created at Rio, and discussed later in this

chapter) have repeatedly focused on the failure of both North and South to hold up their respective ends of the bargain (Bigg and Dodds 1997). Northern financial resources for sustainable development in the South have not only not risen to prescribed new levels, but have actually shrunk by 20 percent since 1992. Southern countries, not surprisingly, have made correspondingly few moves to implement their own promises to make development more sustainable (Osborn and Bigg 1998:2-3). With no additional domestic control from new resources, Southern states have pressed forward autonomously for economic development.

NGOs had signaled their skepticism about the Rio outcome long before the bargain was completed, and were not surprised by these outcomes. During the Fourth PrepCom, NGOs sent a joint message to their governments, asking them to "Save UNCED" by addressing the issue of alternative economic development models directly ("Save UNCED: An Urgent Message to Governments" 1992). In a collective NGO document written and publicized in Rio, NGOs again chided governments of all kinds for failing to secure "the sovereign right and ability of the world's people to protect their economic, social, cultural and environmental interests" ("People's Earth Declaration" 1992:Point 3). Both documents resonate with claims for greater global accountability for states: the "People's Earth Declaration" states firmly that since the world's political leaders have failed to make the choices that will bring truly sustainable government, "the leadership for more fundamental change has fallen by default to the organizations and movements of civil society. We accept this challenge" (Ibid.:Point 2).

National Values: Vienna and Beijing

The cooperative rhetoric and practical bargaining of the Earth Summit, taking place as it did at the first very large global conference after the end of the Cold War, seemed to portend new possibilities for international cooperation on transnational issues. Indeed, the 1993 World Conference on Human Rights was conceived as an opportunity to assess past achievements and chart a new, post-Cold War trajectory for human rights (Korey 1998:274). Despite these expectations, one of the main sovereignty claims expressed at the human rights and women's conferences was for continued autonomy in promoting national or cultural values in the face of universal definitions of rights. At the Vienna conference, many states asserted the desire to choose among conceptions of human rights according to their own national priorities, an assertion made all the more provocative because it challenged a by-then well-established international legal consensus on civil and political human rights. At Beijing, a similar debate focused on the power of governments or nationally based groups independently to determine the structure of gender relations, particularly within the family. Not surprisingly, the countries that argued for particularistic interpretations of human rights and women's rights were those often criticized by NGOs and intergovernmental human rights bodies for concrete violations of universal definitions of rights. Many of those countries were also developing countries, and some of them also asserted that their population's development needs were more urgent than implementation of a Western liberal conception of individual rights.

VIENNA: A coalition of governments used autonomy arguments to attack a certain universalist conception of rights, namely the value placed on individual civil and political rights in the Western liberal tradition. These countries, mostly Asian and some Middle Eastern states, broached pleas for particularistic understandings of human rights, based on different historical, cultural, and religious backgrounds. The cultural relativist position was articulated most strongly in the Final Declaration of the regional preparatory conference for Asia, the Bangkok Declaration, in which governments maintained that universal human rights "must be considered in the context of a dynamic and evolving process of international norm-setting, bearing in mind the significance of national and regional particularities and various historical, cultural and religious backgrounds" (United Nations 1993d:Item 8). Statements that emerged from the African and Latin American regional meetings also implied that human rights standards might vary from country to country and should take economic development into account (United Nations 1992, 1993c; Lewis 1993c). From the regional preparatory meetings for Vienna through the final conference, the strong "particularity" proponents included China, Indonesia, Myanmar, Singapore, Malaysia, Vietnam, Iran, Syria, and Yemen (see Weiss, Forsythe, and Coate 1997:124; also Krauthammer 1993; Lewis 1993b; Riding 1993a; Sciolino 1993).

Many of the countries pushing hard for a relativist conception of human rights had also been subject to strong external human rights criticism. The Bangkok Declaration, in response, emphasized "respect for national sovereignty" and "the non-use of human rights as an instrument of political pressure" (United Nations 1993d:Item 5).

As Vienna opened, the Indonesian Foreign Minister addressed the conference, rejecting Western accusations of cultural relativism, and pleading for recognition of the complexity of human rights "due to the wide diversity in history, culture, value systems, geography and phases of development among the nations of the world," as well as "greater humility and less self-righteousness in addressing human rights issues" (Statement by Ali Alatas 14 June 1993). He parried such accusations by emphasizing the double standard inherent in Western criticism of Asian countries at the same time that ethnic cleansing was happening only "a few hundred kilometers" from Vienna, an allusion to the conflict in Bosnia and Herzegovina (Ibid.). Most observers interpreted the attacks on universalism as "a rather thinly disguised objection to external criticism of the serious human rights violations" (Boyle 1995:87). The arguments for relativism were greeted with some cynicism, due to the fact that many of the same countries had previously signed on to major international human rights treaties without registering official reservations (Weiss, Forsythe, and Coate 1997:124). But at Vienna, states opposing universality on religious or cultural grounds argued that their claims had merit because nation-states should have discretion over how such values were expressed in the context of national life. Thus, the assertion of national values as a component of sovereignty was, at least in part, a bid for renewed recognition of nation-states' autonomy on rights issues.

Human rights bids had certainly met with sovereignty objections before, and even the arguments of states that favored a universal conception of rights at Vienna could hardly be interpreted as proposing a deeper erosion of individual state autonomy. Instead, states affirmed the status quo as expressed in existing global human rights standards, which are strong on universal values in principle but weaker on implementation. Among governments, the United States led the push to reaffirm the universal human rights principle. The United States was backed by other Western nations, Russia and its former satellites, and India and Japan of the Asian region. Although the Latin American and African regional conference statements had expressed some misgivings about the universal applicability of human rights standards, at the final conference in Vienna, "most Latin American and some African countries" also affirmed the principle of universality (Riding 1993a; Boyle 1995:87).

States in favor of universality offered no new incentives to encourage recalcitrant states to change their minds on this issue.

Their offer of legitimacy was not new. By definition, universal rights are assumed to trump other claims, raising principle above pragmatic trade-offs. Proponents of universalism could thus remain rhetorically consistent in their unwillingness to compromise principle for other considerations.[2] Particularity proponents, for their part, were bracketing large portions of text during negotiations over the final document at Vienna. The term *bracketing* refers to the brackets used to mark language that still needs to be negotiated in a draft text. Used tactically, it could completely obstruct agreement on a final document, which would have been an embarrassing outcome for a conference meant to assess and celebrate progress on human rights. Indeed, although the final conference documents were supposed to be well on their way to completion by the time the conferences opened, as the Vienna conference approached, doubt remained as to whether a final document would be achieved at all.

Universality proponents, led by the United States, took a hard line in response. The United States declared that it was willing to do without a final document rather than accept backtracking on universality, pointing fingers at the countries seeking to reverse the universalist status quo (Lewis 1993c). To further pressure the relativists, the United States and its allies used a strategy termed *identify and isolate,* first threatening to name and then actually naming obstructionist governments. China, Syria, Iran, Iraq, Cuba, Myanmar, Sudan, Libya, Vietnam, North Korea, and Malaysia appeared on the United States' list of frequent bracketers (Lewis 1993a).

Significantly, the states arguing for relativism were unable to legitimate their bids for autonomy and control with the claim that their citizens wanted exceptions to the principle of universality, since NGOs at Vienna from all regions were supportive of it. The first substantive section of the declaration that emerged from the NGOs' parallel session at Bangkok, for example, affirmed universality and continued, "While advocating cultural pluralism, those cultural practices which derogate from universally accepted human rights including women's rights must not be tolerated" (Bangkok NGO Declaration on Human Rights of 27 March 1993:124). African NGOs, meeting at their parallel regional conference in Tunis, noted that they had "converged at an inter-cultural consensus on a universal culture of human rights, based on the respect for and the dignity of the human being ... [and] the rejection of all forms of discrimination, intolerance and fanaticism" (Tunis Declaration of

African NGOs of 6 November 1992:122). The NGOs' unity was un-
wavering on this point, despite some differences of approach and
priorities between grassroots NGOs, mostly from the South, and
the older, established human rights NGOs with closer institutional
ties to UN mechanisms (see Korey 1998; Human Rights Internet
1993). Representatives of Asian and Latin American indigenous
groups wanted explicit protection of their ways of life, in recognition and affirmation of what they saw as their special custodial relationship with the earth. A Costa Rican representative told a reporter, "During the Earth Summit . . . we were treated like stars, . .
. [b]ut no declaration was issued on our behalf. We refuse to be used
again, and that is why we need the support of all the NGOs present
here, so that we can put strong pressure on the system" (Pedro Ro-
driguez, quoted in Fernandez 1993:172). Arab NGOs joined in calls
for universality and for extension of human rights guarantees to
women (Bouabid 1993). A Tunisian NGO head noted, "what is ur-
gently needed is to face up to the steps backward announced by
some states which, under the argument of cultural and social particularities, wish to reduce women's rights" (Fred Fennich, quoted
in Bouabid 1993:173). At a coordinating conference in Cairo held
weeks before Vienna, Arab NGOs issued a statement backing particularity arguments where they enhanced respect for human
rights, but opposing "such approaches if they were used to negate
basic human rights or lead to their abrogation" (quoted in Bouabid
1993:173).

The final conference document produced at Vienna upheld universality in principle, tempering the rhetorical bids for increased
autonomy with regard to rights claims (United Nations 1993h). But
autonomy over national values was still used as a justification for
human rights violations. For the states seeking to defend a particularistic approach to rights claims, to yield on the principle of autonomy with reference to national values might have increased legitimacy. However, it also represented a threat to state control,
potentially undermining states' individual trade-offs, real or perceived, between protection of rights and other goals, such as economic development and internal order, without producing a tangible increase in material resources to enhance sovereign control.

BEIJING: States' insistence on autonomy with respect to particular rights claims was renewed at the Fourth World Conference on
Women, where states continued to debate cultural and religious
prerogatives related to gender relations, particularly as manifested
in family structures. As they had at Vienna, the debates at Beijing

focused in large part on autonomy with regard to particularistic understandings of national or cultural rights, rather than on states' material control of resources, territory, or population within their borders. Such legal and ideational understandings do have material effects, but the debates were framed in terms of autonomy over values. These issues had also been discussed at the 1994 International Conference on Population and Development at Cairo, which took place between the Vienna and Beijing conferences (see chapter 5). The most contentious language in Beijing's final document, the Platform for Action, referred to changing gender relations within the family—from women's control over their sexuality to the structure of the family unit itself (United Nations 1996c). A clear coalition of countries emerged in support of national cultural or religious values that depend fundamentally on a traditional conception of gender relations, in particular maintaining a woman's position within the family as a wife and mother and opposing absolute gender equality.

This coalition included governments sensitive to the claims of Catholic or Islamic religious authorities. Kuwait, Egypt, Libya, Mauritania, Oman, Brunei, Yemen, Sudan, the United Arab Emirates, Bahrain, Lebanon, Tunisia, Algeria, Morocco, Djibouti, Qatar, Syria, Comoros, Jordan, and Iran all lodged reservations on paragraphs in the Platform for Action deemed not to be in conformity with Islamic law, or Shariah (United Nations 1996c:723-735). For example, Kuwait registered a reservation "to anything which constitutes a contravention of the Islamic Shariah and the customs and practices of our Islamic society" (Ibid.:729). The issues covered in those paragraphs included reproductive rights (particularly the legality of abortion), control over sexuality, and family inheritance. Although not always explicitly, Latin American countries including Nicaragua, Guatemala, Argentina, Honduras, Peru, and Venezuela, as well as Malta, objected to paragraphs that contradicted the tenets of Catholicism as expressed by the Holy See (Ibid.:723-735). Their concerns overlapped with those of the governments that support Islam: ensuring parental control over children, defining the family as based on a heterosexual couple and their children, restricting sexual activity to heterosexual couples (joined in matrimony or common-law unions), and opposing abortion and homosexuality.

Some states asserted their autonomy through more traditional sovereignty claims that affirmed their own national legal structures as well as the inviolability of their borders. Several countries, including Libya, Japan, Peru, and the United States, lodged reservations or made statements to the effect that their national laws would take precedence over any international agreements implied by the Platform for Action (Ibid.). Developing countries, as represented by the G-77 and China, also referred directly to the need to protect their national boundaries in their invocation of foreign occupation or "alien domination" as a source of harm to women.

There were NGOs that sought to promote the agenda of more religiously oriented governments, even if they did not live in those countries. At the U.S. delegation's NGO briefing, for example, outspoken anti-abortion, pro-traditional "family values" advocates made their objections to the liberal U.S. position loud and clear. Two organizations, the Coalition for Women and the Family, and the Muslim Coalition for Women and the Family, circulated a leaflet entitled "Speak Out or Surrender Your Sovereignty" inside the conference hall a week into the conference. It exhorted all delegates to protect national sovereignty, and religious and cultural values, particularly those regarding the family and reproduction.

But the majority of NGO representatives pressed for a more expansive model of gender relations rather than a traditional one (United Nations Development Programme 1995). NGOs insisted on upholding "women's human rights," using a conceptual foundation that they had carefully laid at the Vienna conference, in collaboration with the United States and sympathetic states from Europe. The final NGO Beijing Declaration called upon all governments not to "misinterpret or impose religious beliefs or traditional practices on women in ways that deny their inalienable human rights." The same document also called for "an end to all laws and customary practices which deny girls and women their equal rights, and deny their equal access to succession and inheritance" (Institute for Global Communications 1995:2). Even NGOs whose governments claimed cultural distinctiveness made these arguments. Many Latin American women's groups, for example, placed their gender agenda before strict Catholic beliefs: a regional NGO spokeswoman praised the Beijing Conference for "the gains made in the face of conservative fundamentalist forces that threaten our dignity" (Vargas 1995). Meanwhile, some Arab NGOs sought a balance between Islamic beliefs and more universal conceptions of women's rights. They pointed out that many violations of Arab women's rights themselves violate Islamic law, noting: "The situation is beyond endurance in certain parts of the Arab world. There is a need to confront fundamentalist efforts to reinterpret the role of women in society" (Fayed 1995).

As at Vienna, NGOs at Beijing were relatively united in asking states to relinquish a conception of sovereign autonomy over values related to women's rights. But their bargaining power was weak. Because control over women is "so often at the base of the social order," thus placing gender relations at the core of what many countries consider their national identity or culture (Yuval-Davis 1998:24), external legitimacy from either state or non-state actors was not a useful enough exchange for what some states perceived as an immediate threat to their external autonomy and an eventual challenge to their internal control. Moreover, in the case of women's rights, the more conservative states had internal forces legitimating values other than the global, liberal "consensus" on individual rights.

Accountability: Rio, Vienna, and Beijing

The prospect of increased international accountability, whether it is strongly enforced or mostly a matter of rhetorical justification, potentially affects several dimensions of a state's sovereignty. It threatens to reduce a state's individual autonomy and places material and administrative demands on the UN and on member states, thus raising the stakes and costs for states as they negotiate new commitments. At the same time, however, cooperation with international monitoring may increase external legitimacy, by buttressing the mutual social regard between states that is necessary for such legitimacy. Granting increased accountability to transnational actors and a larger role for them in global governance potentially also enhances states' standing with such actors. Legitimacy with internal non-state actors may also rise or fall with the signing of the international agreements, depending on the compatibility of domestic and international preferences and values. Finally, control may also be at stake if accountability and implementation agreements create new capacities for transnational actors to act in national territories.

The calculations of costs and accountability reach their peak when compliance with agreements is monitored by new, permanent institutions. Thus, the debates at Rio, Vienna, and Beijing over whether to create a stronger global monitoring or implementation capacity can be analyzed as debates about possible sovereignty bargains. Where effective institutions are established, there is an inherent bargain between the autonomy and legitimacy dimensions of sovereignty. Such debates also help establish whether states recognize that their legitimacy rests in some part on the consent and participation of non-state actors.

At Rio, a Commission on Sustainable Development provided a focal point for arguments about the monitoring of state commitments, as did Vienna's debate over a new High Commissioner for Human Rights. Challenges to make the conference on women a "Conference of Commitments" echoed the theme, as did the demands by some NGOs for a similar High Commissioner on Women's Rights. At all three of the conferences, states debated not only whether to sacrifice autonomy for greater legitimacy through greater accountability, but also to whom they should be accountable.

NGOs were important protagonists in the debates over accountability. Indeed, NGOs were the strongest voices for building monitoring mechanisms at the international level, making fundamental challenges to the sovereign autonomy of nation-states in the UN system. Common to all conferences were NGO demands for better-funded, better-designed, and better-implemented structures to reinforce international accountability, which they expressed in calls for more money, new institutions, and meaningful follow-up on stated conference goals. By mounting such challenges on a foundation of popular consent at the international level, NGOs deliberately invoked a transnational citizenry as their audience. The debates over monitoring institutions were some of the most contentious and last settled.

There were regional differences over whether governments perceived NGOs' advocacy of increased oversight, or their mere participation in the conference process, as a threat to sovereign legitimacy. Northern governments collaborated frequently with NGOs at the three conferences, rarely seeming to perceive NGO participation itself as a threat to sovereignty or to self-determination. The United States and the European Union exhibited great willingness to work with NGOs on shared agendas at all three conferences. Australia joined the NGO-friendly group at Vienna and Beijing, as did Canada at Rio. Overt opposition to NGOs' oversight proposals varied more widely, but even the support of Western governments was not enough to secure participation for NGOs in the most important final meetings of each of the conferences, especially the sessions where final documents were drafted (see chapter 2). Apparently even sympathetic states were not willing to go to the mat to defend NGO participation. Therefore, it appears that NGOs per se still do not have the procedural access required to become *consistently* strong brokers for bargains over sovereign legitimacy, even though states increasingly acknowledge (and sometimes avoid) a role for the consent of the governed on international issues.

RIO AND THE COMMISSION ON SUSTAINABLE DEVELOPMENT: At Rio, open state opposition to intergovernmental monitoring was weaker than at the other two conferences. In principle, states did not oppose creating some accountability at the international level through the mechanism of environmental reporting. Many governments preferred to use existing institutions for any monitoring that might take place, however. Both Northern and Southern countries had reasons to fear a new institution that would focus on monitoring sustainable development: the South, because they would be the main subject of oversight; the North, because of the financial costs of monitoring. Maintaining national autonomy over choices about the use of resources for national development was a concern for some countries on both sides of the North/South divide as well. In the end, states did create a new international monitoring institution. Like the larger Rio bargain on environment and development, however, it has foundered in practice.

At the Rio PrepComs, NGOs made some of the strongest statements favoring the creation of new institutions within the UN to support environmental programs. A report from the Third Prep-Com shows that NGOs were instrumental in keeping new institutions on the agenda at Rio (Goree IV et al. 1991:68-72). NGOs floated several ideas that were much more expansive than those of the governments. The Consortium for Action to Protect the Earth (CAPE), a group of six U.S. NGOs, came up with an extensive set of demands at the Third PrepCom that would have created an auditing agency and an ombudsperson with powers to oversee UN agencies as well as governments, with guarantees of public participation in all international environment and development decision making (Ibid.:69). Even after governments decided to create a new agency, NGOs pushed on for a greater role for themselves. In an article titled "We Need the Equivalent of the International Court of Justice," they explained:

> If the analogy of the UN Commission on Human Rights is anything to go by, the active involvement of NGOs, industry, business and scientific communities in monitoring will

be critical. Otherwise, it will be governments reviewing each other, with the most powerful getting away with murder. Which government, for example, would dare challenge the US report? (Hurtado 1992:41)

States agreed to create the Commission on Sustainable Development (CSD) between the Fourth PrepCom and the Rio Summit, and the General Assembly did so formally in its next session. The new Commission received the mandate of reviewing annual national reports on nation-states' compliance with Agenda 21. The CSD institutionalized the sovereignty bargain reflected in other parts of the Rio process: Southern environmental commitments were to be monitored, in tandem with Northern environmental and financial commitments. Like the vast majority (90 percent) of environmental institutions established since 1973 (Haas and Sundgren 1993:409), the CSD essentially calls for governments to regulate themselves, rather than granting any true independent authority and oversight to the Commission. However, the CSD is to "consider ... periodic communications or national reports" from states (United Nations 1993g:Vol. I:459-460), and reporting requirements are shared by only 7 percent of the post-1973 multilateral environmental treaties (Haas and Sundgren 1993:409).

State opposition to NGO participation in post-conference oversight—and by implication, nontraditional forms of accountability at the international level—was also less galvanized around sovereignty claims than at the other two conferences. The high level of the United States' and Europeans' receptivity toward NGOs was indicated by the fact that they recommended the creation of enduring NGO roles in UN environmental institutions, some of which made their way into final documents. Final discussions over the creation of the CSD were relatively open to NGOs, with an emerging consensus over the need for active involvement by NGOs in the Commission (Chatterjee 1992b). In the end, countries from both the North and South supported this position—although, again, for quite different reasons. Northern states accepted NGO participation as part of their domestic political constituency (non-state legitimacy), while Southern states looked to NGOs more instrumentally, for expertise and support for Southern claims for resource transfers (control). NGOs were allowed observer status in the Commission.

The institutional debates at Rio introduced additional legitimating agents in the form of both a new international institution and new participatory mechanisms for NGOs. To the extent that the CSD commanded respect from its nation-state members, it would have circumscribed the autonomy and control of nation-states. By the late 1990s it was already clear, however, that states had largely failed to meet their obligations as outlined in Agenda 21, and the CSD's annual meetings served primarily to document those failings (Bigg and Dodds 1997).

VIENNA AND A HIGH COMMISSIONER FOR HUMAN RIGHTS: The main practical accountability measure broached at Vienna was the proposal to create a High Commissioner for Human Rights. The idea had been considered from time to time since the 1950s, and the UN's administrative branch for human rights hoped that the Vienna conference would strengthen the UN's authority vis-à-vis states in terms of its capacity to defend human rights (M. Schmidt 1995). According to a UN report, the call for a Commissioner, spear-headed by the major global human rights NGOs, did not explicitly demand "a Commissioner with the authority to intervene in sover-eign states where rights were being violated, but . . . [opened] the way for further negotiations towards that goal" ("Vienna: A Search for Common Ground" 1993:58).

Establishing a Commissioner potentially heightened interna-tional accountability for human rights practices over the preroga-tives of sovereign states. The High Commissioner was envisioned as an office that would coordinate the UN's sprawling variety of human rights procedures and, in addition, use high-profile, inde-pendent authority and good offices to improve state compliance with the full range of human rights concerns. No high-level UN post devoted exclusively to human rights yet existed (Amnesty In-ternational 1992b:6-8).

Most developing country governments opposed a UN Human Rights Commissioner (M. Schmidt 1995), suspecting that they, rather than Western, developed nations, were likely to bear the brunt of new human rights inquiries (see Korey 1998:294). Support for the idea did come mainly from the West, with added support from the African governments of Nigeria, Gambia, and Uganda (Riding 1993a). In conference debate, only 40 of 171 nations spoke in favor of the new post, while opponents called for a delay and fur-ther study (Korey 1998:294). But again, NGOs from all regions ex-pressed strong support. Asian NGOs were the only group explicitly to call for the establishment of the High Commissioner post in their regional declaration (Bangkok NGO Declaration on Human Rights of 27 March 1993:135), but NGOs lobbied governments on the issue to some degree at all three of the regional conferences (Azzam 1993:92-93), and the report of the global NGO Forum at Vienna endorsed the proposal (Nowak 1993:78, Item A.3). After heated debate that continued overnight until the last hour before the conference closed, governmental delegates agreed to call on the General Assembly to consider establishment of a High Commissioner for Human Rights ("Vienna: A Search for Common Ground" 1993:58). The measure was approved at the 1993 General Assembly meeting, where supporting governments included the United States, members of the European Union, Canada, Poland, Australia, Russia, Japan, Costa Rica, Mali, and Mauritius (Lewis 1993d; Korey 1998).

The West and the former USSR favored giving at least some power to the UN to monitor violations; the U.S. delegation provided leadership and strategic cooperation with other states and with NGOs in the fight for universality and for a High Commissioner. However, for many states, opposition to the idea of stronger surveillance over states at Vienna melded with opposition to NGO participation. The vast majority of the approximately fifteen hundred NGOs represented at the Vienna conference, including Asian NGOs, supported broader UN monitoring of human rights, but many states resisted allowing internal or external non-state actors a voice in decisions about states' own international human rights commitments. China proved particularly unfriendly to NGOs at Vienna (Riding 1993c), as well as at Beijing, and was joined by numerous Asian governments, Cuba, and Iran. After the Vienna conference, a bloc of governments including Cuba, Iran, and Malaysia continued to attack NGO privileges by submitting proposals, ultimately unsuccessful, that would restrict future NGO participation in UN human rights bodies (M. Schmidt 1995).[3]

These governments were also the ones making strident arguments for autonomous domestic interpretations of rights issues and state control over domestic populations. In this case, certain states' resistance to trading autonomy and control for accountability to any external legitimating audience, whether state or non-state, was unsuccessful. Their resistance and the debates that ensued, however, indicate that bids for noninterference do not hold sway for all states. Politically, the Western, developed states that possess more de facto sovereign control and legitimacy tended to support ceding some autonomy, in principle, to international notions of human rights—and they did not find it necessary to offer a bargain to states that disagreed. The United States' "identify and isolate" strategy, just mentioned with reference to the debate over universal human rights, is a case in point. The profile of this debate suggests that, on the one hand, sovereignty is defined by powerful states; but on the other hand, the powerful states were listening most closely to the voices of civil society. Thus, it also suggests that these powerful states may be redefining legitimacy not only for other sovereigns, but also for themselves.

BEIJING AND THE "CONFERENCE OF COMMITMENTS": At the Fourth World Conference on Women, an odd set of bedfellows emerged on substantive issues that challenged the legitimacy of states' singular authority over rule-making. The European Union and the United States were adamant about restricting any "new" resources that NGOs sought to have included in the Platform for Action for implementation. They also opposed the Australian idea, heavily backed by NGO supporters, to make the Fourth World Conference on Women a "Conference of Commitments." Their reluctance aligned the United States and Western Europe with the Islamic- and Catholic-influenced governments against international enforcement in the area of women's rights, although the former had disagreed with the latter's claims to cultural autonomy over women's rights and roles.

Australia, consistently an ally of NGOs at Beijing, first promoted the controversial "Conference of Commitments" idea (ENB 18 September 1995), which would require governments to state explicitly what changes they planned to make to fulfill the Platform for Action's mandates by the year 2000. This idea was one of the few offered to ensure some implementation of conference agreements. NGOs, in particular, promoted it. Before the conference they used the idea of commitments as a "key instrument for political mobilization," including it in negotiations between NGOs and governments (Ibid.:6 March 1995). At the conference itself, the NGO Media Caucus hung a "Conference of Commitments" banner in the hallway of the conference building, and released daily updates on commitments they compiled from governmental speeches at the plenary. National NGOs evaluated their own countries' commitments at the daily nongovernmental plenary sessions.

During the governmental negotiations over the Platform for Action, however, the Australian suggestion that governments' specific commitments should be included as an annex of the final document was dismissed. The official objection was that the recording of specific commitments on a limited number of issues would detract from the wider agenda. But the dismissal also indicated states' objections to any binding agreements about their role in implementation that might restrict their autonomy or control over women. Another key NGO demand, that the UN establish a high-level post in the office of the UN Secretary-General to oversee the implementation of the Platform for Action, was heeded, but not acted upon immediately. The Secretary-General was only "invited" to establish such a post (Ibid.:18 September 1995).

States have filed more reservations to the Convention on the Elimination all Forms of Discrimination against Women (CEDAW) than to any other human-rights-related treaty. Accordingly, in other implementation debates, NGOs lobbied for language in the Platform for Action that would urge all governments to review and consider withdrawing their reservations to CEDAW by the year 2000. NGOs also supported the adoption of an Optional Protocol to CEDAW. It would establish a procedure for receiving individual petitions from women asking for protection against abuses within their own states, a procedure that would challenge state control directly (Women's Linkage Caucus 1995:42-43). Governments were not willing to submit to definitive recommendations: no date was assigned to either project, and the language of the draft Optional Protocol was weakened.

The implementation issue was clearly the most significant challenge that the women's conference posed to governmental autonomy. But as has become routine in UN women's conference documents, implementation of the "Commitments" principle was left almost entirely to chance. NGO monitoring of commitments in states' plenary speeches became the primary recording vehicle for any such agreements. NGOs continued to press for accountability and implementation following the conference, with the release of the list of commitments, as well as a follow-up report on governments' progress—or lack thereof—on the issues a year later (Women's Environment and Development Organization 1996).

However, NGOs' challenge to the autonomy of states has garnered some results since the 1995 conference. At least in principle, states seem to be ceding some autonomy and control in the interests of improving legitimacy by agreeing to limited mechanisms for implementation and monitoring. In June 1997 UN Secretary-General Kofi Annan appointed a Special Advisor to the Secretary General on Gender Issues and the Advancement of Women to coordinate implementation of the Beijing Platform in the UN system and to oversee the mainstreaming of a gender perspective in UN activities. The CEDAW Optional Protocol was adopted in October 1999 by the UN's General Assembly. Moreover, the active NGO participation in the UN Beijing + 5 review process included preparatory campaigns and an international electronic "global forum." Onsite lobbying by NGOs at the June 2000 conference can be taken as an ongoing assertion of their role in legitimation.

Conclusion

The conference debates remind us of the continuing strength and diversity of nation-states' claims to state sovereignty. In the face of transnational challenges, particularly from NGO actors, states repeatedly argued for sovereignty in the forms of national control over development processes and for religious and cultural relativism in the standards for treating their citizens, especially women. Many argued against international oversight in the form of mechanisms to enforce whatever commitments were made at these conferences. On the other hand, at all three conferences some state delegations *did* embrace universal conceptions of environmental sustainability, human rights, and women's roles, as well as state accountability to NGOs and international organizations. These compromises appear in Table 4.2.

We began this chapter by categorizing the claims themselves according to their correspondence with different dimensions of sovereignty proposed by Karen T. Litfin (1998): autonomy, control, and legitimacy in the eyes of state and non-state actors. Just as sovereignty cannot be characterized as a theoretic monolith, neither are states' claims to sovereignty absolute. States sometimes find it expedient, profitable, necessary, or socially desirable to compromise. It is the compromises, especially when repeated or repeatedly resisted, that are likely to reveal most about the state of sovereignty itself. We now review the nature of the compromises in the different issue areas, then reflect on the changing nature of sovereignty and who legitimates sovereignty.

Sovereignty Bargains by Issue Area: The Importance of Resources

The tradeoffs among different aspects of sovereignty suggest that all actors still rely on sovereignty, even as they negotiate bargains between different dimensions. Indeed, transnational actors tread a fine line between demanding that states act like legitimate

Table 4.2 Sovereignty in the Balance: Bargains Debated on the Environment, Human Rights, and Women's Rights

	Preferred Element of Sovereignty			
	Autonomy	Control	Legitimacy (Non-state)	Legitimacy (Other States)
Autonomy	—	**environment:** Southern states accepted Northern environmental priorities in exchange for the promise of Northern resources that would enhance their economic control	**human rights:** pressure from domestic NGOs reduced resistance to universal human rights; more powerful states support NGO participation in human rights oversight	**environment:** states adopted at least the rhetoric of emerging sustainable development norms **human rights:** under pressure from Northern states, most states accepted status quo language on universal principles of human rights
Control		—	**environment:** NGO expertise and participation accepted in state-created Commission on Sustainable Development, to oversee implementation of Agenda 21	**all:** partial establishment of accountability mechanisms for conference agreements
Legitimacy (Non-State)	**women's rights:** some religiously oriented states argued for national rather than universal conceptions of women's rights, against the preferences of many of their domestic NGOs	**human rights:** China and others unsuccessfully resisted new roles for non-state actors **women's rights:** most states joined to oppose non-state enforcement and implementation of women's rights at Beijing	—	

Element Considered for Trade

(continues)

Table 4.2 *(continued)*

		Preferred Element of Sovereignty			
		Autonomy	Control	Legitimacy (Non-state)	Legitimacy (Other States)
Element Considered for Trade	Legitimacy (State)	**human rights; women's rights:** Southern states expressed preference for autonomous choices on rights standards	**human rights; women's rights:** Southern states expressed preference for internal "control" instead of accession to universal standards	**women's rights:** Australia broke with other states to voice the demands of NGOs	—

states by signing international treaties and by providing certain social and environmental protections, and simultaneously criticizing states for overemphasizing traditional sovereign prerogatives. In many cases, "progress" on the issues that seem to erode sovereignty also require a capable state for implementation. In some measure, states need autonomy, control, and legitimacy to protect both rights and the environment.

On environmental sustainability issues, the possibility of gaining additional material resources (enhancing control) and recognition (legitimacy) influenced governments' willingness to enter into bargains that restricted their autonomy over natural resources and development. When neither side lived up to its promises after Rio, however, both sides of the bargain collapsed. On the rights issues—especially for women's rights—the benefits of bargains were not as apparent, and legitimacy was not as highly valued by all states as control and autonomy. These patterns are clearly delineated in Table 4.2.

It appears that environmental sovereignty can be "purchased" far more easily than sovereignty over the substance of rights claims, at least at the rhetorical level. In other words, there are tangible ways in which states can gain greater control and legitimacy in exchange for autonomy on environmental issues. Why this difference?

First, international financial and technical resources are especially important for environmental issues. The technical nature of many environmental problems and solutions makes international expertise and assistance—often provided by non-state actors—necessary for achieving environmental control, and states commonly seek and offer such resources. Although international environmental funding failed to materialize as promised after Rio, the rights conferences lacked even such promises. The international community is generally less willing to offer resources in exchange for states to uphold normative goals, and without this incentive states may decide that to give up autonomy for enhanced legitimacy is not worth the price.

Second, rights claims of particular individuals or groups differ from global commons issues in which everyone's enjoyment of a collective good is at stake. Given the ways in which ecosystems ignore nation-state boundaries, individual states often literally cannot control their national territory with respect to the environment but must cooperate with other states. In contrast, it is generally considered possible to achieve human rights for the members of one community even if others outside the community do not enjoy full rights. Although rights claims may be morally compelling, the "excludability" of rights claims removes a compelling common interest in interstate cooperation that is present in global environmental negotiations. A possible exception occurs when poor human rights conditions spill over state borders via extensive refugee movements, as they often do. In such cases, excludability is less clear.

Third, in upholding individual rights states may actually have to cede important aspects of control (over citizens' migration, behavior, etc.) that cannot be easily recompensed by external actors. Moreover, even the opportunity for enhanced control may not compensate for a sacrifice of autonomy, given the salience of rights issues to states' overall sense of themselves as states.

In summary, the sovereignty bargains possible in the environmental issue area as posited by Litfin (1997, 1998) do not extend neatly to other issue areas, but the concept of bargaining itself is useful. While bargains between dimensions of sovereignty do take place on rights issues, they are not likely to be the same bargains as those on environmental issues, which often call for the exchange of material resources. In sovereignty bargains that do not call for the exchange of resources, states may cede a measure of autonomy over internal matters, which have usually been protected by sovereign claims, by signing onto treaties that articulate global norms of protection. On paper, signatories yield the autonomy to violate those norms, calculating that their legitimacy may well be enhanced with both state and non-state actors. Enforcement is a different matter. If states do not adhere to their agreements, as in the years following Rio, there may be little actual loss of autonomy. When a state can manage to accrue external approval without trading off autonomy, the sovereignty bargain turns out to be a steal for the state, at least initially. Whether a state can indeed hold onto both autonomy and legitimacy while cheating on the autonomy/legitimacy bargain depends on, first, the domestic political demands and, second, external pressures to uphold international norms.

It may be that with the advancement of norms and protections inspired by conference negotiations, stronger links between non-state claimants to internal and external legitimacy may compel states to uphold such bargains. Such a link would correspond to the "'boomerang' pattern of influence" described by Margaret E. Keck and Kathryn Sikkink (1998:12-13) and elaborated on by Thomas Risse and Sikkink (1999:13), whereby domestic and transnational NGOs collaborate as part of transnational advocacy networks to target individual states' domestic practices. Furthermore, the non-governmental actors in our study find the participatory limitations imposed by conventional interpretations of sovereign privilege to be inadequate for the political expression of their demands for change. At the international level, they expect a voice in international governance. Neither are domestic and regional NGOs content to leave the representation of their concerns to NGOs with more experience at the UN.

It is important to mention that all types of sovereignty claims came disproportionately from the so-called South, a region united mostly by its subordinate position relative to the so-called North. Relatively secure in their national capacities, with less reason to fear outside influence, Northern states can seek international collaboration and oversight. They are also somewhat more willing to accept NGO participation and oversight, given their extensive familiarity with domestic democracy. Southern states, as a whole, lack these characteristics. Sharing a history of colonial domination and economic underdevelopment, they do not assume that their control and autonomy will remain unscathed by outside influences, whether from governments or from NGOs. Southern states show growing but still widely varying abilities to manipulate UN procedures and norms in ways that would spotlight their own visions of central issues and procedures. Many continue to be plagued by inexperience or budgetary inability to participate fully in UN activities. This means that where additional resources can be made a part of negotiation processes—a step critical to this group of actors—sovereignty bargains are more likely.

Who Legitimates Sovereignty?

Both Northern and Southern states would like to define states as the ultimate arbiters of their own sovereignty, holding on to inward looking definitions of rights even as they hope to share the economic burden of collective action on the environment. Fellow states offer the most sympathetic ears to states invoking sovereign prerogatives and expressing concern about their capacity to provide for their populations. NGOs, in contrast, have tenaciously fought for more broadly conceived forms of international obligation on human rights, women's rights, and environmental responsibilities. While UN conferences privilege state definitions to a great extent, they also point to the growing ability of NGOs to shape the global political agenda through their participation both in collaboration with, and in opposition to, states.

Our study of sovereignty claims at the conferences suggests that the notion of legitimacy is broader than most theories of sovereignty recognize. Sovereign legitimacy now plays not only for a domestic audience, but also for an external one. More dramatically, the external audience now includes NGOs and not just the international community of states. We conclude with a discussion of the NGO role in external legitimation, which has important implications for how sovereignty may be changing and how it should be understood theoretically.

NGOs are attempting to occupy a role as legitimators of state sovereignty in their own right. Our research suggests that at the conferences, NGOs used their own, independent influence to affect sovereign legitimation processes from the outside, thus raising the interesting possibility that state legitimacy is enhanced or diminished by global civil society in some form. NGOs attempted to affect the sovereignty bargains from a transnational standpoint, thus decoupling external legitimacy from states' sole control. External legitimacy, or recognition at a minimum, has traditionally lain within the purview of states. Now, external legitimacy possesses both a state and a non-state dimension. The reassertions of state sovereignty at the conferences were reactions to changes in traditional models of international governance. These reactions reflect shifts in the legitimating audience for sovereignty: some conception of "global popular sovereignty" may become an important rhetorical resource for transnational NGOs as they claim to represent universal values.

State claims about values sometimes responded to differences in national and transnational imperatives, pitting some national and transnational legitimating audiences against one another. While on the whole NGOs involved in the conference processes pushed for more universal definitions of rights, it is clear that some domestic non-state constituencies, such as conservative religious movements, are often interested in upholding particularist social values.

In the bargaining process, state elites clung as tightly to social and cultural practices as to economic models or even models of military security. Such considerations are especially important for understanding the positions of individual states, which is beyond our analysis here. Social and cultural values were used in conference rhetoric as masks or vessels of state power in ways that military and economic self-sufficiency once were. The prominence of sovereignty rhetoric applied to values suggests that states perceive that there is more to sovereignty than coercive power or economic issues.

Significantly, universal social values, more so than economic or military power, are the strongest aspects of global civil society's challenges to state autonomy and legitimacy. But because power and economics are at least hypothetically more fungible aspects of sovereign authority, global civil society, a relatively new source of external legitimacy, will have to seek new ways to transform nonmaterial goals into reality.

CHAPTER 5

Sovereignty Bargains and Challenges at the
Conferences on Population and Development,
Social Development, and Human Settlements

Up to now, we have concentrated on the conferences on the environment, human rights, and women as case studies in the emergence and development of global civil society. In this chapter, we extend the study to three other contemporary UN conferences: the 1994 Conference on Population and Development, held at Cairo, 5-13 September 1994; the World Summit for Social Development, held at Copenhagen, 12-16 March 1995; and the UN Conference on Human Settlements (Habitat II), held at Istanbul, June 1996. Together, these were the six major conferences of the 1990s.

We know that nongovernmental organizations (NGOs) have became routine participants at such conferences. They share many goals and offer diverse interpretations of important issues that often challenge states' own interpretations and interests. While the active presence of NGOs supports the potential for a truly global and social civil society to emerge internationally, there are still significant obstacles to a fully shared democratic sphere of interaction at the international level. Many of these obstacles are created by states, who are likely to use the language of sovereignty to protect issues they see as particularly central to their interests or asserted identities. At the Earth Summit, the human rights conference, and the women's conference, states tried to keep both economic self-determination issues and cultural or religious practices within their sovereign prerogative. However, states were willing to make certain bargains over sovereignty issues when they could gain by it. In our comparison of the conferences on the environment, human rights, and women, the bargains we witnessed suggested that states were more willing to compromise domestic autonomy in order to receive external resources for environmental protection than they were to sacrifice autonomy over cultural values. A brief analysis of the conferences at Cairo, Copenhagen, and Istanbul is useful in providing a broader perspective on those findings.

We examine the following specific propositions generated in chapters 2-4. First, the more states link conference topics to sovereignty issues, the less ready states are to permit the open contestation and mutual accountability at the UN conferences that one would expect of a democratic international system. Conversely, when sovereignty issues are less central, we would expect NGOs to have higher participatory access at the conferences, along with evidence of greater cooperation with states and shared responsibility for implementation and monitoring. Furthermore, where state control might be enhanced by acquiring external resources, we would expect to see sovereignty bargains being negotiated.

When we extend this analysis to the conferences on population, social development, and human settlements, at first glance, the cases seem to encompass topics not traditionally seen as related to core sovereignty questions. In addition, the problems addressed at the conferences appear amenable to the infusion of external resources. In accordance with those observations, on the issues debated at Cairo, Istanbul, and Copenhagen, one might predict a mix of issues and relationships conducive to the emergence of a global civil society—as defined in chapters 1 and 2 and indicated by global attendance and representation, shared rules and procedures for participation by all actors, and shared frames and repertoires for action—and a high potential for sovereignty bargains.

What we found, however, was an articulation of sovereignty claims on social and economic issues that was consistent with the shifts in sovereign claims that we saw at Rio, Vienna, and Beijing. Those conferences revealed the emergence of less traditional articulations of sovereign claims: claims relating to "national" or cultural values. Those sovereignty claims, by their nature, are less available for trade-offs than environmental issues, as discussed in chapter 4. Given the presence of those nontraditional sovereignty claims, we would expect a less favorable climate for either NGO participation or for sovereignty bargains.

Our investigation shows that while the conferences examined in this chapter were quite open to NGOs as participants, the issue dynamics did in fact limit the willingness of states to make bids for non-state legitimacy or other kinds of sovereignty bargains. Cultural values played a prominent role throughout the conference on population. The Habitat conference almost foundered at the very end over the familiar debates about national cultural positions on women and reproductive rights, despite little direct link of the topic to housing issues. In addition, at all three conferences states were reluctant to cede control over economic matters such as aid levels, distribution of aid, and budgets. In spite of the economic and social needs that states and NGOs sought to address through parleys at the global conferences, the sovereignty bargains made at these conferences were rather minimal.

Global Civil Society at Cairo, Copenhagen, and Istanbul

The portion of this chapter in which we treat sovereign claims is organized by issue. But first, it is necessary to provide a brief introduction to the conference cases. In this section, we first describe the subject matter of each conference and the history of UN special meetings on similar topics in previous decades. Then, we summarize our findings concerning how democratic relations were between NGOs and states, by again considering issues of "civil" procedures and "social" values.

The Conferences

THE INTERNATIONAL CONFERENCE ON POPULATION AND DEVELOPMENT (ICPD): The International Conference on Population and Development (ICPD), held at Cairo, was preceded by two expert meetings and two governmental conferences on population; one in each decade since the 1950s. The earliest, held in Rome (1954) and in Belgrade (1965), were meetings of technical and scientific experts. The first convocation of governments took place in Bucharest (1974); the second in Mexico City (1984). Five years after the Mexico City conference, the UN's Economic and Social Council (ECOSOC) called for the ICPD to be the third governmental conference on population (UN ECOSOC Resolution 1989/91). The purposes of the new conference, set for 1994, included assessing the progress made over the last decade on population issues; continuing work on the implementation of prior international agreements; strengthening the international awareness of population issues and their linkage to development; making new recommendations on how to treat population issues in the context of development; and mobilizing the necessary resources, especially for the developing world, to fulfill such recommendations (Johnson 1995:30-31; UN ECOSOC Resolution 1991/93). As was standard practice, preparatory meetings leading up to Cairo focused on drafting the conference document, the Programme of Action, and related issues. Six expert meetings, several roundtables, three PrepComs, and five regional meetings were convened as official preparation for the conference. A parallel NGO Forum was held in Cairo, 4-12 September 1994, immediately prior to the official conference.

NGOs were prominent in numbers and lobbying capacity throughout the preparations for Cairo. Twelve hundred people from 500 NGOs, distributed throughout the global North and South, attended the final PrepCom (ENB 4-22 April 1994). Eleven hundred nineteen NGOs representing 134 countries were accredited to the ICPD,[1] and over 4,000 attended the NGO Forum (Cohen 1994).

NGOs were very active from the first stages of the conference process. Most prominently, women's NGOs started to mobilize for the conference in a Women's Caucus prior to the official process, for the purpose of promoting a women's rights agenda. They were aided by their significant experience in organizing throughout the UN Decade on Women (1975-1985), particularly in working across geographic divides, and they were spurred on by the evidence they had seen at UNCED of an alliance being forged between population control advocates and environmentalists (McIntosh and Finkle 1995:237). Thus, in September 1992, twenty-five international advocates drew up a "Women's Declaration on Population Policies" and formed the "Women's Voices '94 Alliance" to support it. The International Women's Health Coalition circulated the statement internationally, and eventually over 2,200 individuals and organizations from more than 105 countries endorsed it ("Women's Voices '94" 1993; Women's Feature Service 1994). To this document was added the January 1994 Declaration of the Reproductive Health and Justice conference, drafted at what was essentially an NGO PrepCom. Also in 1994, 215 women from 79 countries met for four days in Rio de Janeiro to hammer out NGO positions on population and development to present to the ICPD and to its NGO Forum (International Women's Health Coalition 1994).

An expansive UN Secretariat gave NGOs broad access to the preparatory process, and NGOs made extensive use of it (McIntosh and Finkle 1995:229). "Never before had NGOs been so mobilized, so well-organized and so prepared for the serious and systematic advocacy and lobbying," said a contemporaneous report (*ENB* 4-22 April 1994). From the Second PrepCom onward, NGOs attended even informal consultations, and were allowed to intervene during closed-door sessions. The ICPD Secretariat supported NGO requests for services, but even more remarkably, incorporated their written statements in draft documents (*ENB* 21 May 1993). Throughout the conference process, the Women's Caucus assessed drafts as they progressed from one stage to the next and circulated their own amendments to governmental representatives (Johnson 1995:139-140, 142; Women's Environment and Development 1994). Differences between women's and more population-focused NGOs were mediated during the Second PrepCom (McIntosh and Finkle 1995:238).

NGO unity was stimulated by the strength of the Vatican's opposition to the women's rights agenda advanced at Cairo (DeJong 2000:946). There were also NGOs in support of the Vatican, but they tended to be in the minority. For example, the Pro-Life Caucus assembled at the NGO Forum had only 15 members, while the Women's Caucus had between 400 and 500. Moreover, many mainstream religious groups objected to the media's focus on the most conservative religious positions expressed at the conference, which they felt did not accurately represent the variety of views held by other religious participants (Johnson 1995:144-45).

NGOs were also part of many government delegations (Cowell 1994), and many sympathetic governments, particularly the United States, supported their claims in official meetings. Results of this unprecedented access were seen in the wording of the draft Programme of Action. Going into the Cairo conference, chapter 4 of the conference document, entitled, "Gender Equality, Equity and Empowerment of Women," was almost free of brackets, meaning that the language was uncontested. All definitions of reproductive health throughout the document had been introduced by the Women's Caucus, and an entire chapter devoted to "Partnership with the Nongovernmental Sector," which covers "local, national and international nongovernmental organizations as well as the private sector," was added (*ENB* 4-22 April 1994). The Women's Caucus was by far the largest at the ICPD (Johnson 1995:145). Its power was demonstrated in the reflection of the "Cairo Consensus" throughout the final document of the conference, which had a clear women's rights perspective and highlighted the role of NGOs as well as governments in carrying it out. The fourth "Principle" of the document reads:

> Advancing gender equality and equity and the empowerment of women, and the elimination of all kinds of violence against women, and ensuring women's ability to control their own fertility, are cornerstones of population and development-related programmes. The human rights of women and the girl child are an inalienable, integral and indivisible part of universal human rights. The full and equal participation of women in civil, cultural, economic, political and social life, at the national, regional and international levels, and the eradication of all forms of discrimination on grounds of sex, are priority objectives of the international community. (United Nations 1994c)

THE WORLD SUMMIT FOR SOCIAL DEVELOPMENT (THE SOCIAL SUMMIT): The general theme of Copenhagen's World Summit for Social Development, nicknamed "The Social Summit," was social development, a concern elaborated and promoted by UN development organs as the integral human component of economic development. The organizers, the Social Summit Secretariat, were located in the UN Department for Policy Coordination and Sustainable Development. Three issues were central to the summit: eradicating poverty; increasing employment; and ensuring social integration (United Nations Administrative Committee on Coordination Task Force on Basic Services for All 1998:58). To address the first goal, the conference stipulated the need for a more in-depth understanding of poverty, its root causes, and its social implications. The goal of increasing employment meant not only reducing unemployment, but also increasing *productive* employment. *Social integration* was the term used at the conference to describe a "society for all," respecting human rights, cultural diversity, inclusion of all social groups, and the fostering of democracy and the rule of law.

Thought on economic development as it relates to UN activities has a long and varied history that reached an important turning point in 1987 with the popularization of the idea of sustainable development, which combines concern for economic development with recognition of the need for environmental responsibility (World Commission on Environment and Development 1987). Although the Social Summit was the first-ever UN world conference on the theme of social development, the Social Summit's conference declaration situated itself thematically among the conferences of the 1990s. It looked back to the Earth Summit and to Cairo. In addition, conferees knew that the Fourth World Conference on Women was coming up in six months. Thus, the final document of the Social Summit exhibits an awareness of its place within the context of other conferences and UN programs, and of the need for a departure from "business as usual" if the problems of poverty are to be solved.

The official conference itself was attended by 2,300 NGO official representatives from 811 NGOs. In addition, 12,000 NGO representatives attended the parallel "NGO Forum '95," held 3-12 March at Holmen, a former naval base near Copenhagen (United Nations 1995e:viii). As at Cairo, NGOs were actively involved all stages of conference activity, participating to the extent possible in negotiations over the final document of the conference, criticizing government positions, and putting forth positions of their own.

Although statements at this conference repeatedly emphasized the importance of civil society to the achievement of summit goals, NGOs still had reason to be on their guard against getting shut out of the process. There were just three PrepComs for the Social Summit. NGOs at the First and Second PrepComs made statements and participated in discussions together with governments and intergovernmental organizations. One account of the conference process saw NGOs as instrumental in bringing attention to "three core issues" at the Second PrepCom: "a broader definition of human development; . . . the root causes of poverty; . . . and recognition that the means for implementation must be seriously 'retooled'" (*ENB* 22 August—2 September 1994). NGOs began to express concern about preserving openness in the process as governments got down to business on the actual drafting. In an intersessional meeting between the Second and Third PrepComs, it was agreed that NGOs would be able to observe drafting negotiations. At the Third PrepCom, the working groups regularly briefed NGOs. But at the opening of the summit, while governments were still trying to finish up negotiations over the Final Declaration, NGO access was again called into question. Oxfam, Christian Aid, and Action Aid, all UK-based development NGOs, threatened to pull out of the summit if they were not granted observer access to the sessions. The same report said that Amnesty International had been thrown out of a meeting but allowed back in after protests (Black 1995c). Both the Plenary and the Main Committee (for negotiations on the document drafting) limited NGO access at the Summit. Other meetings effectively limited NGO access when they were held in places only accessible to delegates. After the first sessions, organizers promised to issue daily tickets to NGOs for seats at the Plenary and Main Committee for future sessions (ENB 6 March 1995). In all, the access issues were resolved with less acrimony—and more NGO access—than they had been at some of the earlier world conferences, but not without NGOs' insistence.

The Social Summit was touted as a conference where the importance of NGOs was widely acknowledged, but NGOs were often portrayed by governments as implementation experts, with less acknowledgment of a policy-making or monitoring role. For example, in the final documents, governments used language that includes other societal actors as necessary for the achievement of development goals. "We acknowledge that it is the primary responsibility of states to attain these goals. We also acknowledge that these goals cannot be achieved by States alone," says Copenhagen's declaration (United Nations 1995c:Para. 27). The international community, multilateral financial institutions, regional and local actors, and "all actors of civil society" are cited as potential contributors to development. The civil society language was prominent in conference documents (*ENB* 25 January 1995). Among other roles, NGOs are cited in the Programme of Action, along with educational institutions and the media, as agents in mobilizing public awareness (United Nations 1995c:Ch.2, Para. 34g). Also, NGOs have a role in improving access to reproductive health care (Ibid.:Para. 37e). For care of older persons, NGOs' and governments' services should be integrated (Ibid.:Para. 40c). And, in one policy-making call, governments said NGOs' role in policy formulation and implementation on urban planning to address poverty should be strengthened (Ibid.:Para. 34g).

NGOs put forward their own policy recommendations with vigor. They called for governments to take a stronger role in offering social guarantees to their citizens. Accordingly, strengthening national implementation of economic rights, for example, required strong national institutions. NGOs referred to their own role as essential partners in social development, noting that NGOs should serve as monitors of national efforts to implement conference goals ("Quality Benchmark" 1994). They asserted that citizens were central to social development; therefore, governments should eliminate corruption and construct frameworks for including "local, regional, and national civil society" in social development (Ibid.; Women's Caucus of the World Summit for Social Development 1994; African NGO Caucus nd).

THE CONFERENCE ON HUMAN SETTLEMENTS ("HABITAT II," OR "CITY SUMMIT"): The Conference on Human Settlements, held in Istanbul in June 1996, was the last of the series of six major global conferences. This conference was known as Habitat II, or the "City Summit." The Fourth World Conference on Women had been held in Beijing in September 1995, between the Social Summit and Habitat II. Like other conferences of the 1990s, the agenda of Habitat II was considerably broader than that of its predecessor, Habitat I, held in Vancouver in 1976. While Habitat I had focused on the provision of physical shelter, Habitat II added qualitative considerations to that goal. Its final document endorsed "the universal goals of ensuring adequate shelter for all and making human settlements safer, healthier, and more liveable, equitable, sustainable, and productive"(United Nations 1996b:Ch. 5).

Evaluations of Habitat II conclude that it did produce some significant advances, especially in integrating a fuller range of actors into the governmental conference (Tunali 1996:34; Tosics 1997:366; Bindé 1997:218). The same observers note that the Habitat conference was also marked by significant "summit fatigue": there were fewer participants than expected, the media stayed away, and many of the conference debates recycled controversies from earlier conferences (Bindé 1997:215; Tosics 1997:367). In the words of a UNESCO director,

> In Istanbul, negotiations on urban problems sometimes took on the guise of an international flea market: all the old controversies of Rio, Cairo, Copenhagen and Beijing were brought out again, and given a further airing, to such an extent that one sometimes had the impression of attending some sort of 20th century clearance sale. (Bindé 1997:216)

Opponents moved easily into pre-existing divisions, but many of the debates were eventually settled with language and agreements from the previous conferences.

Two-fifths of the delegates to the conference were from NGOs, 2,400 in all, and they interacted freely with 579 delegates from local authorities and 300 parliamentarians, as well as the national delegations of 185 governments (Strassman 1997:1729; Bindé 1997:215). But in comparison with the tens of thousands of NGOs who had come to Beijing to lobby and network, the Habitat II conference seemed subdued. Only 6,000 NGO participants (Strassman 1997:1729) from 1,500 organizations attended the parallel NGO

Forum. Five hundred of those organizations were based in Turkey, and the remaining 1,000 came from only 60 countries ("Press Release" 6 June 1996). Yet NGOs who wanted to participate in and lobby the official governmental conference found many points of access, at unprecedented levels.

Interestingly, some NGOs felt that the formal participation did not strengthen their capacity to influence governmental proceedings at Istanbul. One commented that "by accepting to be widely recognized as the voice of some abstract 'civil society,' the NGOs condemn themselves to express only their lowest common denominator—they reach the degree zero of speech" (cited in Bindé 1997:220). The wide diversity of NGOs present, oriented toward shelter, women's, environment, and development issues, among others, made it difficult to pick "representatives" to give "representative" positions. In an interesting twist on accountability, both NGOs and governments questioned the representativeness and accountability of NGOs participating in the hearings (UN 1996d: V.B.8.68).

At the Organizational Session in March, 1993, governmental delegates began with the once-innovative NGO Participation Rules from the Rio Conference preparations (GA/RES/47/180, Point 6), and extended them further. NGOs could speak in committee debates, sat as members of at least fifteen national governmental delegations, and were even allowed to seat two representatives on the fifteen-person Drafting Committee, which wrote the Habitat II documents. Other NGOs were also allowed to sit in on the drafting meetings, and could offer advice to those drafting the text, giving NGOs new and very direct influence on the Habitat II agreements (ENB 24 April—5 May 1995; see also *People Toward Habitat II* 1995:no. 2). In another unprecedented step, the UN Secretariat distributed an official conference document to the governmental Working Groups that included proposed amendments by NGOs and local governments. NGOs credited this gesture for some important language changes on women's and environmental issues (*ENB* 5-16 February 1996). Nonetheless, a comparison of NGOs' proposed amendments with the final documents shows that NGOs were usually more successful in retaining existing language than they were in adding new language.

Governments were not uniformly supportive of NGOs' participation. At the First PrepCom, in 1994, India, Brazil, Cuba, and Mexico questioned the role that NGOs should play in national delegations and in the conference preparations, but they accepted a compromise that allowed for more NGO participation without requiring it (*ENB* 11-22 April 1994). At the Second PrepCom, Mexico joined with the United States to try to keep NGOs out of the working groups, but again failed (*People toward Habitat II* 1995).

Instead, it was at the Second PrepCom that delegates accepted the Secretariat's suggestions for a new form of "Partners" in Istanbul. In an effort to formalize the input of participants who were not national governments, the delegates arranged for a series of "Partners Forums" for local and municipal governments (represented by the World Assembly of Cities and Local Authorities), the private sector (World Business Forum), foundations, trade unions, professionals and researchers, national academies of science and engineering, parliamentarians, and NGOs and "community-based organizations" (CBOs) (Wakely 1996:vi). CBOs were acknowledged by states as essential to the purposes of Istanbul; NGOs in that frame of reference could seem less threatening, as "CBOs writ large." Each of the Partners Forums was to meet in advance of the Istanbul conference and to prepare a statement on conference themes. Representatives of each Forum were then to present the statement to Committee 2 of the Istanbul Conference in formal hearings ("Partners Information" 1995).

Gaining space on the official program was an important participatory step, but only a partial one. Committee 2 was a cul-de-sac for the contributions of the Partners Forums: Committee 1 was the one writing the Habitat Agenda for Action. There were no formal links between the two Committees, and, in any case, the hearings were held near the end of the conference process in Istanbul, when it was too late for them to have an impact on the Conference documents. Instead, the statements are published as an Annex to the Agenda, with no official force or commitment (Wakely 1996:vi). Still, at Istanbul we found unprecedented access for NGOs to the important parts of the conference. This increased access seemed to be a result of government understandings that the issues of the conference were less about guarding sovereign prerogatives against global pronouncements, and more about building cooperation at local levels, where NGO input and resources were needed.

On the whole, there was more democratization evident at the transnational level at Cairo, Copenhagen, and Istanbul than at Rio, Vienna, or Beijing. As indicated by global attendance and representation, shared rules and procedures for participation by all actors, and shared frames and repertoires for action, global civil society was active and governments accepted NGO participation.

There was widespread global representation, with mixed levels of civility and shared social understandings among all actors. A partnership frame was prominent, although at all of the conferences NGOs retained their own monitoring frame with regard to states that states did not share at all times.

Sovereignty Claims

In this section we examine the configuration of sovereignty claims at these conferences. In comparison with the conferences on the environment, human rights, and women, the participation of NGOs was less problematic. Whether this would be reflected in the types of actual sovereignty bargains states were willing to make—that is, whether control or autonomy bargains were made in order to gain legitimacy with state and non-state actors—is another question. In addition, while the problems tackled at Cairo, Copenhagen, and Istanbul were potentially more amenable to solutions involving resource transfers between Northern and Southern states, they are much more similar to the rights issues in that there was little collective incentive for the North to offer resources.[2] Thus, bargains involving giving up some autonomy for increased control (the ability to manage population, poverty, and shelter) may have been possible, although those kinds of problems have less obvious spillover into the realm of the global "commons." On the other hand, issues raised at the population conference also intersected with women's rights claims and states' cultural identities, suggesting potential difficulties in achieving sovereignty bargains at Cairo, in particular.

In actuality, sovereignty was asserted less often at these conferences than at Rio, Vienna, or Beijing. The explicit sovereignty references in the conference documents show an awareness of a balance among sovereignty considerations and social needs. In Cairo's final document, the issue of state sovereignty was seemingly resolved textually, by framing sovereignty as control over implementation of conference recommendations that could potentially reduce autonomy. The first paragraph of its "Principles" reserves "the implementation of the recommendations contained in the Programme of Action" as "the sovereign right of each country, consistent with national laws and development priorities, with full respect for the various religious and ethical values and cultural backgrounds of its people, and in conformity with universally recognized international human rights" (United Nations 1994c).

Similar language appears in the Copenhagen declaration, in which the section on "Commitments" is preceded by a statement that states' "common pursuit of social development . . . aims at social justice, solidarity, harmony and equality within and among countries, with full respect for national sovereignty and territorial integrity, as well as policy objectives, development priorities and religious and cultural diversity, and full respect for all human rights and fundamental freedoms" (United Nations 1995c:Para. 27). However, the invocation of particular values is far more common than the invocation of sovereignty in the Copenhagen Declaration and Programme of Action, referring to respect for states' particular religious, ethical, social, or cultural values eight times in the document itself and four times in states' reservations to the document. References to commonly shared values or tolerance for differences as a universal value, on the other hand, appears six times. And "sovereign" or "sovereignty" makes a total of three appearances.

In the Habitat conference process, explicit sovereignty claims of any kind emerged only gradually. NGO observers noted after the First PrepCom that "Habitat II is about national issues that can only be addressed at the national level. Because all governments share these problems, this PrepCom was less like a negotiation and more like a collaborative effort to develop appropriate strategies to deal with a common problem" (ENB 11-22 April 1994). But despite a greater emphasis on the need for global cooperation, at all three conferences the low-key official conference language did not prevent the emergence of sometimes fierce debates on particular topics with implications for sovereign control or autonomy.

We will now separate the sovereignty analysis into the three topics that elicited the most debates in chapter 4: economics, national values, and accountability. At all of the conferences treated in this chapter, sovereignty claims again fell into these categories, although there were slightly different manifestations of the debates. On the issue of resource allocation at these conferences, states refused to trade control over budget directives for promises of more aid for social programs.

Economics: Cairo, Copenhagen, and Istanbul

Discussions over economics centered on how to meet states' funding needs for new social programs. Underlying that debate, however, were conflicts over the kinds of commitments states would make to secure such programs: commitments to other states; to non-state actors; and to their domestic societies. In this respect, the economic debates—potential trades between control and autonomy, in sovereignty terms—blended with accountability questions, and thus, legitimacy, in a way not seen at Rio, Vienna, or Beijing.

CAIRO: Although the population conferences in previous decades had witnessed serious disagreements, the battle lines over issues were redrawn at Cairo. Debates at Bucharest had centered on the nature of the relationship between economic development and population growth (Johnson 1995:18). At Mexico, they had focused on efforts to stabilize population (Ibid.:21). In the 1990s, those discussion were supplanted by debate over the so-called Cairo Consensus: the shift from controlling population growth to emphasizing the need for women's empowerment and reproductive health and rights. The Cairo Consensus was incorporated in the conference's final statement, in large part due to active NGO lobbying, but countries took exception to the parts of it they saw as impinging on their sovereign control or autonomy.

Cairo's Programme of Action gave estimates, albeit contested ones, as to how much funding would be necessary to provide the health services and data collection outlined in the document, as well as how much should be provided by donor countries. A plan called the 20/20 proposal was advanced to require aid recipients (developing countries) to increase social expenditure to 20 percent of their budgets, while donors would designate 20 percent of their aid for social expenditures. By comparison, actual levels in 1995 averaged 13 percent and 7 percent, respectively (Feeney 1995). Developing countries were being asked to cede some autonomy over the budgeting process in exchange for resources that would enhance implementation capability, or control, for those states. Donors, for their part, were also being asked to cede a measure of autonomy in determining budget allocations. The proposal, backed by NGOs and UN agencies, proved to be an unacceptable trade for the majority of both developing and developed states. They deemed budget allocation "a sovereign right" (Johnson 1995:197).

There was some geographic division in discussions over other economic issues, along the lines discussed in chapters 3 and 4. From their regional meeting onward, the Latin American and Caribbean countries sought to put an emphasis on the developing countries' debt burden as an obstacle to funding population programs (Ibid.:35). Overall, the global South and NGOs joined in calling for changes in consumption and production patterns, widely seen as a critique of the profligate (and resource-wasteful) lifestyles of the global North.[3] Australia, Norway, and Sweden backed new resources and unqualified commitments to certain aid levels (Johnson 1995:42; Shepherd nd), but while European countries in particular seemed willing to acknowledge their obligations as donor countries, most were reluctant to make firm financial commitments or agree to structural changes in global development patterns (Johnson 1995:38, 66).

As a result of these debates, Cairo produced no new trades on economic issues. There were "no pledges of additional financial support for population and development programmes and no firm agreement on how bilateral and multilateral aid flows [would] be readjusted to meet the objectives of the Programme of Action" (*ENB* 5-13 September 1994). Moreover, there was no substantial challenge to neoliberal models of development, with "sustained economic growth" linked to "sustainable development" throughout the document (Hartmann 1995:153; Petchesky 1995). Without such changes in global economic models, some have argued, the "almost feminist vision of reproductive rights and gender equality" of the Cairo program cannot be realized (Petchesky 1995:1). At Cairo, resources for empowering women, beyond population-related services, were not included in the estimates of costs (Johnson 1995:195). As for the elements of sovereignty, states chose to retain both autonomy and control over existing resources rather than to make a sovereignty bargain. Although NGOs and UN staff were promoting the 20/20 proposal, the idea was not well accepted by states. First of all, it did not mandate that more resources overall be donated to recipient states, only that priorities be shifted. Without new resource commitments on the part of donor countries, recipient states also had little incentive to make an autonomy-control bargain of the sort that had been possible at Rio. Neither was legitimacy among non-state actors sufficient to entice donor countries to change their resource commitments or their demands on recipient states.

COPENHAGEN: At the Social Summit, as at other conferences, the Bretton Woods institutions and the neoliberal economic model came in for major criticism, particularly from developing countries. The 20/20 proposal of Cairo was floated again at Copenhagen. Although it was included in the final conference document, to the disappointment of NGOs the proposal was made voluntary for "interested" governments. Oxfam called the change "sabotage." As at Cairo, G-77 countries continued to maintain that such a commitment was compromising their sovereignty by directing the use of aid (Black 1995b).

The North also wanted any debt forgiveness to be applied to social development, and Europeans suggested that the UN monitor how aid is spent in less developed countries. These ideas met objections from some nations ("Useful Words but Not Much Action" 1995). The United States was the only country that entered an official reservation on this issue, to reiterate its statements during the conference that it "cannot agree to increase official development assistance," due to "domestic funding constraints" (United Nations 1995b:Ch. 5, Para. 17). Many donor countries also argued against restrictions on the kinds of aid they should give, but sovereignty was not directly invoked. The now-voluntary nature of the 20/20 proposal preserved the potential for an autonomy/control bargain in principle, although developing states continued to resist aid with strings attached, in the name of sovereignty.

ISTANBUL: By the Second PrepCom for the City Summit, familiar sovereignty claims began to emerge on the economic front. The representative of the G-77/China coalition of governments argued at the beginning of the PrepCom that economic globalization and interdependence made developing countries unable to resolve their own habitat issues: "The unjust relationships in terms of trade, debt, and structural adjustment should not be ignored in the context of the conference. The Group of 77 hoped that the Conference would bring about a substantial increase in international cooperation for housing, shelter and development" ("Preparatory Committee" 1995). In this way, the G-77 argued against global economic structures which, they claimed, limited their control of, and autonomy over, housing and urban issues.

A long debate at Istanbul about whether there was a right to housing was resolved in a way that did not *require* governments to provide housing for their citizens, but that allowed them to commit only to "the full and progressive realization of the right to adequate housing" (Istanbul Declaration, Point 8). The language echoes the UN's traditional way of treating economic rights as a matter of nation-state capacity and progressive realization. This language reflects nation-states' resistance to setting shared economic priorities for national implementation, whether they are inspired by international political agreements or by global economic structures. States were reluctant to offer autonomy for any legitimacy to be gained through conformity to standards of economic rights.

To summarize the debates over economics at these conferences as a group, it appears that even when solutions could be purchased, states were not buying. Southern states were unwilling to give up autonomy for any control over social development issues it might bring, since 20/20 did not mandate new resources, just allocation shifts. Northern countries were unwilling to participate in their end of the bargain—not just because of the cost, but because they were being asked to give up some autonomy over decisions on when, where, and how the resources would be applied.

National Values: Cairo, Copenhagen, and Istanbul

National and cultural values took a prominent place in the sovereignty debates at Cairo, given the links between population issues and women's status. At Copenhagen, issues of economic and cultural sovereignty were the subject of debate, reflecting some of the same issue divisions present at Cairo and at the earlier conferences. At Istanbul, the sovereignty objections to conference issues developed slowly. The strongest objections to a global view of values at Istanbul were on the issue of women's rights. When debates and objections were manifest, legitimacy and autonomy were at odds.

CAIRO: At Cairo, countries debated the extent to which national value systems were eroded by the emphasis on women's empowerment and rights throughout the conference. In sovereignty terms, the balance was between legitimacy in the eyes of non-state actors and other states, and autonomy, or the right that states claimed to depart from, or reinterpret, the universals reflected in UN documents and promoted by NGOs and much of the West. From the Third PrepCom on, and especially in the month leading up to the conference, the Vatican sought allies among those countries with either Catholic or Islamic majorities or strong religious leadership. The so-called Unholy Alliance that was struck united Catholic- and Islamic-influenced countries in a "fundamentalist bloc" against what they saw in the Programme of Action as potentially acknowledging or promoting the legality of abortion and harming the traditional family structure (McIntosh and Finkle 1995:246).

This bloc was not monolithic. Brazil, Indonesia, and Malaysia recognized the need to address unsafe abortion as a public health issue, and Islamic-influenced countries tended to be more concerned with traditional family roles than abortion per se (Johnson 1995:108). Although the rhetoric from the Islamic world reached a pitch at which some countries were openly calling for a boycott of the conference, Egypt intervened, with the result that only Iraq,

Lebanon, Saudi Arabia, and the Sudan refused to attend (McIntosh and Finkle 1995:234). Several government representatives, while supportive of more traditional perspectives on gender relations, objected to the way in which the Vatican, in particular, dragged out the debate on abortion over five conference days, effectively precluding discussion of other crucial issues (Ibid.:248-249). In the end, language on abortion as a public health issue, and the need to provide safe abortion services where the procedure is legal, were included in the final document (Johnson 1995:Ch. 6; United Nations 1994c:Section 8.25). Even the Vatican, for the first time in a UN population conference, signed on to the final document.

But the reservations taken to the Programme for Action revealed that cultural or religious prerogatives continued to be at issue for many governments. Led by the Vatican, with its reservations on seven of the sixteen chapters, many countries with a long history of Catholic influence objected to any language that seemed to condone abortion. These included Argentina, the Dominican Republic, Ecuador, El Salvador, Guatemala, Honduras, Malta, Nicaragua, Paraguay, and Peru. Several of them joined with Islamic countries in taking reservations on language that could be construed to support any family structure other than one built on a heterosexual couple, or to sanction extramarital sex by adolescents. This latter group included Afghanistan, Argentina, Ecuador, Egypt, El Salvador, Guatemala, the Holy See, Honduras, Jordan, Libya, Nicaragua, and Paraguay. In a more general statement, Afghanistan, Brunei Darussalam, Djibouti, Jordan, Kuwait, Libya, the United Arab Emirates, and Yemen took reservations on any policies that could be seen as contravening Islamic law.

COPENHAGEN: One news analysis said that the final document of the Social Summit "promised nothing that had not already been agreed" at Rio, Vienna, Cairo, or in the UN General Assembly (Black 1995a). The values debates that did occur, however, were over the by-now standard autonomy-legitimacy trade on the issues of women's rights and labor rights. "Some developing countries tried again" to roll back previous commitments on women's reproductive health and labor practices (Ibid.). But the attempts were unsuccessful, and some new understandings were reached. Language that had been agreed upon at Cairo was preserved on family and reproductive rights, despite "heated debates" and efforts of the Vatican and others to retreat from the Cairo Consensus (*ENB* 25 January 1995). Indeed, the reservations to the Social Summit's final document centered predominantly on phrases like "reproductive health" and "family planning," indicating that reserving governments did not wish to be understood as supporting abortion or, in the case of the Holy See, for example, other forms of contraception or the use of condoms for HIV/AIDS prevention (United Nations 1995e:Ch.5).

ISTANBUL: Assertions of sovereignty on cultural and religious issues developed slowly before exploding near the end of the Istanbul Conference. The most contentious debates were around women's rights and reproductive health care services in particular. The debate was intensified since the Beijing conference had recently occurred, exacerbating differences among the countries on these issues. Delegates stayed up all night on 13 June holding informal consultations, and thought they had an agreement at 6:00 A.M. When that fell apart, a new round of informal consultations at last produced a final report at 9:30 P.M. on 14 June. In a change from usual procedures, countries were allowed to register their reservations immediately, which may have helped spur the final agreement (*ENB* 3-14 June 1996). The differences in language between the Cairo and Beijing conferences provided a context for these debates, as two different precedents for the Habitat conference. The European Union and the United States pushed for strong universal language on women's right to reproductive health, and argued for the Beijing language that insists that states promote all human rights although it notes national differences in implementation. Most of the G-77/China coalition and the Holy See preferred Cairo's language, which stresses national economic, religious, and cultural priorities and laws in the implementation of human rights agreements (Ibid.), a relatively undemanding trade that retained control over such issues while only nominally sacrificing autonomy.

The final Habitat Agenda places a version of Beijing's language in the Preamble, while altering some references to women's reproductive health. As at Copenhagen, the sections on women were the most-reserved in the final document, with 5 Arab countries reserving on the paragraph on gender equality, and 11 delegations—the Holy See, Argentina, Guatemala, and 8 Muslim countries—reserving on a paragraph on reproductive and sexual health. Most of these also took reservations on a paragraph on the family (Ibid.). In contrast, 7 Arab countries took reservations on the clause "living in harmony with nature," and only 5 objected to language on foreign occupation.

Interestingly, only Iran took a reservation on the issue of the right to equal inheritance (Ibid.), which was the issue that most closely linked gender and the Habitat agenda. Some states dropped their opposition to this right after language was adopted from the Beijing Platform for Action. The United States, the European Union, Norway, Australia, and Canada strongly supported the inclusion of the inheritance right.

Accountability: Cairo, Copenhagen, and Istanbul

Neither the population conference nor the social summit saw proposals to establish any new formal accountability mechanisms for follow-up on their purposes. After Cairo, responsibility for follow-up rested within the Economic and Social Council (ECOSOC). Similarly, for the Social Summit, both ECOSOC and the pre-existing Commission on Social Development were charged with follow-up. Habitat participants passed a proposal to create a Commission on Human Settlements, modeled after Rio's Commission on Sustainable Development (CSD). In light of these arrangements, in the next section we address state and non-state sources of legitimacy as items in sovereignty trade-offs at these conferences.

CAIRO: The final document from Cairo has a chapter devoted to "Partnership with the Nongovernmental Sector," which includes two subcategories, "local, national, and international nongovernmental organizations" and "the private sector." Both parts of the nongovernmental sector are asked to enter into "partnerships" with governments (and each other) to achieve the general implementation of the Programme of Action. The recognition of their deep involvement in research and service provision in reproductive health and family planning affirms that the state is far from solely responsible for these areas. However, the nongovernmental sector is to be seen as complementing, not taking on, the responsibility of governments (United Nations 1994c:15.6, 13). At the same time, only the NGO sector, as "important voices of the people" (Ibid.:15.3) is to be included in the "monitoring and evaluation of population and development objectives and activities" and the "present Programme of Action" (Ibid.:15.1, 5). NGO participation is also recognized and encouraged by the recommendation that governments continue to include NGO representatives as delegates to international fora on population and development (Ibid.:15.12).

Thus the effective participation of NGOs (and evidently, representatives of the pharmaceutical industry) resulted in a control/non-state legitimacy trade-off, with states depending on the expertise and resources of the nongovernmental sector in return for at least some acceptance of their role in monitoring state actions.

It is not surprising that no new body was proposed for the specific implementation of the final document from Cairo, given that two UN organs already existed to deal with population and development: the United Nations Population Fund and the Population Division (United Nations 1994c:Ch. 16). ECOSOC was assigned to assist the General Assembly in the implementation of the Cairo Programme.

While in general NGOs did feel that formal participation was effective in influencing governmental proceedings at Cairo, concern was expressed about the extent to which the voices of Southern feminists, and the situation of Southern women, were taken into account. As a result, not enough attention was given to the broader problems of global inequality that affect national population and development decisions—particularly the impact of neoliberal economic reforms on women and poor populations in general (DeJong 2000:947).

COPENHAGEN: The last chapter of the Copenhagen Declaration and Programme for Action, entitled, "Implementation and Follow-Up," emphasizes the need for partnership among states and other actors, including local authorities and nongovernmental organizations, "especially voluntary organizations" (United Nations 1995c:Ch. 5, Para. 82). The document recognizes that, at least at the local level, policy-making and implementation partnerships cannot happen unless NGOs and community organizations are encouraged implicitly, by governments—and the appropriate "legislative and regulatory frameworks are created"—by governmental authorities (Ibid.:para. 83, a, b). Thus, deliberate efforts to involve civil society are called for, and the involvement of NGOs in the process is seen as integral. The tone of such encouragement in the document is one of affirmation but not necessarily a yielding by states of control in exchange for non-state legitimacy. Instead, the outcome is better characterized as a fairly weak autonomy/legitimacy (state and non-state) bargain.

Regarding NGOs' informal role in accountability, the Programme for Action encourages partnering between governments and civil society, but there is a recognition that it has not yet been fully achieved and, moreover, "nothing short of a renewed and massive political will at the national and international levels" will be required. The image that appears of the NGO, in the document, is that of a potential helper of the state. The document's

language is friendly but nonthreatening in offering a list of suggestions for enhancing the potential contribution of NGOs (Ibid.),
emphasizing the need for encouragement of NGO work rather
than acknowledgment of existing NGO initiatives. In short, the
NGO role is muted in the terms of a control/non-state legitimacy
bargain, despite the acknowledged centrality of NGOs in achieving the goals of social development. In the NGOs' alternative declaration, the partnership aspect is acknowledged as well (Copenhagen Alternative Declaration). However, in the governmental
document, there are no explicit nods to NGOs as independent legitimating or monitoring actors as states try to achieve such
goals. In contrast, the NGOs' alternative declaration calls for the
monitoring of transnational corporations and financial institutions
(Ibid.), in addition to the monitoring of states.

At the formal level, the section of the Programme for Action
that focuses on the role of the UN system is most explicit about
arrangements for the monitoring of goals and agreements (United
Nations 1995c:Section D, Paras. 94-100). As at Cairo, no new
agency was proposed for implementation of the Social Summit's
outcome, although existing institutions and norms were invoked.
Instead, the document calls for the General Assembly's follow-up
(Ibid.:Para. 95, a-e). ECOSOC should coordinate implementation,
adding conference follow-up to the mandate of its existing Commission for Social Development (Ibid.:Para. 95, f). Further emphasis on
states' existing treaty commitments under the International
Covenant on Economic, Social and Cultural Rights by the Committee on Economic, Social and Cultural Rights, the treaty body already established for that purpose, should also be "emphasized" by
the UN (Ibid.:Para. 95, i). While the plans for implementation invoked an integrated approach by various parts of the UN, suggesting a weak autonomy/legitimacy trade, states did not bargain away
control in the form of new formal monitoring mechanisms. The suggested arrangements have since received mixed reviews: one participant's comments at a conference hosted by the autonomous UN
Research Institute for Social Development summed up the potential drawbacks of such an approach:

> On the international front, there has been relatively little
> follow-up to the Social Summit, in part because the struc-
> tures and relationships between the relevant bodies have
> not changed. This Summit was unique, among other
> things, in not making specific recommendations for actions

to be taken by individual institutions—though advances
have been seen at the local, national and regional levels.
(Jacques Baudot, comments paraphrased in UN Research
Institute for Social Development 1997)

NGOs have also taken independent monitoring steps. For example, an organization founded to monitor progress on both Social
Summit goals and the goals of the Fourth World Conference on
Women, Social Watch, publishes an annual report on implementation and maintains a web site from its base in Uruguay. The President of the International Council on Social Welfare, an organization also centrally involved in Social Summit follow-up, has noted
that since the conference, "civil society organizations" have directed their own follow-up efforts more toward the G-7, the World
Trade Organizationn and the World Bank than toward ECOSOC
and the Commission on Social Development (Disney 1999:1).

ISTANBUL AND THE COMMISSION ON HUMAN SETTLEMENTS: At
Habitat, NGOs were included in governmental plans for monitoring compliance with the conference agreements, with "enabling"
being the verb chosen to characterize the relations of governments
to nongovernmental actors (*Istanbul Declaration,* Point 12; *Habitat
Agenda,* Point 44). States created a Commission on Human Settlements, modeled on the Earth Summit's Commission on Sustainable
Development. NGOs and local governments were to be included in
the post-conference follow-up, although at least some observers
speculated that this was a strategy for bringing their new resources into an impoverished national governmental process
(Bindé 1997:219). Local governments were particular winners at
this conference, finding a much larger role than they had played in
the other 1990s conferences, or in the Habitat I conference (Wakely
1996:iii). Thus, there was a moderately successful trade of control
for both state and non-state legitimacy at Habitat, perhaps because
NGOs were seen as potential sources of funds (which would, in
turn, enhance state control).

Conclusion

For the conferences analyzed in this chapter, we might have
expected that NGOs' level of inclusion in UN conference proceedings, taken as an indication of the extent of democratization fostered by global civil society, would depend on the relative intensity

of states' claims to sovereignty on the issues pertaining to the conference. The hypothesis is borne out to some degree. At Cairo, Copenhagen, and Istanbul, states tended to look to NGOs for cooperation and, in general, the NGO presence per se did not seem to threaten states on sovereignty grounds.

However, on the whole at these conferences, neither did NGOs exhibit unexpected power in persuading states to change their sovereign claims. First, few new configurations of the elements of sovereignty arose with reference to population, social development, or human settlement. The sovereignty arguments that arose at the conferences referred mainly to resisting rights for women and asserting autonomy over economic decisions. While these topics offered new ways of interpreting sovereignty claims, they were all present early in the 1990s, at Rio and Vienna. They were the subject of intense debate preparatory to Beijing, and both states and NGOs knew that Cairo, in many ways, was preparation for Beijing. But the same debates were more or less rehashed in different ways at Cairo, Copenhagen, and Istanbul. Potential trade-offs among the four elements of sovereignty with regard to the debates at the conferences are summarized in table 5.1.

NGO participation and status were not nearly as threatened or contested at these conferences in comparison with Rio, Vienna, and Beijing, although there was variation among them. For each of the conferences examined in this chapter, the relevant UN Secretariat played an important role in setting procedures permitting NGO access, and its decisions were not overruled. Thus, it should be noted that in the absence of strong objections by states, the UN administration itself can have a significant impact on the relative status of NGOs in the conference process.

Resource offerings available at Cairo and Copenhagen were not attractive enough to bring about trades of sovereign autonomy for enhanced control. While foreign aid was seen as a part of the solution to their economic problems, developing country governments were *not* willing to give up sovereign autonomy regarding decisions over how to allocate resources, as we have seen for some environmental protection issues. This stands in contrast to the control/autonomy bargain that states were willing to strike at Rio. There, the G-77 had made an implicit trade-off, accepting a global economic model of sustainable development in turn for receiving greater economic assistance for achieving sustainable development (see chapter 4). Events at all three conferences remind us that states also continued to demand that the manner in which they attempted to

Table 5.1 Bargains Debated on Population, Social Development, and Habitat

		Preferred Element of Sovereignty		
	Autonomy	Control	Legitimacy (Non-state)	Legitimacy (Other States)
Autonomy	—	**social development:** 20/20 floated again, made "voluntary"	**all three conferences:** UN secretariat opens official conference to NGOs and states permit it to continue (in contrast to "Fourth PrepCom phenomenon" at environment, human rights, and women's conferences) **social development:** NGOs seen as essential partners with governments for achieving social development goals	**all three conferences:** most states preserve universal standards of women's rights and reproductive health (in alliance with non-state actors) over objections of some states **population, social development:** emphasis on existing norms and UN mechanisms for implementation
Control	**population:** potential aid recipients (G-77) refuse 20/20 proposal, retaining autonomy over budget directives in lieu of increased aid for social programs; donors loath to make firm commitments	—	**population:** NGOs included as participants in future monitoring activities **habitat:** NGOs as partners in monitoring	**habitat:** establishment of Commission on Human Settlements
Legitimacy (Non-State)	**population:** some states maintain national rather than universal conceptions		—	

Element Considered for Trade (vertical label on left)

(continued)

Table 5.1 *(continued)*

Element Considered for Trade		Preferred Element of Sovereignty			
		Autonomy	*Control*	*Legitimacy (Non-state)*	*Legitimacy (Other States)*
		of women's rights against own NGOs' lobbying **social development:** no state-recognized monitoring role granted at conference			
	Legitimacy (Other States)	**habitat:** states refuse firm commitments to uphold economic rights on housing **population, social development, habitat:** Catholic- and Islamic-influenced states prefer national values over universal values		**population, social development:** Northern European states argue for mandatory donor commitments, against preferences of other states	

fulfill their own economic obligations to their citizens should be left up to them.

The 20/20 proposal to make a place for social spending in foreign aid and domestic budgets was proposed at Cairo and resurrected at Copenhagen, but was diluted into a voluntary guideline for "interested governments." We see two reasons for the weakening of this initiative. First, the 20/20 proposal differed from the bargaining observed at Rio in that it would have involved ongoing commitments for significantly large trades, rather than a single "purchase." The 20/20 proposal asked for potential change in priorities by developing country governments, threatening continued external interference, rather than simply offering a resource "add-on." Second, more pragmatically, no new resources were being offered. Given developed countries' histories of not even coming close to the G-7's target percentages of foreign aid allocation, the potential trade-off must have looked even less attractive to developing countries. Any legitimacy that might be gained in the eyes of state or non-state actors could not increase the attractiveness of such a bargain.

In conclusion, the relative calm of these conferences should not be seen solely as an "outcome" of earlier, more contentious conferences. For one thing, NGO participation and accomplishments at Rio began broadly, but were challenged later in the conference processes. States did not drop issues between conferences, such as women's rights, if they seemed to be particularly threatening. Such action indicates to us that global civil society does matter to states, so much so that states sometimes see its participation as a threat and will try to quash its growth. However, NGOs were not deterred. We note that over time, NGO participation in world conferences became routine: there was a baseline expectation that organizations nominally part of global civil society would participate early and often in the conference proceedings. Furthermore, NGO participation was not solely at the behest of states. Particularly in the case of rights-based organizations, including women's lobbying groups, NGOs did achieve recognition and some kinds of influence through both confrontation and cooperation, often accruing significant resources and expertise from conference to conference. These achievements were a result of political struggles.

CHAPTER 6

Global Civil Society:
Transforming Sovereignty and
Building Democracy?

In this chapter, we return to our initial queries outlined in chapter 1: does a global civil society exist? If so, has it had an impact on the democratization of world politics, either in the development of an alternative nongovernmental global public sphere or in new global state-society relations? How do changes in global social forces reflect and reinforce changes in statehood and politics at the international level, especially changes in the meaning of state sovereignty? Having examined six global conferences of the 1990s sponsored by the UN, we offer some conclusions here.

The very idea underlying the UN issue conferences is that nation-states cannot and should not try to resolve certain emerging global issues alone, but should do so in the context of collective debate and resolution for action. The format of UN conferences was not designed to mandate the participation of non-state actors, but nongovernmental organizations (NGOs) have been pushing against the limits on their participation at least since the 1972 Stockholm Conference on the Human Environment. Certainly by the Rio conference in 1992, states had to understand that calling a global conference among states also issued a shadow invitation to a plethora of non-state actors who would show up in droves to work against nation-state prerogatives and for universal values. Some did so by lobbying governmental representatives, while others preferred to devote their energies to networking among themselves.

In these ways, simply calling and participating in a global UN conference posed inherent challenges to the sovereignty and centrality of nation-states. Some states embraced these challenges to varying degrees, while others strongly resisted them. In our investigation we have found the following patterns of participation and responses, which we will evaluate with regard to their broader implications for the developments of global civil society, sovereignty, and democracy.

A Global Civil Society?

The *global* dimension of global civil society queries whether NGO participants in world politics are geographically diverse, based in multiple world regions and countries. This dimension is important for assessing the nature of any emerging global civil society. A "global" civil society dominated by just one world region would raise serious questions about the representativeness of this new sector.

At the UN conferences of the 1990s, this component was the one that was most nearly achieved. NGOs from all over the world indeed made their way to regional and global preparatory conferences as well as to the final conferences themselves. Total numbers of participants varied, with the largest numbers in Rio in 1992 (18,000) and in Copenhagen (12,000) and Beijing (30,000) in 1995. Few government delegations from any part of the world could hope to avoid pressures from domestic NGOs even as they met far from home, and the parallel NGO fora showcased a diverse array of languages, traditions—and preoccupations. As discussed in chapter 2, Northern NGOs often numerically predominated and took a leading role in lobbying government delegations. But NGOs from other regions also strongly presented their sometimes opposing positions, and the ensuing debates and networks among a wide variety of NGOs provided much of the spark and innovation of the global gatherings.

Chapter 3, which focuses on Latin American participation, shows that the increasingly global nature of NGO participation was not accidental and suggests ways in which even more representative participation could be achieved. The overwhelming presence of Latin Americans at the only conference in their region—they formed 40 percent of NGO participants in Rio de Janeiro—endorses the UN strategy of locating its conferences and activities in different parts of the world. In addition, the regional preparatory conferences were important for early articulations among regional NGOs, who typically went home to recruit more participants for subsequent meetings. Finally, chapter 3 stresses the important role that NGOs from other world regions played in encouraging Latin American NGO participation and in supporting their positions. A variety of governments also supported specific NGO positions or insisted on greater NGO access, which helped legitimize and encourage broader NGO participation. Together, chapters 2 and 3 offer strong evidence against characterizations of global civil society as "heavily concentrated in north-western Europe" (Anheier, Glasius, and Kaldor 2001:7).

The *civil* component of global civil society is the one that is most focused on the opportunities for interaction among the actors and the quality of nongovernmental access to global forms of governance. With respect to state-led international governing spheres, our criteria for civility mandate that NGOs have clear mechanisms for participation in, and influence on, state-led politics—both during the conference processes and in provisions for implementing conference agreements. Yet while states are important potential guarantors of civility, NGOs retain the ability to choose between a variety of responses to state-created opportunities. They may engage them directly or may resist or ignore them. In addition, NGOs may display varying levels of civility in their interactions with each other, with development of an alternative nongovernmental public sphere dependent on balanced and inclusive relations in their networking activities.

The advances in NGO-state civility emerge most clearly when we compare the conferences of the 1990s with their predecessors of the 1960s and 1970s. Not only did the numbers of NGO participants increase dramatically over two decades, but so did the variety of ways in which they were allowed to participate. Governments at the earlier conferences could virtually ignore the presence of NGOs, both at the conferences and in implementation of conference agreements. By the 1990s, this was no longer possible, especially as NGOs were allowed to freely observe and lobby many governmental sessions. By the time of the Habitat conference in 1996, the last one we consider here, governments put NGOs on the drafting committee and granted NGOs and subnational governments summit time to present their positions on conference themes.

Nonetheless, NGO-state civility was far from completely achieved at any of the conferences. While the UN conferences opened new opportunities for NGOs to participate and partner with states, states also used conference proceedings to close those opportunities unilaterally—especially as negotiations reached important and sensitive points. Even at the Habitat conference, the special sessions allowing NGOs to speak for themselves happened only after governments had already largely shaped their agenda and documents. Throughout the 1990s conferences, a number of different states regularly argued to limit NGO access to governmental negotiations and sought to restrict their future participation in overseeing conference agreements. Other states sometimes countered those arguments. Individual states also took inconsistent positions, with Latin American governments, for example, accepting NGO participation at the conferences themselves but less enthusiastic about their participation in conference implementation.

Overall, our investigation of the civility of current global civil society offers partial support for the view of NGOs as regular and consistent influences on states in world politics (Foster and Anand 1999; Willetts 2000). NGOs were clearly present and engaged in new roles at the UN conferences. At all of them, NGOs helped put new issues on the agenda, as in the role of women's groups in raising gender concerns at all of the other conferences. NGOs lobbied states for stronger commitments and stronger institutions. Even when they lost, their arguments and presence put governments on the defensive and moved the terrain of debate. In final conference documents, governments recognized the fact that NGOs would be crucial for enhancing their ability to live up to their conference commitments. In these ways, the participation of NGOs at the UN conferences does present a partial model for peaceful and significant NGO-state interactions that could transform and legitimize other intergovernmental fora if introduced there. Yet governments continued to control the points of access and decision making and, as discussed in the next section, many continued to question the right of NGOs to have such access and influence.

With respect to civility among NGOs themselves, they often split into playing two different kinds of roles, which we refer to as the lobbier and networker roles, with varying levels of antagonism. Lobbiers took advantage of any opportunities for participation with states, and pushed hard to expand them. Networkers, in contrast, focused more of their attention on building connections with other NGOs, a position more compatible with the view of NGOs as formulators of alternative types of non-state-based, global politics. Occasional differences among NGOs about appropriate strategies—divided along North-South lines at the Rio conference, for example—illustrate incomplete civility of NGO-NGO relations. Nonetheless, NGOs were willing to work on bridging their differences in ways that governments often were not. At all six of the conferences discussed here, many more NGOs attended the NGO-only parallel fora than accompanied the governmental conferences, illustrating their commitment to building alternative global meeting places. They worked out mechanisms for representation and inclusiveness, even as the range of participating NGOs expanded to an unprecedented extent. Many NGOs traveled from conference to conference through the 1990s, broadening their agendas and connections. Their networks have spilled over from the conferences themselves to ongoing advocacy and mobilizing efforts that cross national boundaries. The regular face-to-face contacts facilitated by the ongoing conference schedules both reflected the emergence of a more truly global citizens' network and reinforced it in turn.

Finally, we claim that global civil *society* exists when members of the global society (states and NGOs) act with reference to their ongoing relationships, based on the construction over time of their identities, relations, and substantive issues. We do find evidence of a deepening society of global NGOs, which offers some confirmation of the presence of global civil society defined as alternative forms of non-state-based politics (Lipschutz 1996; Shaw 1994; Wapner 1996). While NGOs continue to disagree on some specific substantive issues, they do so in a context of intense interaction and debates that places value on their interrelationship, as discussed in the previous section. Ongoing interactions among NGOs have helped to narrow the distance between them on substantive issues. Overall, NGOs presented the most consistent and consensual voices for emerging universal values of sustainable development, human rights, women's rights, the right to development, and so on. In fact, NGOs often directly countered their own governments' arguments that those values were not truly universal, as when women's organizations from states with conservative Catholic or Islamic influence supported more expansive freedoms for women. Broad areas of agreement coexisted with continuing contention, however. Certainly, NGOs' extended exposure to NGOs coming from other world regions and possessed of varying experiences revealed as many differences as agreements. Many nonprofit NGOs disagreed with the United Nations' historic inclusion of business and manufacturing associations as nongovernmental participants, for example. Holding all NGOs together was their conviction of their right to be a part of the conference processes and, by extension, global decision-making on critical issues.

In contrast, states were much less willing to acknowledge a clear right of NGOs to be present as central participants. This unwillingness points to a much less fully realized society of states *with* NGOs at the global level. States only provisionally accepted NGOs' contributions to UN conference processes. They stood firm on their claims to ultimate sovereignty over the issues that most affect their ability to control the distribution of power and resources, whether at home or abroad. When NGOs sought to engage states, many states seemed to respond by calculating their interests rather than by cultivating an intimate and ongoing relationship with NGOs. Thus we sometimes find rather different orientations by the same state to NGO influence and participation at different conferences, reflecting the ways in which its interests were recalculated in different issue areas. When alliances with NGOs promised potential resources, for example, NGO participation was more welcomed than when it simply meant more international accountability. Some states did show more principled commitment to NGO participation and influence, typically if they were also committed to active civil society participation at home. As such, these examples do not necessarily reflect a fully transformed conception of state-NGO relations at the global level, although they may suggest a possible mechanism for establishing the groundwork for future developments.

Global Civil Society and Democracy

The preceding discussion suggests that there is somewhat better evidence for the existence of a transnational democratic sphere of interaction conceived as one among non-state actors alone than as one that includes states and NGOs. The more demanding standard of social interaction among state and non-state actors that we posed at the beginning of our study is not fully met. A sphere of global debate has been emerging among NGOs, however, even as it remains strained with tensions and inequality. The 1990s conferences aided this development, as they thrust NGOs into ever-greater prominence both globally and as they returned home. The conferences also provided focal points for networking and interaction that multiplied linkages among diverse NGOs. Few other events have spurred such large gatherings of NGOs—as many as thiry thousand for over a week at a time—and the impact of the gatherings is likely to last as long or longer as any substantive achievements of the conferences.

In considering the impact of global civil society in promoting democratic interactions between states and NGOs at the international level, we see a substantial new lobbying force, with equally strong resistance from states. As a result, we are reluctant to argue that changes in NGO-state interactions over time from Rio to Istanbul represent a fully democratic sphere of state-based governance of the sort envisioned by some at the end of the Cold War. In fact, the terms of NGO access were renegotiated at every one of the 1990s conferences, so that while NGOs always were able to participate, they had to struggle for that right each time. That indicates to us that some states were significantly threatened by the emergence of the new lobbying force, and willing to risk the wrath of NGOs to confine their new roles. However, they were able to do so only at the margins of a new set of rules established by a coalition of other states and NGOs that allowed more NGO participation than was possible before the 1990s. Finally, we see emerging changes in the nature of states themselves, and in the nature of their sovereignty in particular. These changes suggest that we have not yet reached the limits of the transformations in world politics that may come.

Sovereignty

Sovereignty is one of the constitutive principles of modern statehood. As such, it is not surprising that states defended their sovereignty against emerging global civil society actors and purported universal norms throughout the 1990s world conferences. The strength of the objections of at least some states shows the level of threat they felt to their traditional claims to sovereignty. Straightforward reassertions of sovereignty were not the only state response to the new challenges, however. Sometimes states responded by trying to manage various dimensions of their sovereignty, reasserting one dimension of sovereignty while bargaining away another, and so on. And sometimes they responded by accepting new limits on their individual sovereignty. The patterns of these sovereignty assertions and bargains show potentially important changes in how states define their expectations for themselves and for other states, and are somewhat surprising in what they reveal about states' priorities and nonnegotiables.

In examining these patterns, we found it helpful to identify four different dimensions of sovereignty. The first, autonomy, asserts an individual state's right to make its own decisions, against possible interference from other states or from non-state actors. The second, control, is linked to the ability of states to achieve their desired aims internally. The final two dimensions are both linked to the concept of state legitimacy, which can be understood as the power that states receive from being recognized as having the authority to act and decide in a particular domain. This legitimacy, we argue, is granted not only by other states, building upon the mutual recognition assumed in the traditional conception of legitimate sovereignty, but also by non-state actors—a potential global popular sovereignty.

In the international interactions we study, states are floating arguments about their preferences. A few may stand unchallenged, a few may be bolstered by the actions of other states, and others may stimulate debate among fellow states and nongovernmental actors. Nongovernmental organizations do not have sovereignty and do not seek it. Instead, to the extent that they acknowledge states' sovereign power, they tend to place demands upon it, asking that states use it for the ends that they, NGOs, see fit. However, in suggesting that states bargain while trying to maintain the different forms of authority that sovereignty supposedly protects, we do not mean to imply, paradoxically, that sovereignty is thereby always "national, instrumental, and total."[1] It is, for the most part, national, and used instrumentally, but it is almost never total. The empirical observations in this study defy such a characterization. The implications of sovereignty are contested by multiple actors in ways that sovereign privilege cannot fully circumscribe.

A critic might assert that characterizing sovereignty as a bundle of exchangeable attributes still assumes that states hold sovereignty in totality, because states are always in charge of shaping sovereignty themselves. In this view, sovereignty, like clay, may be stretched thin or pulled into nearly unrecognizable shapes, but it is so malleable that it never breaks. Our response is that while states, as states, possess the rights now associated with external legal sovereignty as a result of mutual recognition, sovereignty in other respects is a de facto rather than a de jure condition. Although sovereignty is key to the current understanding of what makes a state, states do not always maintain control of the terms of the argument. Furthermore, as this study has shown, external non-governmental actors are new participants in such manipulation, and sovereign autonomy cannot always be redeemed when states are ready to reclaim it. This is an important change in sovereignty's underpinnings in that it expands the basis of authority to both domestic and international civil society.

Substantively, states vocally asserted and negotiated their sovereignty on a set of issues that remained surprisingly consistent at all six of the conferences. First, women's rights remained the most vigorously contested sovereignty referents across the conferences studied, even at conferences as seemingly unrelated to women's rights as the social development and habitat conferences. The strong cultural or national defenses of traditional family structures and gender relations more generally may seem surprising at first glance, but their emergence as a central division between countries at these conferences demands serious consideration. It may be that, as some countries realize that they have relatively less leeway in economic development matters, they look to aspects of national life that are under their legal control. Moreover, gender relations are at the core of what most countries consider their national identity. Not only are women often seen as the "bearers of culture," but the family is conceived of as the building block of society. Thus, threats to alter the gender relations underpinning men's and women's roles in society have the potential, in the view of many countries, to fundamentally change all social structures (Friedman 2003). Resolution of such differences is complicated even further if certain structures of gender relations are also promoted as fundamental to religious practice, as evidenced by the negotiating positions of some Catholic- and Islamic-influenced governments at the conferences. States showed similar resistance to bargaining away control over other kinds of human rights as well.

A second consistent referent for claims of national sovereignty was autonomy over national economic decisions. The G-77, or Southern countries, made this claim most consistently. At the Rio conference in 1992, the final conference documents indicated a willingness of Southern countries to bargain away economic autonomy over certain sustainable development decisions in exchange for new resources from the North that would allow them greater control over their national economies. Nonetheless, this bargain was not repeated at any of the subsequent conferences for a variety of reasons discussed in chapters 4 and 5: fewer resources were offered for other conferences' issues; a significant subgroup

of the South refused to relinquish any autonomy over rights issues; and, perhaps most importantly, Northern countries failed to
deliver the new resources they had promised at Rio. Northern
countries also protected their national autonomy over economic
decisions, with strong resistance by many to any mandatory foreign aid targets in particular. States from all of the world regions
were willing to jeopardize their legitimacy with NGOs and with
states upholding universal values if autonomy over economic issues was at stake. This was especially clear at the Cairo and
Copenhagen conferences, where both donor and recipient states
exhibited great reluctance to restrict their national governmental
financial autonomy, despite pleas from non-state actors to commit
foreign aid and government budgets to social issues through the
20/20 proposal.

Finally, on accountability issues, states displayed varying degrees of willingness to build new mechanisms of accountability to
other states and to NGOs. Formal institutions for implementation
and monitoring indicate an implicit or explicit trade of reduced autonomy for increased legitimacy with state and non-state actors, as
discussed in chapter 4. Once again, there is little evidence of a
steady expansion of such new mechanisms across the conferences.
States created entirely new institutions to oversee implementation
of conference agreements only at the first and last of the six 1990s
conferences we studied. Rio's Commission on Sustainable Development and Istanbul's Commission on Human Settlements were
structured in similar ways to allow for oversight by both NGOs and
other states. The Office of the High Commissioner for Human
Rights was created as a result of Vienna, to be a more authoritative
and more centralized version of the former UN Centre for Human
Rights, but no new oversight by NGOs was incorporated. Finally,
two years after Beijing, UN Secretary General Kofi Annan created
the Special Advisor to the Secretary General on Gender Issues and
the Advancement of Women to oversee implementation of the Platform for Action.

New institutions are not the only measure of states' willingness to accept accountability for new commitments, however, as existing institutions can also play such a role. The social development
conference at Copenhagen redefined the mandate of the existing
Commission on Social Development, and focused on integrating existing UN programs. Population and human rights issues already
had an extensive international institutional structure, and the
human rights institutions had established procedures for NGO

oversight and reporting, but within the existing UN guidelines for consultation with NGOs.

To evaluate states' willingness to acknowledge transnational actors as a source of legitimacy, we also examined the provisions for NGOs that were outlined in final conference documents. According to one model, prominent in the Rio, Vienna, and Copenhagen documents on the environment, human rights, and social development, respectively, NGOs are instrumental in helping states that continue to stand alone as the primary actors. For Rio and Vienna, this secondary role is somewhat balanced by NGOs' ability to contribute to global monitoring and reporting on states' behavior. Other conference documents used stronger language for the NGO role, with Cairo, Beijing, and Istanbul final documents calling NGOs "partners" with states. The partnership is invoked most frequently for assistance with implementing conference agreements, but partnership in policy making and monitoring of states is also mentioned.

Finally, one of the strongest pieces of evidence for the emergence of important relationships of mutual accountability in global politics is the fact that agreements were reached at all, given the continuing strength of sovereignty claims at all the conferences. States increasingly recognize that they are accountable to a larger global community that includes NGOs as well as other nation-states. In this context, many state delegations did embrace non-state actors and/or universal conceptions of environmental sustainability, human rights and women's rights, and the right to development and housing—at least in the form of general, rhetorical commitments to these principles. Hundreds of pages of documents and literally months of negotiations chronicle their willingness to set out new global goals and models of action. Their intense debates and sometimes intransigent positions on language in these documents suggest a certain level of seriousness to these commitments, as do the resources states from all over the world committed to participation.

The conferences were both less than, and more than, simply functional ways for states to interact. Kenneth W. Abbott and Duncan Snidal (1998) have noted that international relations scholars need to pay more serious attention to international organizations, because states see them as places to get things done. The fluid nature of the conference process had portended something more—at the beginning of this new round of conferences in the early 1990s, the possibilities for increased cooperation looked bright. But as the 1990s wore on and the century turned, it became harder to profess

that the end of the Cold War had ushered in a new age of cooperation. As a practical matter, for the most part, states have not garnered new autonomy or control over the conferences' issues. If individual states had not participated in any of the conferences, they
might not have lost much. Once states entered the conference
venue, they played to win—but to win may have meant something
different than measureable gains in many cases. As we noted, some
issues could be bought but most could not, and it was difficult to get
states to ante up post-conference money and resources in all cases.
Playing a role in the conferences, we think, reinforced states' desire
for gains in legitimacy with other states and with non-state actors
through the give-and-take of political interactions on the issues at
hand. In this regard, we see that the UN as an international organization did "teach" states their interests in the sense that Martha
Finnemore (1996) elaborates for standing international organizations. Because these were dynamic conference processes, however,
state representatives were also creating and articulating their interests to an even greater degree on new issues, through interaction and through the recognition that the words of the conference
documents were also creating expectations for the future. Thus, we
would contend that even if the conferences have reached their end
point as UN funds are stretched and fully committed participation
by some countries becomes unpredictable (e.g., Barr 2002; Meyerson 2002), the conference processes established a pattern and basis
of interaction that will persist.

Perhaps more significantly, the sovereign limits of global civil
society have expanded in ways that newly incorporate NGOs as social actors. Our study reinforces the conclusions of many recent
works that emphasize the importance of nongovernmental organizations and their links with other parts of international society
(e.g., A.M. Clark 2001; Foster and Anand 1999; Keck and Sikkink
1998; Smith, Pagnucco, and Chatfield 1997; Wapner 2000). NGOs
did make a difference. More so than states, the NGOs did have incentives to make each conference a "conference of commitments,"
as NGOs at Beijing did explicitly. While at the official level NGOs
were allowed in or not by states, states themselves were not fully in
control of such relationships. NGOs themselves saw their own potential impact in different ways, both in a traditional capacity as
pressure groups on states and in their ability to form global social
and communicative bonds with each other. Politically, NGOs have
managed to make some progress on their policy issues and on the
creation and maintenance of their networks. Furthermore, as we

have demonstrated, sovereignty has also been under construction throughout the conference processes on the issues considered here. The full implications of such changes—and whether or not they are reversible—remain to be seen. However, the changes themselves manifest a new conception of what it means for states and non-state actors to engage in global politics.

Global Civil Society: Future Directions?

Clearly, the UN World Conferences have not ended with the experiences we study here. Further research on the so-called +5 and +10 follow-up conferences and others that followed Habitat would provide an important contribution to our understanding of how global civil society is developing, as well as the extent to which states are, or are not, accepting NGOs as ongoing partners in global developments. Moreover, the UN world conferences are not the only arenas in which issues of global democratization, non-governmental participation, and state sovereignty are at stake. There are various other arenas of NGO/state interaction that could be fruitfully explored to see how far the findings of this work travel, and to continue to explore various facets of global civil society.

How might these conclusions about global civil society at UN conferences transfer to an analysis of the sphere of global economic governance? The actors of civil society interested in economic governance are clearly a global group, perhaps even more so than at the UN conferences. Southern actors such as the Mexican Zapatistas have pushed economic globalization activism forward, as has the Southern-dominated World Social Forum of Porto Alegre, Brazil (J. D. Clark 2003). The levels of civility in relations between state and non-state actors are dramatically different between economic institutions, such as the World Trade Organization (WTO), and the UN, and we propose that that difference originates in the incompletely realized social dimension. The failure of states to accord NGOs continuous and respected—if nonsovereign—participatory status in global politics creates the observed arbitrariness of rules for non-state participation. This is manifested both in the way in which NGOs had to struggle anew for favorable terms of participation in every UN conference and in their inability to enter the sphere of global economic governance, except on the streets in opposition. Without mutual social regard by states and NGOs, global democratization seems quite distant. The example of the UN conferences does suggest, however, that greater openness on the part of states to NGO participation contributes to less oppositional NGO participation. This kind of practical reasoning may result in more civil relations in the economic institutions even without a principled commitment by states to broad consultation and participation.

Any analysis of global civil society in the economic sphere would need to give more attention than we do to the distinctions within the non-state sector as well. In this book, we have concentrated on NGOs as not-for-profit members of social movements. This was possible in part because the nonprofit NGOs dominated the civil society sector in the UN conferences in both number and levels of activism. In the economic sphere, for-profit actors are much more active and the two sets of actors are more directly opposed, and so we would expect to find rather different characterizations of civility and sociability within civil society itself. As one recent study observes, global civil society is already densely populated by transnational business entities engaging in formal and informal modes of association (O'Brien et al. 2000:15), and it is open to conflict and competition as well as sociability.

The nature of sovereignty bargaining is also likely to be different in the economic sphere. Economic actors can drive direct bargains with states on policy matters at home. They have their own resources to exchange with states and, for that matter, with NGOs. Therefore they do not have to rely as centrally on the kinds of legitimacy arguments that we saw NGOs making at the UN conferences. However, we might expect that issue-oriented, not-for-profit NGOs would attempt to use legitimacy bargains as a form of leverage against for-profit influence. Given states' propensity to guard their sovereignty over economic decision-making, any bargaining over collective economic decision-making is likely to be especially contentious.

Another possibly fruitful extension and evaluation of this book's conclusions could come from observing relationships between states and global civil society in contexts that are more sustained and concentrated. One obvious place to turn is to the examination of NGO-state interactions at other venues within the UN system, such as ECOSOC, the Commission on Human Rights, the Commission on the Status of Women, and the Security Council (Alger 2002; Cooper, English, and Thakur 2002; Weiss and Gordenker 1996; Weiss 1998; Willetts 1996). Many of these institutions have venerable histories of NGO lobbying: what does comparison across institutions and over time reveal in terms of patterns of NGO engagement and state response? Is the social dimension more fully developed when relationships are continuous rather than occasional? Is there truly global representation among civil society participants? What kinds of relationships exist between the civil society organizations that take part in these sustained relationships and those who do not? Such studies would help us to understand the dynamics of more regularized and sustained global civil society exchanges with UN institutions.

Regional economic institutions somewhat resemble these other global fora, but differ from them in interesting ways, so that systematic comparisons could prove fruitful. Like the WTO, they address economic issues, where we have seen states try to preserve their autonomy and control. Yet in institutions like the European Union, and to a lesser extent, the North American Free Trade Agreement and the Common Market of the South (Mercosur), NGOs have made strong claims for access to governmental negotiations over issues that cut to the core of those sovereignty claims (Bouget and Prouteau 2002; Cason 2000; Hochstetler 2002; MacDonald and Schwartz 2002). Those claims rest in part on the stronger and more sustained relationships between citizens and state governments in a particular world region. Research that examines state-society relations at the regional level can reveal the extent to which citizens are gaining a voice in regional governing and how that affects both regional democracy and state sovereignty.

Finally, another approach would be to reverse the angle of analysis and look at what happens after the participants in the UN conferences return home. Explorations of "transnationalism reversed" have revealed that these conferences have varied impacts on national states and social movements, often lending the pressure of world opinion to domestic actors, but sometimes distracting NGO members and agendas from pressing local and national problems (Alvarez 2000; Friedman 1999). In some cases, advocates have found their work on national issues jeopardized, "tainted" by association with conference declarations that domestic actors find illegitimate. Again, comparison across countries—or within countries across conferences—would yield important findings about the effects of global civil society on national norms and development. Similarly, exploring the relationship between prominent NGOs and decision makers in the capital cities of powerful states in the world system would enhance our understanding of how decisions get made before, during, and after conferences.

As this last section is intended to suggest, there are many questions still to be answered about global civil society as a collection of actors and activities outside the circumscribed arena of the UN conferences. Beyond an analysis of the existence and dynamics of global civil society within the UN conference framework, we hope that this study has also established a set of questions relevant to identifying and understanding global civil society's broader impact. To assess broader manifestations, further research on the topic should ask the following questions. Descriptively, how can we recognize global civil society and its effects? Does global civil society make world politics more or less democratic? And, how does its presence affect the nature and capabilities of the nation-state? We would not expect global civil society to have exactly the same importance or impact in all settings of global, regional, or national governance. After all, domestic civil society is also multifaceted, with different channels of access to national decision makers for different groups and different issues at different times (Tarrow 1994). What is to be expected, however, is that as global interactions of all kinds become more numerous and frequent, global civil society will become more complex, prominent, and perhaps more institutionalized, despite its present limitations. Continued study of the characteristics and limits of global civil society is an essential component of a complete understanding of global politics.

Notes

Chapter 1

1. Others have observed that further investigation is necessary. Shaw (1994:648) finds that "too little attention has been paid" to the "empirical analysis of [social movements in civil society] and their relevance to the global/interstate contexts." Weiss, Forsythe, and Coate (1997:252-253) note that "the differences, conflicts, and tensions in the interstate order are relatively well documented and discussed; this is not true for the non-state order."

2. We use *official* to distinguish governmental proceedings from the *parallel* NGO fora, the gatherings of nongovernmental groups that are held in tandem with the governmental activities.

3. On *NGO* and related terms, Gordenker and Weiss (1996:18-19) provide a good definitional overview.

4. The focus on a final set of formal documents was lessened at the Johannesburg conference in 2002 (Rio + 10). This conference produced a Plan of Implementation, but the main focus was on setting up voluntary partnerships to implement earlier agreements and dialogue among the state and non-state participants. See the conference reports on-line at <http://www.johannesburgsummit.org/html>.

5. Organizations falling into the latter category sometimes call themselves social movements, but we have chosen to use the term *nongovernmental organization* (NGO) to refer to groups with both types of aims. Smith, Pagnucco, and Chatfield (1997:60) refer to all such groups as "social movement organizations," defined as "formal groups explicitly designed to promote specific social changes." We use NGO in this study since it is also the UN designation for such groups.

6. Many NGOs, of course, use both simultaneously. Works that address social movements' political roles directly are Hochstetler (1997) and Wapner (1995). See also A. M. Clark (1995).

7. Friedman observed Vienna's NGO Forum; the NGO Forum of the Latin American Regional Preparatory Meeting for Beijing at Mar de Plata, Argentina; and attended both the NGO Forum and the official conference at Beijing as an accredited NGO representative. Hochstetler observed four preparatory meetings of the Brazilian NGO Forum for UNCED; a Latin American NGO preparatory forum in São Paulo, Brazil; and the official and parallel meetings of UNCED's Fourth PrepCom.

Chapter 2

1. The International Commission of Jurists estimated over 1,400 in "Preliminary Evaluation of UN World Conference on Human Rights," Statement issued 1 July 1993, *Review of the International Commission of Jurists* 50 (1993):109; an estimate of 1,500 appears in "Human Rights Groups Take Centre Stage," *Amnesty International Newsletter* 23, no. 9 (September 1993):8.

2. E.g., only two representatives per accredited NGO were permitted to participate on a limited basis in the governmental conference at Mexico City.

3. MacBride was Secretary-General of the International Commission of Jurists (ICJ) from 1963 to 1970, and chaired the International Executive Committee of Amnesty International from 1964 to 1974 (Tolley 1994:105-109).

4. For more on North/South tensions between NGOs, see the following section on "Unaligned Frames."

5. For more on the efforts to establish a High Commissioner post, see chapter 4.

6. The women's organizational strategies were carried to other conferences as well. In preparing for the 1994 UN Conference on Population and Development in Cairo, the women's NGOs decided to focus on gaining access to official delegations and working with the media, as well as preparing lobbying strategies. NGOs again used the Women's Caucus to coordinate lobbying, convening daily meetings at the Forum and at the conference site. The interaction between NGOs and official delegations contributed to consensus on the conference document. Similar strategies were repeated at the 1995 UN Social Summit in Copenhagen.

7. In the preparatory process for the Rio conference and for others, the

official meetings received one of three designations, which provided for different levels of NGO participation. "Formal" meetings, with governmental statements for the record, allowed NGOs to be present, to give presentations if asked or allowed by the meeting Chair, and to lobby. "Formal informal" meetings allowed the presence of NGOs at the discretion of the Chair. "Informal" meetings involved many kinds of gatherings. Most of the actual governmental negotiating sessions were scheduled as officially "Informal" meetings, meaning that NGOs had no systematic access to them.

8. For a full discussion of the problems that NGOs faced in participating throughout the Beijing process, see Amnesty International et al. (1996). The report finds that access was denied through

> restrictions on, and politically motivated interference with, NGO participation and access during official preparatory meetings; government interference in the process of NGO accreditation to the governmental conferences and a lack of transparency in that process; the denial of visas to participants registered and accredited to the NGO Forum and/or the government conference; and de facto exclusion of participants with disabilities through the failure to provide adequate and accessible facilities. (Ibid.:3)

It also describes "arbitrary restrictions on participation" and "restrictions on freedom of expression and association" (Ibid.).

9. Amnesty International published a book on women's rights in March 1995 at the launch of a campaign on women's rights in the lead-up to Beijing (Amnesty International 1995). Human Rights Watch began a research and monitoring project on women's human rights in 1990, and published the results of its five years of work in 1995 (Human Rights Watch Women's Rights Project 1995).

10. Working Group D did consider "the relationship between human rights, development and democracy" (see Nowak 1993:Section D).

11. Compare the three-page statement by Amnesty International, *Our World: Our Rights,* December 1992, AI Index: IOR 41/19/92, with *World Conference on Human Rights: Facing Up to the Failures,* the 39-page document issued the same month by Amnesty International.

12. Final Document, Vienna Plus Five Global NGO Forum on Human Rights, 22-24 June 1998, Ottawa, Canada, online at <http://www.hri.ca/fortherecord1998/documentation/final-report.htm>; "A Statement from the NGOs of the Linkage Caucus" (New York, 10 June 2000) online at <http://www.cwgl.rutgers.edu/b5/linkage.htm>.

13. "Vienna: A Search for Common Ground" (unsigned) 1993. *UN Chronicle* 30 (3):59.

14. Nowak and Schwartz (1994:8) estimate that over 70 percent of

NGOs at Vienna were small, Southern NGOs participating at the global level for the first time.

15. O'Dea, Director of Amnesty International-USA's Washington Office, spoken comments delivered 2 September 1993 at "The 1993 World Conference on Human Rights and the Politics of Identity," roundtable panel, Annual Meeting of the American Political Science Association, Washington DC. See also Gaer (1996:58). According to a survey of 500 NGOs that "go to, or wish to go to UN conferences in the 1990s," 76 percent felt "restricted" by larger NGOs; 75 percent by English-language NGOs, and 71 percent by Northern NGOs (Benchmark Environmental Consulting 1996:26-28).

16. Uvin (1996:167) makes the point, however, that Southern NGOs have a good deal to gain from cooperating with larger Northern NGOs. "Third World NGOs increasingly attempt to link up with Northern INGOs [International NGOs] in order to influence rich country governments . . . Northern INGOs increasingly serve as lobbyists for their Southern partners, working with them to promote policy change at the summit."

17. ECOSOC Resolution 1996/31 (passed 25 July 1996) replaced ECOSOC Resolution 1296 (1968), which formerly governed NGO consultative status.

18. ECOSOC Resolution 1996/31, Paras. 5, 6, 7, 20.

19. Section IX, Paras. 68-70. Also see Willetts (2000).

Chapter 3

1. The report also admits that the official delegates had little time to present their positions, since too many NGOs had talked for too long.

2. Author observation of the VI Brazilian NGO Forum in São Paulo, 27-29 September 1991.

3. "Statistics on NGO-Participation in the World Conference on Human Rights," *NGO-Newsletter,* no. 4 (July 1993), reprinted in Nowak (1994:224). This statistic refers to organizations registered with the Ludwig Boltzman Institute of Human Rights, which helped to facilitate NGO participation in the conference process.

4. A detailed list of state and nongovernmental attendees is found in United Nations (1993e).

5. *NGO-Newsletter,* no. 2, (February 1993), in Nowak (1994:212).

6. This paragraph draws from "Annex I: Recommendations and Pro-

posals Submitted by the Non-Governmental Organizations Present in San José," 22 January 1993, in United Nations (1993f:3-17).

7. See "UN General Assembly Acts on the World Conference," *NGO Newsletter,* no. 2 (February 1993), in Nowak (1994:210).

8. Accredited NGOs were officially allowed to lobby and inform governmental delegates. Calculations based on "List of Accredited Non-Governmental Organizations Who Were Represented at the Fourth World Conference on Women."

9. One official delegate who came from an NGO named this new sort of "female" participation: gossips (mujeres del chisme) who assembled to discuss the platform regularly (León 1995).

10. At the official plenary, indigenous women presented their own declaration, much of which focused on general demands of indigenous peoples, such as international and national recognition and protection of their particular rights, and increased allotment of development resources.

11. As they put it in their closing statement at the NGO Forum, "Put the Vatican in Brackets" ("Declaración de América Latina y del Caribe").

12. As a whole, Ecuador took seven reservations, Argentina six, the Dominican Republic, El Salvador, Guatemala, and Peru five, Nicaragua and Honduras four, and Venezuela one (United Nations 1996c:723-735).

Chapter 4

1. In practice, as well as in theory, the degree to which this aspect of sovereignty has rested on normative criteria has varied. See Litfin (1997:190-192) for a discussion.

2. The United States did, for the first time, recognize the "right to development" at Vienna. This was a significant nod to the positions of developing states, although we have not found evidence to show whether this recognition was part of any explicit bargain.

3. In 1997, the Office of the UN High Commissioner for Human Rights was consolidated with the UN Human Rights Office at Geneva, which had previously been known as the Centre for Human Rights (United Nations High Commissioner for Human Rights nd). The High Commissioner oversees the UN's human rights programs and related treaty bodies and reports directly to the Secretary-General.

Chapter 5

1. A region-wide breakdown of accredited NGOs finds 18 percent from Sub-Saharan Africa, 11 percent from the Arab States, 19 percent from Asia, 35 percent from the Americas and the Carribean, and 12 percent from Europe. India, Egypt, and the United States sent the most, at 6 percent, 7 percent, and 17 percent of the accreditees, respectively, with many NGOs from the United States registering as "international" (see United Nations 1993a, 1994a, 1994b).

2. See the discussion in chapter 4 on the relative excludability of rights versus environmental issues.

3. The first three points of the Rio Declaration stress the consequences of inequitable development and poverty on women and access to basic services (International Women's Health Coalition 1994). See also Johnson (1995:145).

Chapter 6

1. Thanks to an anonymous reviewer for highlighting this question.

Bibliography

Abbott, Kenneth W. and Duncan Snidal. 1998. Why States Act through Formal Organizations. *Journal of Conflict Resolution* 42, 1:3-32.

Acta de las Reuniones del Foro Paralelo de la UNCED Celebrada entre los Grupos Latinoamericanos y del Caribe. 1992. New York, 15 March 1992. Mimeo.

Acuerdo de los Andes. 1991. Las Leñas, Argentina, 14-20 April, 1991. In *Earth Summit: The NGO Archives.*

Addendum 1 to the Final Report of the NGO-Forum. 1993. Preamble, UN Document. A/CONF.157/7/Add.1, Para. 4, 17 June 1993. In *The World Conference on Human Rights: Vienna, June 1993: The Contribution of NGOs: Reports and Documents,* edited by M. Nowak. Vienna: Manz, 1994.

African NGO Caucus. N.D. Position Paper of the African NGO Caucus on the Draft Declaration and Draft Programme of Action. Prepared for the Second PrepCom of the World Summit for Social Development, Meeting in New York, 22 August-2 September 1994. On-line at <gopher://gopher.undp.org:70/00/unconfs/wssd/pc2/ ngo/african.ngos>.

Agüero, Felipe and Jeffrey Stark, eds. 1998. *Fault Lines of Democracy in Post-Transition Latin America.* Miami: North-South Center Press at the University of Miami.

Aguila, Elena. 1995. Las Unas, las Otras, y las Otras-Otras. *Fempress* 165:15-16.

Alatas, Ali. 1993. Statement by H. E. Mr. Ali Alatas, Minister of Foreign Affairs, Head of the Delegation of the Republic of Indonesia to the Second World Conference on Human Rights, Vienna, 14 June 1993.

Originally published at web site of Republic of Indonesia, Department of Foreign Affairs.

Alger, Chadwick. 2002. The Emerging Roles of NGOs in the UN System: From Article 71 to a People's Millennium Assembly. *Global Governance* 8, 1:93-117.

Alternative Non-Governmental Agreement on Climate Change. 1992. Rio de Janeiro. In *Earth Summit: The NGO Archives*.

Alvarez, Sonia E. 1998. Latin American Feminisms 'Go Global': Trends of the 1990s and Challenges for the New Millennium. In *Cultures of Politics Politics of Cultures: Re-visioning Latin American Social Movements,* edited by S. E. Alvarez, E. Dagnino, and A. Escobar. Boulder: Westview.

———. 1990. *Engendering Democracy in Brazil.* Princeton: Princeton University Press.

Alvarez, Sonia E., Evelina Dagnino, and Arturo Escobar, eds. 1998. *Cultures of Politics Politics of Cultures: Re-visioning Latin American Social Movements.* Boulder: Westview.

Amado, Ana Maria. 1995. El Neo Papismo de Menem. *Fempress* 167:3.

Amnesty International. 1997. Statute of Amnesty International, Appendix II of *Amnesty International Report 1997*. London: Amnesty International Publications.

———. 1995. *Human Rights Are Women's Right.* New York: Amnesty International.

———. 1992a. *Our World: Our Rights.* London: Amnesty International, International Secretariat, December 1992. AI Index: IOR 41/19/92.

———. 1992b. *World Conference on Human Rights: Facing Up to the Failures.* London: Amnesty International, International Secretariat, December 1992. AI Index: IOR 41/16/92.

———. N.D. About AI. On-line at <http://web.amnesty.org/web/aboutai.nsf>.

Amnesty International, Human Rights in China, Human Rights Watch, the International Human Rights Law Group, and the Robert F. Kennedy Memorial Center for Human Rights. 1996. NGO Participation at the UN Fourth World Conference on Women: Report on Barriers to Access, With Recommendations for Change. Copy in authors' possession.

Anheier, Helmut, Marlies Glasius, and Mary Kaldor. 2001. Introducing

Global Civil Society. In *Global Civil Society 2001,* edited by H. Anheier, M. Glasius, and M. Kaldor. Oxford, UK: Oxford University
Press.

Annex I: Recommendations and Proposals Submitted by the Non-Governmental Organizations Present in San José. 1993. San José, 22 January 1993. In UN Document *Regional Meetings,* Doc. No.
A/CONF.157/PC/72.

Annex II: Declarations Submitted by Two Groups of Non-Governmental
Organizations Present in San José. 1993. San José, 19 January
1993. In *The World Conference on Human Rights: Vienna, June
1993: The Contribution of NGOs: Reports and Documents,* edited by
M. Nowak. Vienna: Manz, 1994.

A Statement from the NGOs of the Linkage Caucus. 2000. New York, 10
June, 2000. On-line at <http://www.cwgl.rutgers.edu/globalcenter/
ngorespondw2000.html>.

Asturias, Laura E. 1995. El Presidente y las Conferencias Mundiales. *Fempress* 166:2.

Azzam, Fateh. 1993. Nongovernmental Organizations and the UN World
Conference on Human Rights. *Review of the International Commission of Jurists* 50, Special Issue:89-100.

Bangkok NGO Declaration on Human Rights of 27 March 1993. 1993. In
*The World Conference on Human Rights: Vienna, June 1993: The
Contribution of NGOs: Reports and Documents,* edited by M. Nowak.
Vienna: Manz, 1994.

Barr, Bob. 2002. Protecting National Sovereignty in an Era of International Meddling: An Increasingly Difficult Task. *Harvard Journal
on Legislation* 39, 2:299-324.

Benchmark Environmental Consulting. 1996. *Democratic Global Governance: Report of the 1995 Benchmark Survey of NGOs.* Oslo, Norway: Royal Ministry of Foreign Affairs.

Berlusconi Says 'No Cover-up' Over Summit Violence. 2001. *Deutsche
Presse-Agentur,* 27 July.

Bichsel, Anne. 1996. NGOs as Agents of Public Accountability and Democratization in Intergovernmental Forums. In *Democracy and the Environment,* edited by W. M. Lafferty and J. Meadowcroft. Brookfield,
VT: Edward Elgar.

Bierstecker, Thomas J. and Cynthia Weber. 1996. The Social Construction
of State Sovereignty. In *State Sovereignty as Social Construct,* edited by T. J. Biersteker and C. Weber. Cambridge: Cambridge University Press.

Bigg, Tom and Felix Dodds. 1997. The UN Commission on Sustainable Development. In *The Way Forward: Beyond Agenda 21,* edited by F.
Dodds. UK: Earthscan Publications.

Bindé, Jérôme. 1997. The City Summit—The Lessons of Istanbul. *Futures*
29, 3:213-227.

Black, Ian. 1995a. Development: Hot Air for the Have Nots. *Guardian*
(UK), 15 March:4.

———. 1995b. Diplomats Sink Hopes for Aid Plan at Summit. *Guardian*
(UK), 10 March:13.

———. 1995c. Charities Lambast 'Poverty' Summit. *Guardian* (UK), 8
March:10.

Bohman, James. 1998. The Globalization of the Public Sphere: Cosmopolitan Publicity and the Problem of Cultural Pluralism. *Philosophy
and Social Criticism* 24, 2/3:199-216.

Bouabid, Ihsan. 1993. Arab NGOs in Agreement on Women's Rights. *Terra
Viva.* 12 June. Reprinted in *Human Rights—The New Consensus,*
edited by R. Reoch. London: Regency Press, 1994.

Bouget, Denis and Lionel Prouteau. 2002. National and Supranational
Government-NGO Relations: Anti-Discrimination Policy Formation
in the European Union. *Public Administration and Development* 22,
1:31-37.

Boyle, Kevin. 1995. Stock-taking on Human Rights: The World Conference
on Human Rights, Vienna 1993. *Political Studies* 43:79-95.

Brysk, Allison. 1994. *The Politics of Human Rights in Argentina.* Stanford,
CA: Stanford University Press.

Bunch, Charlotte, Mallika Dutt, and Susana Fried. N.D. Beijing '95: A
Global Referendum on the Human Rights of Women. Rutgers, NJ:
Center for Women's Global Leadership.

Bunch, Charlotte and Niamh Reilly. 1994. *Demanding Accountability: The
Global Campaign and Vienna Tribunal for Women's Human Rights.*
Rutgers, NJ and New York: Center for Women's Global Leader-
ship/UNIFEM.

Butler, William J. 1996. A Global Advocate of Freedom. *Review of the International Commission of Jurists,* Special Edition: *In Memoriam:
Niall MacDermot* 57:19-22.

Cason, Jeffrey. 2000. Democracy Looks South: Mercosul and the Politics of
Brazilian Trade Strategy. In *Democratic Brazil: Actors, Institutions,
and Processes,* edited by P. R. Kingstone and T. J. Power. Pittsburgh:
University of Pittsburgh Press.

Center for Women's Global Leadership, the Conference of NGOs, the European Women's Lobby, and the Women's Environment and Development Organization. 2003. Fifth World Conference on Women and the 2005 CSW Review of the Beijing Platform for Action: Discussions by NGOs at the 47th Session of the Commission on the Status of Women, 3-14 March 2003. On-line at <http://www.cwgl.rutgers.edu/globalcenter/policy/bio/index.html>.

Centre for Applied Studies in International Negotiations Issues and Non Governmental Organizations Programme. 1992a. Report on the Participation of Non-Governmental Organizations in the Preparatory Process of the United Nations Conference on Environment and Development. In *Earth Summit: The NGO Archives.*

———. 1992b. NGO Activities at the United Nations Conference on Environment and Development and the Global Forum. In *Earth Summit: The NGO Archives.*

Chatterjee, Pratap. 1992a. F, F, F, Report for Ryan. *CrossCurrents* PrepCom 4, 3:24-25. In *Earth Summit: The NGO Archives.*

Chatterjee, Pratap. 1992b. Bigger UN Role for NGOs Recommended. *CrossCurrents* PrepCom 4, 5:13-14. In *Earth Summit: The NGO Archives.*

Chen, Martha Alter. 1996. Engendering World Conferences: The International Women's Movement and the UN. In *NGOs, The UN and Global Governance,* edited by T. G. Weiss and L. Gordenker. Boulder: Lynne Rienner.

Ching, Frank. 1994. Is It an NGO, or a GONGO? *Far Eastern Economic Review* 7 (July 1994):34.

Chow, Esther Ngan-ling. 1996. Making Waves, Moving Mountains: Reflections on Beijing '95 and Beyond. *Signs* 22, 1:185-191.

Clark, Ann Marie. 2001. *Diplomacy of Conscience: Amnesty International and Changing Human Rights Norms.* Princeton: Princeton University Press.

———. 1995. Non-Governmental Organizations and Their Influence on International Society. *Journal of International Affairs* 48, 2:507-525.

Clark, Ann Marie, Elisabeth J. Friedman, and Kathryn Hochstetler. 1998. The Sovereign Limits of Global Civil Society: A Comparison of NGO Participation in Global UN Conferences on the Environment, Human Rights, and Women. *World Politics* 51, 1:1-35.

Clark, John D. 2003. *Worlds Apart: Civil Society and the Battle for Ethical Globalization.* Bloomfield, CT: Kumarian Press.

Cohen, Jean L. and Andrew Arato. 1992. *Civil Society and Political Theory.* Cambridge: The MIT Press.

Cohen, Susan. 1994. International Community Hails Cairo Accord. *Washington Memo:* 1-2 (14 October 1994).

Colás, Alejandro. 2002. *International Civil Society.* Cambridge, UK: Polity Press in Association with Blackwell Publishers.

Comeau, Pamela. 1994. Partnership in Action. In *Human Rights—The New Consensus,* edited by Richard Reoch. London: Regency Press.

Cook, Helena. 1996. Amnesty International at the United Nations. In *"The Conscience of the World": The Influence of Non-Governmental Organisations in the U.N. System,* edited by P. Willetts. Washington, DC: Brookings.

———. 1993. International Human Rights Mechanisms: The Role of the Special Procedures in the Protection of Human Rights—The Way Forward after Vienna. *Review of the International Commission of Jurists* 50, Special Issue:31-55.

Cooper, Andrew Fenton, John English, and Ramesh Chandra Thakur. 2002. *Enhancing Global Governance: Towards a New Diplomacy?* Tokyo and New York: United Nations University Press.

The Copenhagen Alternative Declaration: Declaration of Civil Society Organizations Participating in The NGO Forum of the Social Summit. 1995. Prepared by Participants in the NGO Forum of the United Nations World Summit for Social Development, held in Copenhagen, Denmark, 6-12 March 1995. On-line at the web site of the International Institute for Social Development at <http://www.pcdf/1995/cpendecl.htm>.

Cowell, Alan. 1994. The Hidden Population Issue: Money. *New York Times,* 12 September.

Cox, Robert. 1999. Civil Society at the Turn of the Millenium: Prospects for an Alternative World Order. *Review of International Studies* 25:3-28.

Cronin, Bruce. 2002. The Two Faces of the United Nations: The Tension between Intergovernmentalism and Transnationalism. *Global Governance* 8, 1:53-71.

CrossCurrents, various issues. In *Earth Summit: The NGO Archives.*

Cuales, Sonia. 1994. Desarrollo: Ajuste Estructural. Pre-Informe. Foro de ONGs Beijing '95. Mar de Plata, Argentina. Mimeo.

da Costa, Peter. 1993. Probing Rights Violations. *Terra Viva.* 24 June.

Reprinted in *Human Rights—The New Consensus,* edited by R. Reoch. London: Regency Press, 1994.

da Costa, Peter and Lucy Johnson. 1993. Human Rights: Carter Shouted Down at Keynote NGO Address. Inter Press Service, 12 June.

DeJong, Jocelyn. 2000. The Role and Limitations of the Cairo International Conference on Population and Development. *Social Science and Medicine* 51, 6:941-953.

Declaración de América Latina y del Caribe. 1995. Huairou, China, 8 September, 1995. Document in authors' possession.

Declaración de la delegación de Chile. N.D. Statements made upon the adoption of the Vienna Declaration and Programme of Action, World Conference on Human Rights, Meeting in Vienna, Austria, 14-25 June 1993. On-line at the web site of the UN Office of the UN High Commissioner for Human Rights, <http://www.unhchr.ch/html/menu5/d/statement/chile.htm>.

Declaración del Pacto Acción Ecologica de América Latina. 1992. Rio de Janeiro, 13 June, 1992. In *Earth Summit: The NGO Archives.*

Diamond, Larry. 1994. Rethinking Civil Society, Toward Democratic Consolidation. *Journal of Democracy* 5, 3:5-17.

Diamond, Larry, Jonathan Hartlyn, Juan J. Linz, and Seymour Martin Lipset, eds. 1999. *Democracy in Developing Countries: Latin America,* 2d ed. Boulder: Lynne Rienner.

Disney, Julian. 1999. The Copenhagen Commitments and Geneva 2000. *UNRISD News* 21:1-3.

Dolgopol, Ustinia. 1996. Niall MacDermot, A Life Exemplifying Courage and Vision. *Review of the International Commission of Jurists,* Special Edition *In Memoriam: Niall MacDermot* 57:29-41.

Dryzek, John. 2000. *Deliberative Democracy and Beyond: Liberals, Critics, Contestations.* Oxford: Oxford University Press.

Earth Negotiations Bulletin (ENB), various issues. In *ENB* Archives, on-line at <http://www.iisd.ca/voltoc.html>.

Earth Summit: The NGO Archives. 5. Montevideo, Uruguay: NGONET. Note: This CD-ROM compiles primary documents pertaining to NGO participation at the Rio conference. Where possible, locations, dates, and pages cited are from the original documents.

ELCI Global Meeting on Environment and Development for NGOs—Nairobi. N.D. In *Earth Summit: NGO Archives.*

Earth Summit Battle Opened by Greenpeace. 1992. *Independent* 30 May: 14.

Earth Summit Bulletin. 3 March 1992. In *Earth Summit: The NGO Archives.*

Elliot, Rebecca. N.D. The NGO Forum, Report on the World Conference on Human Rights, 14-25 June 1993. Geneva: Quaker United Nations Office, Geneva, doc. no. 252/93.

Encuentro de los Andes/Taller del Cono Sur. 1991. São Paulo, Brazil, 26-27 February 1991. In *Earth Summit: The NGO Archives.*

Faccio, Alda. 1995. Muchos Caminos Hacía Beijing. *Fempress* 153:4.

———. 1994. Paz: El Derecho a Una Vida Sin Violencia. Pre Informe Foro de ONGs Beijing '95. Mar de Plata, Argentina. Mimeo.

Fayed, Amal Mahmoud. 1995. Excerpt from Press Release, Arab Organization for Human Rights. Document in authors' possession.

Feeney, Patricia. 1995. Fair Shares for the Rich. *Guardian* (UK), 11 March:24.

Fernandez, Carmen Alicia. 1993. Indigenous People Plead for Attention and Sensitivity. *Terra Viva.* 12 June. Reprinted in *Human Rights— The New Consensus,* edited by R. Reoch. London: Regency Press, 1994.

Ferreira, Lúcia da Costa. 1992. El Papel de Brasil en las Negociaciones Internacionales de la CNUMAD. *Revista Interamericana de Planificación* 25:45-55.

Final Document, Vienna Plus Five Global NGO Forum on Human Rights. 1998. Ottawa, Canada, 22-24 June 1998. On-line at <http://www.hri.ca/fortherecord1998/documentation/final-report.htm>.

Fine, Robert and Shirin Raj, eds. 1997. *Civil Society: Democratic Perspectives.* London and Portland, OR: Frank Cass.

Finger, Matthias. 1994. Environmental NGOs in the UNCED Process. In *Environmental NGOs in World Politics: Linking the Local and The Global* edited by T. Princen and M. Finger. London and New York: Routledge.

Finnemore, Martha. 1996. *National Interests in International Society.* Ithaca: Cornell University Press.

Foley, Michael W. and Bob Edwards. 1996. The Paradox of Civil Society. *Journal of Democracy* 7, 3:38-52.

Fomerand, Jacques. 1996. UN Conferences: Media Events or Genuine Diplomacy? *Global Governance* 2, 3:361-375.

Fórum de ONGs Brasileiras. 1992. *Meio Ambiente e Desenvolvimento: Uma*

Visão das ONGs e dos Movimentos Sociais Brasileiros. Rio de Janeiro: Fórum de ONGs Brasileiras.

Foster, John W., ed. with Anita Anand. 1999. *Whose World Is it Anyway? Civil Society, the United Nations and the Multilateral Future.* Ottawa: United Nations Association in Canada.

Franco, Jean. 1998. Defrocking the Vatican: Feminism's Secular Project. In *Cultures of Politics Politics of Cultures: Re-visioning Latin American Social Movements,* edited by S. E. Alvarez, E. Dagnino, and A. Escobar. Boulder: Westview.

Fraser, Arvonne. 1987. *The U.N. Decade for Women: Documents and Dialogue.* Boulder: Westview.

Friedman, Elisabeth Jay. 2003. Gendering the Agenda: The Impact of the Transnational Women's Rights Movement at the UN Conferences of the 1990s. *Women's Studies International Forum* 26, 4:313-331.

Friedman, Elisabeth J. 1999. The Effects of 'Transnationalism Reversed' in Venezuela: Assessing the Impact of UN Global Conferences on the Women's Movement. *International Feminist Journal of Politics* 1, 3:357-381.

―――. 1995. Women's Human Rights: The Emergence of a Movement. In *Women's Rights, Human Rights: International Feminist Perspectives,* edited by J. Peters and A. Wolper. New York: Routledge.

Friedman, Elisabeth Jay and Kathryn Hochstetler. 2002. Assessing the "Third Transition" in Latin American Democratization: Representational Regimes and Civil Society in Argentina and Brazil. *Comparative Politics* 35, 1:21-42.

Friedman, Elisabeth Jay, Kathryn Hochstetler, and Ann Marie Clark. 2001. Sovereign Limits and Regional Opportunities for Global Civil Society in Latin America. *Latin American Research Review* 36, 3:7-35.

Gaer, Felice D. 1996. Reality Check: Human Rights NGOs Confront Governments at the UN. In *NGOs, The UN and Global Governance,* edited by T. G. Weiss and L. Gordenker. Boulder: Lynne Rienner.

Gordenker, Leon and Thomas G. Weiss. 1996. Pluralizing Global Governance: Analytical Approaches and Dimensions. In *NGOs, The UN and Global Governance,* edited by T. G. Weiss and L. Gordenker. Boulder: Lynne Rienner.

Goree IV, Langston James, Johannah Bernstein, Pam Chasek, and Richard Jordan. 1991. PC3: A Compilation of the Four Weekly Synopses, 9 September, 1991. In *Earth Summit: The NGO Archives.*

Goree IV, Langston James, Pamela Chasek, and Johannah Bernstein. 1992. In the Corridors. *Earth Summit Bulletin from PrepCom IV* 1, 24:5-6. In *Earth Summit: The NGO Archives*.

Grubb, Michael, Matthias Koch, Abby Munson, Francis Sullivan, and Koy Thomson. 1993. *The Earth Summit Agreements: A Guide and Assessment.* London: Earthscan Publications.

Guest, Iain. 1993. NGOs Face Exclusion from Crucial Drafting Committee. *Terra Viva.* 12 June. Reprinted in *Human Rights—The New Consensus,* edited by R. Reoch. London: Regency Press, 1994.

Guidry, John A., Michael D. Kennedy, and Mayer N. Zald, eds. 2000. *Globalizations and Social Movements: Culture, Power, and the Transnational Public Sphere.* Ann Arbor: University of Michigan Press.

Haas, Peter M. 2002. UN Conferences and Constructivist Governance of the Environment. *Global Governance* 8, 1:73-91.

Haas, Peter M. with Jan Sundgren. 1993. Evolving International Environmental Law: Changing Practices of National Sovereignty. In *Global Accord: Environmental Challenges and International Responses,* edited by N. Choucri. Cambridge: The Massachusetts Institute of Technology Press.

Hall, John A., ed. 1995. *Civil Society: Theory, History, Comparison.* Cambridge, MA: Blackwell and Cambridge, UK: Polity.

Hartmann, Betsy. 1995. *Reproductive Rights & Wrongs: The Global Politics of Population Control.* Boston: South End Press.

Hecklers Stop Carter Speech at Vienna Rights Discussion. 1993. *New York Times* (Reuters), 13 June:23.

Held, David. 1999. The Transformation of Political Community: Rethinking Democracy in the Context of Globalization. In *Democracy's Edges,* edited by I. Shapiro and C. Hacker-Cordón. Cambridge: Cambridge University Press.

———. 1995. *Democracy and the Global Order: From the Modern State to Cosmopolitan Governance.* Stanford: Stanford University Press.

Hernández Carballido, Elvira. 1995. Tergiversan Información. *Fempress* 170.

Hinsley, F. H. 1986. *Sovereignty,* 2d ed. Cambridge: Cambridge University Press.

Hochstetler, Kathryn. 2002. After the Boomerang: Environmental Movements and Politics in the La Plata River Basin. *Global Environmental Politics* 2, 4:35-37.

————. 1997. The Evolution of the Brazilian Environmental Movement and Its Political Roles. In *The New Politics of Inequality in Latin America: Rethinking Participation and Representation* edited by D. A. Chalmers, C. M. Vilas, K. Hite, S. B. Martin, K. Piester, and M. Segarra. New York: Oxford University Press.

Holmes, Steven A. 1993. Clinton Reverses Policies at U.N. on Rights Issues. *New York Times,* 8 May:1.

Human Rights Groups Take Centre Stage. 1993. *Amnesty International Newsletter* 23, 9:8.

Human Rights Internet. 1993. "States Stand Pat While NGOs Face a Revolution," *Human Rights Tribune* (November), 2, 2:5-9. On-line at <www.hri.ca/vienna+5/1993/index.shtml>.

Human Rights Watch Women's Rights Project. 1995. *The Human Rights Watch Global Report on Women's Human Rights.* New York: Human Rights Watch.

Hurtado, María Helena. 1992. The Commission: 'We Need the Equivalent of the International Court of Justice.' *CrossCurrents* in *Terra Viva* 5, 8 (June):40-41. In *Earth Summit: The NGO Archives.*

Imber, Mark. 1994. *Environment, Security and UN Reform.* New York: St. Martin's.

Information on the '92 Global Forum 6. Rio de Janeiro. Pamphlet.

Informe "R." 1992. In *Earth Summit: The NGO Archives.*

Institute for Global Communications. 1995. *Non Governmental Organisation Beijing Declaration,* 15 September, interim version. Beijing: Institute for Global Communications. On-line at <http://www.igc.org/beijing/ngo/ngodec.html>.

Inter Press Service staff and Internet. 1993. NGOs Rebuff UN Rights Conference. *Terra Viva.* 11 June. Reprinted in *Human Rights—The New Consensus,* edited by Richard Reoch. London: Regency Press, 1994.

International Commission of Jurists 1993. Preliminary Evaluation of the UN World Conference on Human Rights. Statement issued 1 July 1993, Printed in *Review of the International Commission of Jurists* 50:110.

International Women's Health Coalition. 1994. Reproductive Health and Justice: International Women's Health Conference for Cairo '94. International Women's Health Coalition. Self-published Report.

Jackson, Robert H. 1990. *Quasi-states: Sovereignty, International Relations and the Third World.* Cambridge: Cambridge University Press.

Jacobsen, Michael and Stephanie Lawson. 1999. Between Globalization and Localization: A Case Study of Human Rights versus State Sovereignty. *Global Governance* 5, 2:203-219.

Jaquette, Jane S., ed. 1994. *The Women's Movement in Latin America: Participation and Democracy.* Boulder: Westview.

Joachim, Jutta. 2003. Framing Issues and Seizing Opportunities: The UN, NGOs, and Women's Rights. *International Studies Quarterly* 47, 2:247-274.

Johnson, Stanley. 1995. *The Politics of Population: The International Conference on Population and Development.* London: Earthscan Publications.

Kari-Oca Declaration of the World Conference of Indigenous Peoples on Territory, Environment and Development. 1992. Rio de Janeiro, 25-30 May 1992. In *Earth Summit: The NGO Archives.*

Keck, Margaret E. and Kathryn Sikkink. 1998. *Activists beyond Borders.* Ithaca: Cornell University Press.

Kingham, Ron, ed. 1991. *Agenda Ya Wananchi: Citizens' Action Plan for the 1990's.* Nairobi: Environment Liaison Centre International.

Knight, W. Andy. 1999. Engineering Space in Global Governance: The Emergence of Civil Society in Evolving 'New' Multilateralism. In *Future Multilateralism: The Political and Social Framework,* edited by M. G. Schechter. New York: New York University Press.

Kocs, Stephen A. 1994. Explaining the Strategic Behavior of States: International Law as System Structure. *International Studies Quarterly* 38, 4:535-556.

Korey, William. 1998. *NGOs and the Universal Declaration of Human Rights: "A Curious Grapevine."* New York: St. Martin's.

Krasner, Stephen D. 1999. *Sovereignty: Organized Hypocrisy.* Princeton: Princeton University Press.

Krauthammer, Charles. 1993. Human Rights Shell Game. *Washington Post,* 18 June:A25.

Lamas, Marta, Alicia Martínez, María Luisa Tarrés, and Esperanza Tuñon. 1995. Building Bridges: The Growth of Popular Feminism in Mexico. In *The Challenge of Local Feminisms: Women's Movements in Global Perspective,* edited by A. Basu. Boulder: Westview.

Latin American and Caribbean Commission on Development and Environment. 1990. Our Own Agenda (Extracts). Reprinted in *Environment and Diplomacy in the Americas,* edited by Heraldo Muñoz. Boulder: Lynne Rienner, 1992.

León, Magdalena. 1995. Report from the 5th World Congress on the Status of Women, Beijing. Paper read at XIX International Congress of the Latin American Studies Association, 28-30 September, at Washington, DC.

Lewis, Paul. 1993a. Differences Are Narrowed at UN Talks on Rights. *New York Times,* 21 June:A5.

———. 1993b. Differing Views on Human Rights Threaten Forum. *New York Times,* 6 June:14.

———. 1993c. Splits May Threaten Rights Conference. *New York Times,* 6 June:1.

———. 1993d. U.S. and Others Press Fight for U.N. Rights Chief. *New York Times,* 11 November:A15.

Lipschutz, Ronnie. 1996. *Global Civil Society and Global Environmental Governance: The Politics of Nature from Place to Planet.* Albany: State University of New York Press.

List of Accredited Non-Governmental Organizations Who Were Represented at the Fourth World Conference on Women. 1995. Document in authors' possession.

Litfin, Karen T. 1998. The Greening of Sovereignty: An Introduction. In *The Greening of Sovereignty in World Politics,* edited by K. T. Litfin. Cambridge: Massachusetts Institute of Technology Press.

———. 1997. Sovereignty in World Ecopolitics. *Mershon International Studies Review* 41:167-204.

Lynch, Marc. 2000. The Dialogue of Civilisations and International Public Spheres. *Millennium* 29, 2:307-330.

Lumsdaine, David Halloran. 1993. *Moral Vision in International Politics: The Foreign Aid Regime, 1949-1989.* Princeton: Princeton University Press.

MacDonald, Gordon J. and Daniel L. Nielson. 1997. Conclusion: Latin American Foreign Policy and International Environmental Regimes. In *Latin American Environmental Policy in International Perspective,* edited by G. J. MacDonald, D. L. Nielson, and M. A. Stern. Boulder: Westview.

Macdonald, Laura. 1994. Globalising Civil Society: Interpreting International NGOs in Central America. *Millennium* 23, 2:267-285.

MacDonald, Laura and Mildred A. Schwartz. 2002. Political Parties and NGOs in the Creation of New Trading Blocs in the Americas. *International Political Science Review* 23, 2:135-158.

McAdam, Doug, John D. McCarthy, and Mayer N. Zald. 1996. *Comparative*

Perspectives on Social Movements: Political Opportunities, Mobilizing Structures, and Cultural Framings. New York: Cambridge University Press.

Martin, Ian. 1998. Hard Choices after Genocide. In *Hard Choices: Moral Dilemmas in Humanitarian Intervention,* edited by Jonathan Moore. Lanham, MD: Rowman & Littlefield.

McIntosh, C. Allison and Jason L. Finkle. 1995. The Cairo Conference on Population and Development: A New Paradigm? *Population and Development Review* 21, 2:223-260.

Mello, Fatima Vianna. 1994. Aceptar o no Aceptar el Dinero:? Is That the Question? *Fempress* 148/49.

Meyerson, Frederick A. B. 2002. Burning the Bridge to the 21st Century: The End of the Era of Integrated Conferences? *PECS News* 7:1, 12-13.

Middleton, Neil, Phil O'Keefe, and Sam Moyo. 1993. *Tears of the Crocodile: From Rio to Reality in the Developing World.* London and Boulder: Pluto Press.

Mitchell, Ronald B. 1998. Discourse and Sovereignty: Interests, Science, and Morality in the Regulation of Whaling. *Global Governance* 4, 3:275-293.

Moravcsik, Andrew. 1997. Taking Preferences Seriously: A Liberal Theory of International Politics. *International Organization* 51, 4:513-553.

Morgan, Robin. 1996. The NGO Forum: Good News and Bad. *Women's Studies Quarterly* 24, 1 and 2:12-21.

Morphet, Sally. 1996. NGOs and the Environment. In *"The Conscience of the World": The Influence of Non-Governmental Organisations in the U.N. System,* edited by P. Willetts. Washington, DC: Brookings.

Navarro, Marysa. 1995. Report from the Fifth World Congress on the Status of Women, Beijing. Paper Read at XIX International Congress of the International Studies Association, 28-30 September, at Washington, DC.

NGO Forum on Women. 1995. Final Report: Look at the World Through Women's Eyes. Beijing: NGO Forum on Women.

NGO-Newsletter, no. 2. 1993. In *The World Conference on Human Rights: Vienna, June 1993: The Contribution of NGOs: Reports and Documents,* edited by M. Nowak. Vienna: Manz, 1994.

Nike. N. D. Company overview. On-line at <http://www.nike.com/nikebiz/nikebiz.jhtml?page=3&item=facts>.

Nowak, Manfred, ed. 1994. *The World Conference on Human Rights: Vi-*

enna, June 1993: The Contribution of NGOs: Reports and Documents. Vienna: Manz, 1994.

―――. 1993. Written Report by the General Rapporteur, Manfred Nowak, as adopted by the Final Plenary Session of the NGO-Forum. UN Document A/Conf.157/7, 14 June 1993. In *The World Conference on Human Rights: Vienna, June 1993: The Contribution of NGOs: Reports and Documents,* edited by M. Nowak. Vienna: Manz, 1994.

Nowak, Manfred and Ingeborg Schwartz. 1994. Introduction to The Contribution of Non-Governmental Organizations. In *The World Conference on Human Rights: Vienna, June 1993: The Contribution of NGOs: Reports and Documents,* edited by M. Nowak. Vienna: Manz, 1994.

O'Brien, Robert, Anne Marie Goetz, Jan Aart Scholte, and Marc Williams. 2000. *Contesting Global Governance: Multilateral Economic Institutions and Global Social Movements.* Cambridge, UK: Cambridge University Press.

O'Dea, James. 1993. Spoken Comments Delivered 2 September 1993 at "The 1993 World Conference on Human Rights and the Politics of Identity," Roundtable Panel, Annual Meeting of the American Political Science Association, Washington DC.

On the Record. On-line at <http://www. advocacynet.org/news_view/news_129.html>.

Ortiz Monasterio, Fernando. 1992. La Deuda Externa, Políticas de Ajuste Estructural y su Impacto sobre el Deterioro del Ambiente y la Sostenibilidad del Desarrollo. *Cuadernos Verdes Sobre Eco 92―Habla la Gente* 6:7-11.

Osborn, Derek and Tom Bigg. 1998. *Earth Summit II: Outcomes and Analysis.* London: Earthscan Publications.

Ottaway, David R. 1993. Women Having their Way at Rights Conference. *Washington Post,* 17 June.

Panario, Daniel H. 1992. Informe Oficial de Uruguay Ante Eco 92: Un Pesimo Anual Escolar. *Tierra Amiga* 4:19-23.

Paolini, Albert J., Antony P. Jarvis, and Christian Reus-Smit, eds. 1998. *Between Society and Global Governance: The United Nations, the State, and Civil Society.* New York: St. Martin's.

Partners Information. 1995. *Countdown to Istanbul,* 5. On-line at <http://www.undp.org/un/habitat/>.

Pasha, Mustapha Kamal and David L. Blaney. 1998. Elusive Paradise: The Promise and Peril of Global Civil Society. *Alternatives* 23:417-450.

Payne, Douglas W. 1993. Human Rights vs. Aspiring Autocrats. *Washington Post,* 2 June:A19.

People Toward Habitat II. 1995. Document in authors' possession.

People's Earth Declaration. 1992. Rio de Janeiro, June 1992. In *Earth Summit: The NGO Archives.*

Pérez-Díaz, Víctor M. 1993. *The Return of Civil Society: The Emergence of Democratic Spain.* Cambridge: Harvard University Press.

Petchesky, Rosalind Pollack. 1995. The Programme of Action of the International Conference on Population and Development Treads on Thin Ice between Feminism and Old Population Theory. *Reproductive Health Matters* 6:152-161.

Peterson, M. J. 1992. Transnational Activity, International Society and World Politics. *Millennium* 21, 3:371-388.

Poggi, Gianfranco. 1990. *The State: Its Nature, Development and Prospects.* Stanford, CA: Stanford University Press.

Posner, Michael and Candy Whittome. 1994. The Status of Human Rights NGOs. *Columbia Human Rights Law Review* 269:283, as excerpted in Henry J. Steiner and Philip Alston, *International Human Rights in Context.* Oxford: Clarendon, 1996.

Preparatory Committee for Istanbul Human Settlements Conference Begins Two-Week Session. 1995 (5 March). UN Press Release no. HAB/103. On-line at <http://www.undp.org/un/habitat/>.

Preparatory Meetings: Latin American and Caribbean Regional Meeting, Costa Rica in *NGO-Newsletter,* no. 2. 1993. In *The World Conference on Human Rights: Vienna, June 1993: The Contribution of NGOs: Reports and Documents,* edited by M. Nowak. Vienna: Manz, 1994.

Press Release [re: Habitat II]. 1996. 6 June. Document in authors' possession.

Princen, Thomas. 1994. NGOs: Creating a Niche in Environmental Diplomacy. In *Environmental NGOs in World Politics: Linking the Local and the Global,* edited by T. Princen and M. Finger. London and New York: Routledge.

Prinze, Roland. 1993. Former President Carter's Speech Drowned Out by Protests. Associated Press. 12 June.

Putnam, Robert. 1988. Diplomacy and Domestic Politics: The Logic of Two-Level Games. *International Organization* 42:427-460.

The Quality Benchmark for the Social Summit: An NGO Statement for the Third Session of the Preparatory Committee of the Social Summit.

1994. On-line at <http://www.socialwatch.org/en/acercaDe/anexos/benchmark.htm>.

Ramírez, Socorro. 1995. Desde Las Mujeres Organizadas. *Fempress* 167:8.

Raustiala, Kal. 1997. States, NGOs, and International Environmental Institutions. *International Studies Quarterly* 41, 4:719-740.

———. 1996. Democracy, Sovereignty, and the Slow Pace of International Negotiations. *International Environmental Affairs* 8, 1:3-15.

Reoch, Richard, ed. 1994. *Human Rights—The New Consensus*. London: Regency Press (Humanity).

Riding, Alan. 1993a. Bleak Assessment as Rights Meeting Nears. *New York Times*, 25 April 1993:11.

———. A Rights Meeting, but Don't Mention the Wronged. *New York Times,* 14 June 1993:23.

———. Human Rights: The West Gets some Tough Questions. *New York Times,* 20 June 1993, Section 4:5.

Risse, Thomas, Steven C. Ropp, and Kathryn Sikkink, eds. 1999. *The Power of Human Rights: International Norms and Domestic Change.* Cambridge, UK: Cambridge University Press.

Risse, Thomas and Kathryn Sikkink. 1999. The Socialization of International Human Rights Norms into Domestic Practices: Introduction to *The Power of Human Rights: International Norms and Domestic Change,* edited by T. Risse, S. C. Ropp, and K. Sikkink. Cambridge, UK: Cambridge University Press.

Rodríguez A., María Lis. 1995. Agua Fría Camino a Beijing. *Fempress* 167:5.

Rosenau, James N. 1998. Powerful Tendencies, Enduring Tensions and Glaring Contradictions: The United Nations in a Turbulent World. In *Between Sovereignty and Global Governance,* edited by A. J. Paolini, A. P. Jarvis, and C. Reus-Smit. Great Britain: MacMillan Press and New York: St. Martin's.

———. 1997. *Along the Domestic-Foreign Frontier: Exploring Governance in a Turbulent World.* Cambridge, UK: Cambridge University Press.

Rosow, Stephen J. 2000. Globalisation as Democratic Theory. *Millennium* 29, 1:27-45.

Rowland, Wade. 1973. *The Plot to Save the World: The Life and Times of the Stockholm Conference on the Human Environment.* Toronto: Clarke, Irwin, and Co.

Salazar Ramírez, Hilda. 1992. El Medio Ambiente y la Participación Ciudadana: El Foro Mexicano de la Sociedad Civil para Río 92. *El Cotidiano* 47:11-15.

Samuel, Kumudini. 1994. Contest in Vienna. In *Human Rights—The New Consensus,* edited by R. Reoch. London: Regency Press.

Sandbrook, Richard. 1997. UNGASS Has Run Out of Steam. *International Affairs* 73, 4:641-654.

Sané, Pierre. N. D. AI: Governments on Trial. In *APCDOC II, Background Documents from the World Conference on Human Rights* (DOS computer file, floppy disk). Speech Delivered to Foreign Press Association, London, 1993. Hanover, Germany: Association of Progressive Communications (APC)/ ComLink e.U, 1993.

Sanger, David E. 2001. Genoa Summit Meeting: The Overview. *New York Times,* 23 July.

Sant'Anna, Wania. 1994. Mujeres Brasileñas Camino a Beijing. *Fempress* 156.

Save UNCED: An Urgent Message to Governments. 1992. In *Earth Summit: The NGO Archives.*

Schmidt, Brian C. 1998. *The Political Discourse of Anarchy: A Disciplinary History of International Relations.* Albany: State University of New York Press.

Schmidt, Markus. 1995. What Happened to the 'Spirit of Vienna'? The Follow-up to the Vienna Declaration and Programme of Action and the Mandate of the UN High Commissioner for Human Rights. *Nordic Journal of International Law* 64:591-617.

Schmitter, Philippe C. 2000. Designing a Democracy for the Euro-Polity and Revising Democratic Theory in the Process. In *Designing Democratic Institutions,* edited by I. Shapiro and S. Macedo. New York: New York University Press.

Scholte, Jan Aart. 2002. Civil Society and Democracy in Global Governance. *Global Governance* 8, 3:281-304.

Sciolino, Elaine. 1993. At Vienna Talks, U.S. Insists Rights Must Be Universal. *New York Times,* 15 June:A1.

Seligman, Adam B. 1992. *The Idea of Civil Society.* New York: Free Press.

Shapiro, Ian and Casiano Hacker-Cordón, eds. 1999. *Democracy's Edges.* Cambridge, UK: Cambridge University Press.

Shaw, Martin. 1994. Civil Society and Global Politics. *Millennium* 23, 3:647-667.

Shepherd, Anne. N.D. Abortion Debate Deferred as More Voices Join the Vatican. Women's Feature Service. Document in authors' possession.

Sikkink, Kathryn. 1993. Human Rights, Principled Issue-Networks, and Sovereignty in Latin America. *International Organization* 47, 3:411-432.

Smith, Jackie. 2001a. Transnational Mobilizations against Global Trade Liberalization: Challenges for Global Institutions. Paper Prepared for the 2001 Meeting of the International Studies Association, 23 February, Chicago.

———. 2001b. Globalizing Resistance: The Battle of Seattle and the Future of Social Movements. *Mobilization: An International Journal* 6, 1:1-19.

Smith, Jackie, Ron Pagnucco, and Charles Chatfield. 1997. Social Movements and World Politics: A Theoretical Framework. In *Transnational Social Movements and Global Politics: Solidarity beyond the State,* edited by J. Smith, C. Chatfield, and R. Pagnucco. Syracuse: Syracuse University Press.

Smouts, Marie-Claude. 1999. Multilateralism from Below: A Prerequisite for Global Governance. In *Future Multilateralism: The Political and Social Framework,* edited by M. G. Schechter. New York: New York University Press.

Snow, David A. and Robert D. Benford. 1992. Master Frames and Cycles of Protest. In *Frontiers in Social Movement Theory,* edited by A. D. Morris and C. M. Mueller. New Haven: Yale University Press.

Socialist International. N.D. The International. On-line at <http://www. socialistinternational.org/1What/info.html>.

Statistics on NGO-Participation in the World Conference on Human Rights. 1993. In *NGO-Newsletter,* no. 4 (July 1993). In *The World Conference on Human Rights: Vienna, June 1993: The Contribution of NGOs: Reports and Documents,* edited by M. Nowak. Vienna: Manz, 1994.

Stephenson, Carolyn M. 1995. Women's International Nongovernmental Organizations at the United Nations. In *Women, Politics, and the United Nations,* edited by A. Winslow. Westport, CT: Greenwood Press.

Sternbach, Nancy Saporta, Marysa Navarro-Aranguren, Patricia Chuchryk, and Sonia E. Alvarez. 1992. Feminisms in Latin America: From Bogotá to San Bernardo. In *The Making of Social Movements in Latin America: Strategy, Identity, Democracy,* edited by A. Escobar and S. E. Alvarez. Boulder: Westview.

Strassman, W. Paul. 1997. Avoiding Conflict and Bold Inquiry—A Recapitulation of Habitat II. *Urban Studies* 34, 10:1729-1738.

Tarrow, Sidney. 1995. Cycles of Collective Action: Between Moments of Madness and the Repertoire of Contention. In *Repertoires and Cycles of Collective Action,* edited by M. Traugott. Durham: Duke University Press.

————. 1994. *Power in Movement: Social Movements, Collective Action and Politics.* Cambridge, UK: Cambridge University Press.

Tempest, Clive. 1997. Myths from Eastern Europe and the Legend of the West. In *Civil Society: Democratic Perspectives,* edited by R. Fine and S. Raj. London and Portland, OR: Frank Cass.

Terra Viva 12, 15 June 1992. In *Earth Summit: The NGO Archives.*

Thomson, Janice E. 1995. State Sovereignty in International Relations: Bridging the Gap Between Theory and Empirical Research. *International Studies Quarterly* 39, 2:213-233.

Tolley, Howard. 1994. *The International Commission of Jurists: Global Advocates for Human Rights.* Philadelphia: University of Pennsylvania.

Tosics, Ivan. 1997. Habitat II Conference on Human Settlements, Istanbul, June 1996. *International Journal of Urban and Regional Research* 21, 2:366-372.

Traugott, Mark, ed. 1995. *Repertoires and Cycles of Collective Action.* Durham, NC: Duke University Press.

Tunali, Odil. 1996. Habitat II: Not Just Another 'Doomed Global Conference.' *World Watch,* 9, 3:32-34.

Tunis Declaration of African NGOs of 6 November 1992. 1992. In *The World Conference on Human Rights: Vienna, June 1993: The Contribution of NGOs: Reports and Documents,* edited by M. Nowak. (Translated from French original.) Vienna: Manz, 1994.

United Nations. 1996a. The Habitat Agenda. From Report of the United Nations Conference on Human Settlements (Habitat II), Istanbul, 3-14 June 1996. UN Doc. A/Conf. 165/14. On-line at <http://www.unhcs.org/declarations/habitat_agenda.asp>.

————. 1996b. Istanbul Declaration on Human Settlements. United Nations Conference on Human Settlements (Habitat II), Istanbul, 3-14 June 1996. On-line at <http://www.unchs.org/declarations/Istanbul.asp>.

————. 1996c. Report of the Fourth World Conference on Women, held in

Beijing from 4 to 5 September 1995; including the Agenda, the Beijing Declaration, and the Platform for Action (extract)—including country reservations. In *The United Nations and the Advancement of Women 1945-1996.* New York: United Nations Department of Public Information.

———. 1996d. Report of the United Nations Conference on Human Settlements (Habitat II), Istanbul, 3-14 June 1996. UN Doc. A/CONF. 165/14.

———. 1995a. Accreditation of NGOs to the FWCW. Resolution of Commission on the Status of Women [ECOSOC], 10 April 1995, UN Doc. E/CN.6/1995/l.20.

———. 1995b. Adoption of the Copenhagen Declaration on Social Development and the Programme of Action of the World Summit for Social Development. Report of the World Summit for Social Development, A/Conf.166/9, 19 April 1995.

———. 1995c. The Copenhagen Declaration and Programme of Action, World Summit for Social Development. UN Doc. A/Conf.166/9, 19 April 1995.

———. 1995d. Regional Programme of Action for the Women of Latin America and the Caribbean, Sixth Regional Conference on the Integration of Women into the Economic and Social Development of Latin America and the Caribbean, held at Mar del Plata, Argentina, from 20 to 25 September 1994, UN Doc. E/CN.6/1995/5/Add.3.

———. 1995e. World Summit for Social Development. New York: UN Department of Public Information.

———. 1994a. Accreditation of Non-Governmental Organizations to the Conference and Its Preparatory Process. UN Doc. A/CONF.171/ PC/6, Add. 1-4. 10 February 1994-April 1994.

———. 1994b. Organization of Work, Including the Establishment of the Main Committee of the Conference. UN Doc. A/CONF.171/7, Add. 1. 17 August 1994.

———. 1994c. Report of the International Conference on Population and Development. UN Doc. A/CONF.171/13, 18 October 1994.

———. 1993a. Accreditation of Non-Governmental Organizations to the Conference and Its Preparatory Process. UN Doc. E/CONF.84/ PC/10, Add. 1-3. 22 April-12 May 1993.

———. 1993b. Annotations to the Provisional Agenda, World Conference on Human Rights, Regional Meeting for Latin America and the Caribbean, Meeting in San José, Costa Rica, 18-22 January 1993. UN Doc. A/CONF.157/LACRM/1/Add.1 of 11 January 1993, Item 3.

———. 1993c. Final Declaration of the Regional Meeting for Latin America and the Caribbean of the World Conference on Human Rights, Meeting in San José, Costa Rica, 18-22 January 1993. UN Doc. A/CONF.157/LACRM/15 of 11 February 1993.

———. 1993d. Final Report of the Regional Meeting for Asia of the World Conference on Human Rights. Bangkok, 2 March-2 April 1993. UN Doc. A/CONF.157/ASRM/8, Cross-listed as A/CONF.157/PC/59. 7 April 1993.

———. 1993e. List of Attendance, World Conference on Human Rights, Regional Meeting for Latin America and the Caribbean, Meeting in San José, Costa Rica, 18-22 January 1993. UN Doc. no. A/CONF.157/LACRM/INF.1, of 1 February 1993.

———. 1993f. A Report of the Regional Meeting for Latin America and the Caribbean of the World Conference on Human Rights, San José, Costa Rica, 18-22 January 1993. UN Doc. A/CONF.157/LACRM/15 of 11 February 1993.

———. 1993g. Report of the United Nations Conference on Environment and Development, Vols. I-III, UN Doc. A/CONF.151/26/Rev.1. New York: United Nations.

———. 1993h. Vienna Declaration and Programme of Action, UN Doc. A/CONF 157/24. Adopted on 25 June 1993 by the World Conference on Human Rights on 25 June 1993, meeting in Vienna, Austria, 14-25 June 1993.

———. 1993i. *Yearbook of the United Nations 1993,* Vol. 47. Dordrecht (Netherlands): Martinus Nijhoff.

———. 1992. Tunis Declaration on Human Rights, Final Declaration of the Regional Meeting for Africa of the World Conference on Human Rights. In Report of the Regional Meeting for Africa of the World Conference on Human Rights, Tunis, 2-6 November 1992. UN Doc. A/CONF.157/AFRM/14 of 24 November 1992, chapter I.

———. 1991. The Tlatelco Platform [Report of the Latin American and Caribbean Governmental Representatives to the Regional Preparatory Meeting of the United Nations Conference on Environment and Development, Mexico City. Conference Room Document MIN/5/Rev. 1 of 7 March, 1991.] In *Environment and Diplomacy in the Americas,* edited by Heraldo Muñoz. Boulder: Lynne Rienner, 1992.

———. 1975. World Plan of Action for the Advancement of Women. Adopted in Mexico City. In *The United Nations and the Advancement of Women 1945-1996.* New York: United Nations Department of Public Information, 1996.

————. 1968. Final Act of the International Conference on Human Rights, Tehran, 22 April to 13 May 1968. UN Doc. A/CONF.32/41.

UN General Assembly Acts on the World Conference. 1993. *NGO Newsletter,* no. 2 (February 1993). In *The World Conference on Human Rights: Vienna, June 1993: The Contribution of NGOs: Reports and Documents,* edited by M. Nowak. Vienna: Manz, 1994.

United Nations ACC Task Force on Basic Social Services for All. 1998. *Compendium of Social Issues from the United Nations Global Conferences in the 1990s.* New York: United Nations Population Fund. UN Doc. E/3000/1998.

United Nations Development Programme.1995. *NGO Statements at the Plenary Sessions of the Fourth World Conference on Women.* Beijing: United Nations Development Programme and UN Fourth World Conference on Women Secretariat. Document in authors' possession.

United Nations Economic and Social Council. 1991. ECOSOC Resolution 1991/93.

————. 1989. ECOSOC Resolution 1989/91.

United Nations High Commissioner for Human Rights. N.D. Office of the High Commissioner for Human Rights: Mandate. On-line at <http://www.unhchr.ch/html/hchr.htm>.

UN Research Institute for Social Development (UNRISD). N.D. *Advancing the Social Agenda: Two Years after Copenhagen.* Report of the UNRISD International Conference and Public Meeting, Geneva, 9-10 July 1997. Geneva: UNRISD. On-line at <http://www.unrisd.org/>.

United Nations Administrative Committee on Coordination Task Force on Basic Social Services for All. 1998. *Compendium of Social Issues from the United Nations Global Conferences in the 1990s.* New York: United Nations Population Fund. UN Doc. E/3000/1998.

Useful Words, but Not Much Action. 1995. *St. Louis Post-Dispatch* 15 March:6B.

Uvin, Peter. 1996. Scaling Up the Grassroots and Scaling Down the Summit: The Relations Between Third World NGOs and the UN. In *NGOs, The UN and Global Governance,* edited by T. G. Weiss and L. Gordenker. Boulder: Lynne Rienner.

Valdés, Teresa. 1995. Report from the 5th World Congress on the Status of Women, Beijing. Paper read at XIX International Congress of the Latin American Studies Association, 28-30 September 1995, at Washington, DC.

Vargas Valente, Virginia. 1996. Disputando el Espacio Global: El Movimiento de Mujeres y la IV Conferencia de Beijing. Nueva Sociedad 141:43-54.

Vargas, Virginia. 1995. Presentation by Virginia Vargas, Coordinator of The Latin American and Caribbean Forum, 13 September 1995 Plenary Statement. On-line at <http://www.un.org/esa/gopher=data/conf/fwcw/conf/ngo/141232Z1.txt>.

———. N.D. Discurso de Inauguración, Foro de ONGs Mar de Plata. Mimeo.

Vienna: A Search for Common Ground. 1993. UN Chronicle 30, 3:59.

———. 1995. Presentation by Virginia Vargas, Coordinator of the Latin American and Caribbean NGO Forum, 13 September 1995 plenary statement. On-line at <http://www.un.org/esa/gopher-data/conf/fwcw/conf/ngo/14123221.txt>.

Wakely, Patrick. 1996. Viewpoint: Building on the Success of Habitat II. *Third World Planning Review* 18, 3:iii-viii.

Waltz, Kenneth N. 1999. Globalization and Governance. *PS: Political Science and Politics* 32, 4:693-700.

Wapner, Paul. 2000. The Normative Promise of Nonstate Actors: A Theoretical Account of Global Civil Society. In *Principled World Politics: The Challenge of Normative International Relations,* edited by P. Wapner and E. J. Ruiz. Lanham, MD: Rowman and Littlefield.

———. 1997. Governance in Global Civil Society. In *Global Governance: Drawing Insights from the Environmental Experience,* edited by O. R. Young. Cambridge: Massachusetts Institute of Technology Press.

———. 1996. *Environmental Activism and World Civic Politics.* Albany: State University of New York Press.

———. 1995. Politics Beyond the State: Environmental Activism and World Civic Politics. *World Politics* 47, 3:311-340.

Weber, Cindy. 1998. Performative States. *Millennium: Journal of International Studies* 27:77-95.

Weiss, Thomas George. 1998. *Beyond UN Subcontracting: Task-Sharing with Regional Security Arrangements and Service-Providing NGOs.* New York: St. Martin's.

Weiss, Thomas George, David P. Forsythe, and Roger A. Coate. 1997. *The United Nations and Changing World Politics,* 2d ed. Boulder: Westview.

Willetts, Peter. 2000. From 'Consultative Arrangements' to 'Partnership': The Changing Status of NGOs in Diplomacy at the UN. *Global Governance* 6, 2:191-222.

———. 1996. From Stockholm to Rio and Beyond: The Impact of The Environmental Movement on the United Nations Consultative Arrangements for NGOs. *Review of International Studies* 22:57-80.

———. 1989. The Pattern of Conferences. In *Global Issues in the United Nations' Framework,* edited by P. Taylor and A. J. R. Groom. New York: St. Martins.

Women's Caucus of the World Summit for Social Development. 1994. The Women's Caucus Statement: Compilation of Comments and Suggestions on the Overview Report of the Secretary-General and Working Papers Prepared During PreCom I. 10 February. Document in authors' possession.

Women's Environment and Development Organization (WEDO). 1996. *Beyond Promises: Governments in Motion One Year after the Beijing Women's Conference.* New York: WEDO.

———. 1995a. A Brief Analysis of The UN Fourth World Conference on Women Beijing Declaration and Platform for Action. Report, New York, 30 November 1995.

———. 1995b. Cover Letter for WEDO 1995a.

———. 1994. WEDO Fact Sheet on Women's Caucus (12 September) On-line at <http://www.iisd.ca/linkages/Cairo/wedofac2.txt>.

Women's Feature Service. 1994. The Legacy of the Women's Caucus, 7 September. On-line at <http://www.iisd.ca/linkages/Cairo/wfslegac.txt>.

Women's Linkage Caucus. 1995. Recommendations on Bracketed Text in the WCW Draft Platform for Action. Mimeo.

Women's Voices '94—A Declaration on Population Policies. 1993. *Population and Development Review* 19, 3:637-640.

World Commission on Environment and Development. 1987. *Our Common Future.* Oxford and New York: Oxford University Press.

Yole, Steve. 1992. The '92 Global Forum: 14 Incredible Days in June. *Brundtland Bulletin* 16:8-12. In *Earth Summit: The NGO Archives.*

Young, Iris Marion. 2000. Self-Determination and Global Democracy: A Critique of Liberal Nationalism. In *Designing Democratic Institutions,* edited by I. Shapiro and S. Macedo. New York: New York University Press.

Yuval-Davis, Nira. 1998. Gender and Nation. In *Women, Ethnicity and Nationalism,* edited by R. Wilford and R. L. Miller. New York: Routledge.

Zheng, Wang. 1996. A Historic Turning Point for the Women's Movement in China. *Signs* 22, 1:196.

Index

SUNY series in Global Politics
James N. Rosenau, Editor

List of Titles

American Patriotism in a Global Society—Betty Jean Craige

The Political Discourse of Anarchy: A Disciplinary History of International Relations—Brian C. Schmidt

Power and Ideas: North-South Politics of Intellectual Property and Antitrust—Susan K. Sell

From Pirates to Drug Lords: The Post–Cold War Caribbean Security Environment—Michael C. Desch, Jorge I. Dominguez, and Andres Serbin (eds.)

Collective Conflict Management and Changing World Politics—Joseph Lepgold and Thomas G. Weiss (eds.)

Zones of Peace in the Third World: South America and West Africa in Comparative Perspective—Arie M. Kacowicz

Private Authority and International Affairs—A. Claire Cutler, Virginia Haufler, and Tony Porter (eds.)

Harmonizing Europe: Nation-States within the Common Market—Francesco G. Duina

Economic Interdependence in Ukrainian-Russian Relations—Paul J. D'Anieri

Leapfrogging Development? The Political Economy of Telecommunications Restructuring—J. P. Singh

States, Firms, and Power: Successful Sanctions in United States Foreign Policy—George E. Shambaugh